SAGE was founded in 1965 by Sara Miller McCune to support the dissemination of usable knowledge by publishing innovative and high-quality research and teaching content. Today, we publish over 900 journals, including those of more than 400 learned societies, more than 800 new books per year, and a growing range of library products including archives, data, case studies, reports, and video. SAGE remains majority-owned by our founder, and after Sara's lifetime will become owned by a charitable trust that secures our continued independence.

Los Angeles | London | New Delhi | Singapore | Washington DC | Melbourne

FEDERAL
FISCAL
RELATIONS
IN INDIA

Thank you for choosing a SAGE product!
If you have any comment, observation or feedback,
I would like to personally hear from you.

Please write to me at **contactceo@sagepub.in**

Vivek Mehra, Managing Director and CEO, SAGE India.

Bulk Sales

SAGE India offers special discounts
for purchase of books in bulk.
We also make available special imprints
and excerpts from our books on demand.

For orders and enquiries, write to us at

Marketing Department
SAGE Publications India Pvt Ltd
B1/I-1, Mohan Cooperative Industrial Area
Mathura Road, Post Bag 7
New Delhi 110044, India

E-mail us at **marketing@sagepub.in**

Subscribe to our mailing list
Write to **marketing@sagepub.in**

This book is also available as an e-book.

FEDERAL
FISCAL
RELATIONS
IN INDIA

Imperatives for Restructuring

J. V. M. Sarma

Los Angeles | London | New Delhi
Singapore | Washington DC | Melbourne

First published in 2020 by

SAGE Publications India Pvt Ltd
B1/I-1 Mohan Cooperative Industrial Area
Mathura Road, New Delhi 110 044, India
www.sagepub.in

SAGE Publications Inc
2455 Teller Road
Thousand Oaks, California 91320, USA

SAGE Publications Ltd
1 Oliver's Yard, 55 City Road
London EC1Y 1SP, United Kingdom

SAGE Publications Asia-Pacific Pte Ltd
18 Cross Street #10-10/11/12
China Square Central
Singapore 048423

Published by Vivek Mehra for SAGE Publications India Pvt Ltd. Typeset in 10.5/13 pt Berkeley by Zaza Eunice, Hosur, Tamil Nadu, India.

Library of Congress Cataloging-in-Publication Data Available

ISBN: 978-93-5388-266-2 (HB)

SAGE Team: Abhijit Baroi and Vandana Gupta

CONTENTS

LIST OF ILLUSTRATIONS

FIGURES

TABLES

ACKNOWLEDGEMENTS

This book is based on the Indian Council of Social Science Research National Fellowship No. 1-04/2014-15/N-Fel (Ref. Lr. 18 November 2014). I am grateful to all the concerned officers and staff of the organization for timely responses and encouragement.

I am grateful to the University of Hyderabad for providing all the necessary facilities during the national fellowship period.

A brief version of the book was presented at the seminar conducted by Ernst & Young (EY) and the Madras School of Economics on 22–23 February 2019 on 'Fiscal Federalism in India: Contemporary Perspectives'. I am immensely benefited from the comments and suggestions made, especially by the following people:

- Dr C. Rangarajan, Chairman, Madras School of Economics; formerly Governor, Reserve Bank of India; and Chairman, Twelfth Finance Commission
- Dr Ashok Lahiri, Member, Fifteenth Finance Commission; Director, National Institute of Public Finance and Policy
- Dr D. K. Srivastava, Chief Policy Adviser, EY India; formerly Member, Twelfth Finance Commission; and Director, Madras School of Economics

- Dr M. Govinda Rao, Member, Fourteenth Finance Commission; Director, National Institute of Public Finance and Policy; and Member, Prime Minister's Advisory Council
- Dr V. Bhaskar, Economic Advisor to the Fourteenth Finance Commission; and Principal Secretary, Government of Andhra Pradesh

I am grateful to all the stalwarts for the encouraging comments.

INTRODUCTION

The system of federal fiscal relations in India has come a long way over the past six decades. Yet, the system remains imperfect. Also, with the changing economic structure, there is a need to completely revamp the mechanism and methods used. The purpose of this study is, first, to examine the present system's evolution, developments and need for change. The institutional mechanism was set up by the British government to suit their own purposes. Post Independence, some changes were made, which have become outdated now. Therefore, the second purpose of this study is to indicate what kind of changes are required and how these can be brought about.

FEDERAL FORM OF GOVERNANCE

The federal form of governance is best suited to maintain democratic characteristic and inculcate decentralized governance, especially appropriate for a society with a vastly diverse economic and cultural background. A federal system is preferred to a unitary system of governance not only for political and administrative reasons but also for economic benefits. It involves a multilayer governance structure and has proximity advantage safeguarding the local ethnic and cultural diversities with freedom to adopt local specific policies. Though the federal form of governance involves more expenditure and might lead to unnecessary competition between subnational government (SNG) units, its advantages override such disadvantages.

Originated in Britain sometime in the late 18th century, the federal form is shaped by the American Revolution. Currently, it covers about

40 per cent of the world population in 25 countries. India, with its diverse social, economic and cultural background, is an ideal case of adopting the federal form of the government and has its roots in the pre-Independence era itself. The necessary institutional structure has been evolving over the past six decades.

Yet, the system remains imperfect: first, in view of certain unresolved issues in the operationalization, and second, due to the changing contours in the economy and the resultant policy changes in the fiscal governance. Especially, in recent years, with the landmark changes such as the replacement of the Planning Commission with the National Institution for Transforming India (NITI) Aayog, implementation of the Direct Tax Code, introduction of the goods and services tax (GST), which might alter the revenue positions of the centre, state and local level governments. All these developments signal that it is time for revamping of the system of federal fiscal arrangements for intergovernmental transfers in India.

There exist several thorny issues in the federal fiscal management and fiscal-sharing mechanism, which are further aggravated by other economic policy side effects, such as the shift towards liberalization in 1991, the introduction of the Fiscal Responsibility and Budgetary Management (FRBM) Act, the introduction of goods and services tax (GST), changes in monetary policies and so on. In short, the economy has come a long way, and there have been major changes in the nature and structure of the economy. The federal fiscal institutional structure, therefore, needs fundamental revamping.

The overall purpose of the present study is to identify the need and suggest suitable alterations in the federal fiscal system in India taking into account the possible changes in the structure of the economy and the potential revenue generation at different levels of government.

FEDERAL FISCAL SYSTEM: BROAD REQUIREMENTS

The adaptation and operationalization of the federal system of governance involve certain basic choices.

The Nature of the Federal System

The world over, the consensus seems to have on three levels of governments: federal, provincial and local.

The Division of Powers

The constitutional division of revenue and expenditure powers between national and SNGs is one of the fundamental requirements for adopting the federal form.

An important consideration for the division of fiscal powers—vertical or horizontal—is the management of 'spillover effects'. As per this theory, public goods and services have spillover effects with different 'spans'—local, provincial, regional, national and international. Ideally, fiscal powers relating to public goods with larger spans of spillover effects should be assigned to higher levels of governments. Further, in the literature, it is suggested that the assignment of expenditure functions should precede the division of revenue-raising powers so that the latter can be determined by the requirements of different spending agencies.

The world over, the division of functions and responsibilities varies from one federation to the other depending upon the basic preference as to whether to have a centripetal federation or 'cooperative' federation. For example, India follows the centripetal federalism, where the central government holds more powers than the states either directly or indirectly.

Need for Intergovernmental
Fiscal Transfers

The inadequacy of resources to meet expenditure functions makes the SNGs dependent on the federal government. The central tax revenues need to be shared between the three levels of governments.

Nature of Fiscal Imbalances and Methods of Alleviation

In federal systems, two types of fiscal imbalances can occur: vertical fiscal imbalance (VFI) and horizontal fiscal imbalance (HFI). When the fiscal imbalance occurs between two levels of government (such as centre and states, or states and local), it is called VFI. When the fiscal imbalance occurs between the governments at the same level, it is called HFI. This imbalance is also known as regional disparity. While HFI requires equalization transfers, VFI is a structural issue and thus needs to be corrected by the reassignment of revenue and expenditure responsibilities between national and SNGs.

Vertical Fiscal Imbalances

VFI is a structural issue and might arise by design. Generally, expenditure responsibilities assigned to SNGs would require a larger share of revenue resources. The raising of taxes, however, must be largely centralized for efficiency and economic reasons. Thus, a large part of the VFI is by design. Among the established federal countries, Australia seems to have a higher vertical imbalance.

VFI is justified on the basis of the following reasons. First, central government functions are to provide public goods with a larger span of externalities ('spillovers') such that they serve the 'national' interests as opposed to the narrower regional interests. The functions such as defence, border security and integrated planned macroeconomic development require huge resources. Second, the central government needs to meet the equity objectives through tax and expenditure policies. The horizontal fiscal equalization needs greater access to revenue sources. Third, certain national taxes such as income tax and manufacturing tax require a centralized uniform administration. Also, the centralized tax administration reduces scope for needless 'tax competition' among the SNGs.

At the same time, there are certain arguments for minimizing the VFI. First, there is the accountability argument. The fact that the central government collects most of the revenues, and provincial governments collect less but spend more, which requires vertical transfers from the centre to the provinces, may reduce the accountability of provincial governments. Second, a large VFI makes the central government financially very powerful and the provinces to be weak. Apart from the intended VFI, there could be other undesired components of VFI caused by several factors, some of which are as follows:

1. The nature and extent of actual fiscal autonomy;
2. Conflicting or uncoordinated federal and state priorities (e.g., education, agriculture, social welfare and infrastructure expenditures);
3. Shortcomings in the existing revenue-sharing arrangements; and
4. Political conflicts.

More than the tax revenue sharing, tax power sharing could also cause VFI. It depends upon the degree of discretionary change to tax rates or tax bases required for generating additional revenue. This point can be illustrated by contrasting two governments: one (say, the central government) raises its revenue from progressive income taxation and the other (say, a state government) from sales tax. In a period of high inflation accompanied by correspondingly high increases in money incomes with little growth in output, the central government would experience high and automatic growth in its tax revenue without having to increase the rate of tax or broaden the tax base while the state's revenue would remain static. The basic idea in correcting the VFI is that 'government at each level can command the financial resources necessary for them to carry out their expenditure responsibilities'.

Vertical transfers should be fixed in such a way that SNGs should be able to meet their assigned expenditure functions. There are two options to reduce the revenue gaps through vertical transfers:

- **Option A** is to completely reduce the fiscal gaps of SNGs to zero. This may result in a wider fiscal gap at the central government level, which can be met through new borrowings. In this case, the vertical share should be made equivalent to the aggregate of subnational fiscal gap. There will not be any need for states to go for borrowing.

- **Option B** is to partially fill the fiscal gaps of federal and state governments keeping them at equal level, and allowing SNGs, especially state governments, to go for borrowing. This is a policy issue. In this case, the vertical share should be determined in such a way that the fiscal gaps at the national and subnational levels are equal. In this case, additional fiscal gaps will have to be filled up with borrowings by the central and state governments individually.

Under option B, a measure of VFI can be developed given the constitutional division of revenue and expenditure responsibilities. The positive difference between the central and state-level fiscal balances is as follows:

$$VFI = (R_c - E_c) - (R_s - E_s) \neq 0$$

where R_c and R_s denote revenues of the centre and states, respectively, before devolution and transfers and E_c and E_s are respective total expenditures.

As Bird and Tarasov (2002, p. 6) put it, if imbalance is the problem, balance is the solution. Therefore, the transfer needed from the centre to states should be such that VFI = 0. Let T be such transfers that

$$(R_c - E_c) - T = (R_s - E_s) + T.$$

Therefore, the required amount of transfers to the states is

$$T = [(R_c - E_c) - (R_s - E_s)]/2.$$

A part of the VFI is a policy issue over the desired degree of dependence of SNGs on the federal government. As and when the VFI policy changes, the part of the VFI that is consciously built can be corrected to a manageable level by reassignment of revenue and expenditure responsibilities between the two governments. (More details are given in Appendix B.)

Clearly, the policy option A is suitable in the initial stages of federal governance where states by themselves may not be in a position to borrow from the market and have to look up to the centre to help them out. The second policy option requires less transfers from the centre and gives more independence to the states to borrow to manage their fiscal gaps.

Vertical transfer options:
Revenue sharing versus grants

Basically, there are two broad channels of transfers from the federal government to the SNGs: tax sharing and grants. Once the vertical share is determined, a decision needs to be taken as to how much should be the tax sharing and how much should be the grants. The issue to be resolved is how to apportion the vertical transfer to be channelled through tax sharing and grants.

The merits of tax sharing are as follows: First, the transfer amount through tax sharing is in line with the productivity and growth of the central taxes, unlike grants which are usually not linked to tax revenue collections. Therefore, tax share being a fixed percentage of the tax revenue collections of the federal government would mean the SNGs can be assured of reasonably growing amount. Second, transfers through tax sharing could reduce uncertainty for the SNGs. SNGs can be fairly sure of the amount of revenue they are going to get and accordingly make suitable spending plans in advance. Third, although the federal government collects the taxes, the bases for the central taxes lie within the states. Therefore, state governments do get a feeling of re-claiming a portion of the central tax.

The disadvantages of tax sharing could be: First, the federal government might be lax in collecting taxes, being aware that the revenue needs to be shared. Second, transfers in the form of grants give flexibility to determine the form, method of transfers with and without certain conditions. Conditional grants, matching grants and so on give control over the expenditure management of the SNGs.

An issue pertaining to tax sharing that needs attention is whether the sharing should be from all the taxes collected by the federal government or should it be only from selective taxes. International experience shows that the tax sharing from all the tax revenues collected by the federal government is better than sharing specific tax revenues because experience shows that selective tax-wise sharing biases tax policy over time as federal governments invariably tend to focus more on those taxes which they do not have to share. This issue has been discussed in detail in the literature. For example, Bird and Smart (2002) conclude:

> On the whole, the best way to provide both some degree of stability to local governments and some degree of flexibility to the federal government is to establish a fixed percentage of all central taxes (or current revenues) to be transferred as is (more or less) done, for example, in Colombia and Argentina. Sharing specific national taxes is less desirable than sharing all national taxes because experience shows that it biases tax policy over time as federal governments invariably tend to increase more those taxes which they do not have to share. Sharing all taxes also ensures that the 'pain' as well as the 'gain' of cyclical variations in central revenue is shared. (p. 900)

In some countries, the tax base sharing is in vogue. Tax base sharing could occur when the federal and state governments tax the same base with different rates. This has become common especially in the case of value-added tax or GST as in Australia, Canada and India. For example, in Canada, Australia and, more recently, in India, the introduction of GST in July 2017 that provides for sharing of the GST base between the federal and state governments might require major adjustments in the tax devolution mechanism.

Horizontal Fiscal Imbalances

The horizontal tax shares are usually determined on the basis of a formula which is a weighted linear combination of selected criteria (suitably quantified). Three kinds of criteria are used for the purpose: (a) those representing need factors; (b) those representing the equity factors; and (c) those representing the fiscal effort and fiscal management factors. Usually, certain proxy variables are selected as representing each of these basic criteria, and the revenue share of the lower tier government is determined as

$$S_i = \sum_{j=1}^{n} w_i X_{ij} \cdots j = 1 \text{ to } n \text{ states,}$$

where S_i are the shares of the ith states/SNGs; X_i are the selected criteria variables suitably proxied; and w_i are the appropriate weights.

It is important to analyse the factors that cause the fiscal gap. Differences in the fiscal gap can be partly attributable to structural differences among the states, leading to differential costs of providing public goods and services, and partly to differences in the effort in raising the revenues. Each of the criteria is to be represented by one or more proxies depending upon the available data and converted to a relative index. The important drawbacks of this method are the arbitrariness in identifying the factors, difficulties in choosing the right proxies and quantifying them, and objectively assigning the weights before combining them into a composite index. Utmost caution is needed as the resultant share pattern could be highly sensitive to even small alteration in quantifying the factors.

A more refined procedure could be to express the fiscal gap as a function of all possible factors and estimate the function through regression method on cross-section or panel data as suggested by Sarma (1997). This has been explained in more detail in Appendix C.

The advantage of this method is, first, that it is possible to objectively identify relevant factors or their proxies. For example, if variations in urbanization (measured as a share of the urban population in total) are not relevant for variations in the fiscal gap, its regression coefficient tends to become statistically insignificant. If, on the other hand, if they are responsible for variations in the fiscal gap, then the regression coefficient will be statistically significant. The final regression will contain only be those factors which are significant, implying that those factors are responsible for the size of the fiscal gap. Of course, caution needs to be exercised in properly identifying the fiscal gap, identifying the factors, specifying and quantifying the proxies and estimating the regression. An important advantage of this method is that the weights of the factors emerge as regression coefficients. What is more, when a more refined weighted least-squares method is used, the resultant weights reflect the relative importance of the factors. The estimated fiscal gaps can be used to derive the horizontal shares for each state. The development of the method is given in Sarma (1997) in more detail. The regression (more specifically, the weighted least-squares regression) can be estimated based on the pooled cross-section and time-series data of the states. Estimated fiscal gaps of the states can indicate the size of the tax shares.

Options for Grants

The other broad channel of federal fiscal transfers is grants. International experience shows there are certain common features regarding grant systems. For example, virtually all federations have certain equalization grants. In addition, there are grants with conditions that induce the SNGs to meet certain national objectives. The following are the types of grants provided to SNGs in different countries. In some countries, the equalization objectives are combined with the tax sharing.

General-purpose unconditional bloc grants

In the case of unconditional grants, no restriction is imposed on the use of funds. However, experience with the general-purpose unconditional grants shows that these grants are prone to a phenomenon referred to as the 'flypaper effect'. It implies that grants to SNGs tend to result in more local spending than they would have, had the same transfers been made directly to local residents for political and bureaucratic reasons.

Equalization grants

Adapting the federal system with decentralization of expenditure and revenue raising invariably creates different fiscal capacities across regions, making it impossible to provide comparable levels of public services at comparable rates of taxation (Alm & Jorge Martinez, 2015). This is so because, to provide a given level of public goods and services, different states require different amounts of expenditure per capita for various reasons. Since tax sharing might not eliminate inequity, additional grants can help to further reduce horizontal inequity (Dogra, 2018).

There are two broad types of fiscal equalization: fiscal capacity equalization (FCE) and horizontal equity equalization (HEE). FCE is the traditional interpretation, widely used in Canada, Australia, Germany and Switzerland. This model calls for transfers from states with high per capita income and low per capita needs to those of opposite characteristics. HEE is an alternative view which seeks to apply the rule of horizontal equity (equal treatment of individuals in equal positions) across the fiscal operation of states and does so on a nationwide basis. The fiscal treatment given by lower level jurisdictions should be the same for individuals in equal positions, independent of the jurisdiction in which they reside. Usually, FCE grants are easier to determine and are more popular. Across the Organisation for Economic Cooperation and Development (OECD) countries, fiscal equalization transfers average around 2.5 per cent of GDP, 5 per cent of general government spending and 50 per cent of intergovernmental grants (OECD, 2004).

In Canada, as a federal system of government, there is also a commitment to fiscal equity within the Canadian economic union (Government of Canada, 2017). In Nepal, the new constitution provides for the distribution of fiscal equalization grants to the state and local governments, on the basis of two main criteria: expenditure need and revenue capacity (Government of Nepal, 2015, p. Art 60(4) and (5)). To some extent, the formula-based tax sharing can achieve the same objective. Yet, the fiscal equalization grant should aim at further reducing the horizontal imbalances in the administrative and other costs.

Conditional/Specific-purpose grants

Conditional grants are specific-purpose grants or categorical grants, wherein the federal government specifies the purpose for which the recipient local body can use the funds. Conditional grants can be matching or non-matching. In the case of conditional matching grant, the federal government asks local bodies to match certain portion of the expenses on specific programmes as a condition to receive the grant.

Matching grants

Certain grants may incorporate matching provisions—requiring grant recipients to finance a specified percentage of expenditures using their own resources. Matching grants differ from permanent public transfers, such as subsidies for inputs and services or safety nets as well as equalization grant. Matching requirement encourages greater scrutiny and local ownership of grant-financed expenditures and is helpful in ensuring that the grantor has some control over the costs of the transfer programme.

Special grants

Special-purpose grants are project based relating to supply of basic services such as health education, drinking water and so on. A reason for the use of special grant is to promote and consolidate the relation between the federation province and local level and encourage to work commonly with proper coexistence and coordinated way for national and subnational interest.

Performance-based grants

Another category of grants that can be useful are the performance-based grants (PBGs). PBGs can be used towards providing SNGs with tangible incentives to improve their overall institutional, organizational and functional performance, thus making the grant more effective, efficient and responsive as a strategy for the delivery of public goods and services. By linking the level of funding that SNGs receive in the form of fiscal transfers to their performance, such grants can provide incentives to improve their activities such as revenue collection, planning, budget execution, accountability, financial management and good governance in general.

In countries such as India, PBGs take the form of incentives under the FRBM system. Under this, states are required to keep the fiscal deficit and revenue deficit under certain limits, failing which they attract certain penalty, which is then distributed among those states that manage the deficits within limits. There could be other types of PBGs.

The minimum conditions and performance measurement (MCPM) grants

MCPM is a performance-based system providing incentives to improve local governance, financial management, participation, revenue mobilization, planning, and budgeting, service delivery, among others. In Nepal, the government believes that MCPM system has helped promote accountability at the local level and ensure basic local service delivery.

MCPM grants are based on an objective evaluation of local bodies and a measuring tool to assess their accountability, transparency and responsiveness.

Capital grants

Federal governments have two reasons to be interested in what state and local governments do in financing infrastructure. First, some local infrastructure projects may involve significant externalities; second, some such projects may constitute essential elements of national development programmes; and third, some of the capital projects may be part of the overall national development plans and therefore need federal government interventions and plan-related grants.

ANALYSIS OF THE INDIAN EXPERIENCE

In India, Article 246 of the Constitution divides the lawmaking powers under three lists—the Union List (List I), the State List (List II) and the Concurrent List (List III)—each assigning expenditure responsibilities and revenue sources of respective governments. As regards revenue sources, most broad-based taxes have been assigned to the centre, and among the taxes assigned to the states, only the tax on the sale and purchase of goods has been significant for state revenues. The centre has also been assigned all residual tax powers. The central government has the power to collect tax and non-tax revenues to the extent of 68–70 per cent of the total combined revenue collections. However, the states undertake nearly 67 per cent of the expenditure functions. Thus, the required extent of transfers would be about 34 per cent on average.

In India, fiscal transfers are essentially of three types: from current revenues as determined by the Finance Commission (FC), capital transfers for financing investment by the erstwhile Planning Commission (PC) and transfers under centrally sponsored schemes (CSS).

The FC transfer formulae in India appear to follow an incremental approach. The objective of successive FCs seems to increase the share of the states, albeit marginally. There is no evidence of any scientific derivation of the share. An important improvement has been the combining of all the central taxes for revenue sharing as recommended by the Tenth Finance Commission (10FC), excluding cesses and surcharges. The aggregate share of states in the net proceeds of all union taxes and duties, excluding surcharge, cesses and the cost of collection during the last two decades has fluctuated between 26 and 30 per cent (Table 3.3).

Vertical Sharing Issues to Be Resolved

Some issues pertaining to the vertical revenue sharing between the central and state governments that remain to be solved are as follows:

1. For example, it has been argued that the power to levy surcharges, instead of meeting any emergent requirements of a specific nature, is used as a normal source of revenue.
2. Similarly, although there is no explicit mention of services in the Seventh Schedule, taking cue from entry 97 that the central government to levy taxes on the residual items, the central government has been levying taxes on services under this entry. The

introduction of the GST to some extent solved the problem of sharing the service tax proceeds.

3. Further, the non-tax revenue is not sharable. Hence, the union government is now better equipped, financially, to meet with its expenses, and therefore there is a scope for higher devolution of union taxes to the states.

Issues Pertaining to Horizontal Sharing

Intergovernmental transfers are also needed to reduce possible inequalities across the SNGs with respect to their revenue capacities and unit costs of providing public goods and services. With regard to the horizontal revenue sharing, however, not much attention seems to have been paid.

1. One aspect that remains a source of controversy is the near-subjective use of the criteria determining the horizontal shares and arbitrary assignment of weights to them.
2. Further, the proxying and quantification of the criteria such as the population, the poverty and economic backwardness used have been sources of controversy.
3. Even if one is in broad agreement with the selected criteria for horizontal transfers, the assignment of weights to these factors still poses a problem. The weights assigned by the FCs do not seem to flow from any comprehensive theoretical framework.
4. Of late, the formula used for the purpose tends to be more complex and less transparent, the specification of the criteria subjective and the exact form of the criteria incomprehensible.

NEED FOR REVAMPING

There is, thus, a need for fundamental revamping of the federal fiscal-sharing system. Over the last two decades, the Indian economy has been experiencing significant growth along with structural transformation necessitating vital economic reforms. To some extent, realizing this fact the FC is being increasingly entrusted with many other tasks including that of overall macroeconomic and fiscal management of the country. Instead of such cosmetic changes as in the terms of reference (ToR), it is time for fundamental institutional changes in the form and working of the Finance Commission.

Three important milestones in the economic reforms that can have deep impact on the federal fiscal relations and therefore calling for revamping of the relevant institutions are the economic liberalization in 1991, the abolition of PC and setting up of NITI Aayog in 2014 and the introduction of GST in 2015.

The Economic Liberalization, 1991

The changeover to a more liberalized and open economy in 1991 involved designing and sequencing of the reforms and redefining the governmental role. In the new situation, the governments at the central, state and local levels need to shift their focus from direct participation in production and distribution activities to strengthening the regulatory mechanism. It, in turn, has necessitated relatively more active participation of the sub-central governments in the regulatory setup than during the earlier era. This is because the market regulation is more effective when implemented at decentralized levels. At the same time, the SNGs will have to continue to provide quasi-public goods.

NITI Aayog

In May 2014, the Government of India abolished the PC and instituted the NITI Aayog. The main idea for this step appears to be to strengthen the role of the states in the process of economic development.

Goods and Service Taxation

An important milestone in the Indian economy is the introduction of GST. India has been making efforts towards transforming its indirect tax system into a full-fledged VAT system in line with the worldwide trends. However, being a federal country where the constituent states enjoy independent fiscal powers, countrywide tax system reform involves coordinated and harmonized changes across the country to minimize the likely distortions in the centre–state and interstate economic relations. The introduction of GST required the states to surrender their power to tax sales, which has been their most important revenue source. This would compel them to depend more on federal fiscal tax-sharing arrangements. Although the loss in revenue of the states due to introduction of GST is promised to be compensated by the centre (as provided for in the GST Bill) for some time, yet, it does not make good a state's loss of the political right to fix its own tax rates. The states will have no power to decide what rates to impose on which goods, including luxuries and necessities.

Thus, with the tax powers of states severely limited, fiscal decentralization would be seriously undermined. Further, if the revenue is collected by the states but pooled and distributed through a revenue-sharing formula, there would be little incentive for the states to take the responsibility for administering it unless the distribution is made largely based on collection. The state governments will be left with negligible control over funds for the working of their states and will be dependent on the centre for means to fund disasters and welfare programmes. In the light of the introduction of GST and the possible increase in the states' dependence on the centre, the sharing responsibility of the FC increases. This would call for reviewing the sharing formulae, making it less arbitrary and more acceptable.

Expanding FC Responsibilities

Further, it can be observed that over time, there has been steady widening of the commission's mandate and the change in the ToR. Of late, the FC has been entrusted with many tasks of macroeconomic and fiscal management. Besides the macroeconomic management, it deals with issues such as calamity relief to states, need for ensuring reasonable returns on investments in power, transport and industrial enterprises (Government of India, 1988). More notably, the last four commissions were required to go into the fiscal management aspects more deeply.

Permanent Finance Commission

An aspect that has received persistent attention is whether the FC should be a permanent body like the PC or continue to be in the present form. The functioning of the FCs suffers from two major handicaps. The first is the absence of a permanent secretariat with cells for collection and maintenance of databases and for undertaking research studies on issues coming within the purview of the commissions. The second is lack of mechanism to keep a vigil on the states' performances round the year.

TOWARDS RATIONALIZATION OF THE FEDERAL FISCAL SYSTEM

The main duty of the FC relates to the sharing of central taxes under Article 270 and determination of grants for the states as provided for under Article 275. Over time, the principles and methods adopted have undergone substantial changes and rightly so in keeping with the changing economic structure and policy environment. However, there is a need to bring more fundamental changes in the approach to make it more objective and scientific.

VFI Measurement

The measure of VFI should be such that it preserves the basic idea that 'government at each level can command the financial resources necessary for them to carry out their expenditure responsibilities'. Given the constitutional division of revenue and expenditure responsibilities, a measure of VFI can be defined as the positive difference between the central and state-level fiscal balance. The suggestions for better management of fiscal sharing are as follows.

1. Employ scientific methods to derive the optimal vertical transfers to the states.
2. Surcharges/cesses should be treated as normal source of central tax revenue and included in the divisible pool. Various commissions have observed that surcharges/cesses should not be levied by the centre except to meet emergent requirements only for limited

periods but still the centre raises revenue through this measure for longer periods.

3. A minimum guaranteed devolution of central taxes from the centre to the states should be fixed to restore predictability in the devolution of share of central taxes to the states and provide necessary stability in fiscal management of the states.

Horizontal Sharing

As regards the horizontal sharing, the approach adopted so far reflects some inherent confusion: whether and to what extent states' efficiency should be rewarded, to what extent equity should be built, and to what extent the state-specific factors and circumstances should be taken into account while assessing the fiscal management of the states and so on.

It is only fair that the criteria and the weights for horizontal distribution should be related to the basic economic motivations of the federating units for coming together. To be more specific, federal fiscal efficiency requires offsetting of the inequity among the federating units (hereafter referred to as states) with respect to the net marginal benefit due to federating (NMBF). The NMBF of each federating unit can be understood as the difference between the marginal fiscal benefit and marginal fiscal costs of federation (Breton, 1965; Gramlich, 1987; Rao & Chelliah, 1991). The fiscal costs to a state for agreeing to be in the federation are in terms of tax powers and revenue forgone, while the fiscal benefits are the gains in terms of increases in the government revenues (owing to possible rise in the tax base due to lower trade barriers across the states and so on), and increased supply, and/or lower unit costs, of providing the public goods.

Operationalization of this principle requires, as a first step, the measurement and comparison of the NMBF of each state which, in a way, is likely to be reflected in its own revenue—total expenditure gap (hereafter referred as 'fiscal gap').

Make FC a Permanent Body

As a permanent body, the role and powers of the FC need to be specified more carefully. The permanent FC can be expected to be the country's macroeconomic manager, as an apex instrument body to monitor the economy of the country as well as of the states and local bodies, and as the think tank for the design of the important economic policies.

Revamp the Taxing Powers of the Centre and States

An important question is whether a permanent commission will be able to inspire the states to put in a little more effort to mobilize resources. A permanent commission can take up these matters with the states, and make them implement reforms such as the tax reforms and GST. The GST Council will be part of the FC.

Merge All Economic Advisory Councils with the FC

The FC should be an apex body advising the finance ministry with sufficient fiscal management plan. Entrust it with the duty of not only making recommendations for revenue sharing but also closely monitoring it, and with the overall macroeconomic management.

SUMMARY OF RECOMMENDATIONS

The art of federalism lies in designing institutions with appropriate assignment of powers and functions among different orders of government and rules to regulate their relationship especially in the fiscal arena that can strike the right balance among different objectives and resolve tensions. According to many, the Indian federal system, though decentralized, is quasi-federal at best and does not allow enough room for the states to function freely. The restricted decentralization has been the problem of the Indian economy and a major factor responsible for its stunted growth. In China, on the other hand, growth has been propelled greatly by the 'market preserving federalism' practised there, allowing autonomy to provinces in running their economies.

This study recommends revamping of the federal fiscal transfer system in India. Basically, to make the fiscal transfers more acceptable and to consider the changing structure of economic and fiscal governance, our major recommendations are as given below.

Recommendation 1: Permanent Finance Commission

Make the FC permanent. The setting up of the FC at five-year intervals has been leading to a variety of immature acts.

Recommendation 2: Converge the Relevant Bodies into the Finance Commission

Merge all the bodies concerned with economic and fiscal policy design, such as the Economic Advisory Council to the Prime Minister (PMEAC) and NITI Aayog, with the FC. This will reduce possible duplication, conflicts and coordination problems.

Recommendation 3: Extended ToR and Expanded Membership

The FC will have expanded membership and expanded ToR. It will also take care of macroeconomic planning and management. There has already been substantial diversification in the ToR given to the FC. The additional ToR include the tax design, macroeconomic stabilization, fiscal monitoring, public debt management and dealing with natural calamities and so on.

Recommendation 4: Involve the National Development Council for States Cooperation

Before submitting the quinquennial report to the President as required and deliberated in the Parliament, the FC will present it to the National Development Council (NDC) with proper representation from the states and make it acceptable. This will reduce the possible dissent from the states and make the system closer to cooperative federalism.

Recommendation 5: Federal Fiscal Sharing Should Be from All Revenues of Centre

Federal fiscal sharing should be from all the revenues of the central government and not just the tax revenues alone. This will include not only the taxes, but also the surcharges and cesses, as also the non-tax revenues of the central government. This will eliminate the room for allegations of biases in raising the revenues by the centre.

Recommendation 6: Transfer Share (Revenue Share + Grants) to Be Consensus-Based

The total transfers (tax devolution + grants) from the centre to the states can be fixed on the basis of consensus, for example, 50 per cent of the centre's total revenues.

Recommendation 7: Vertical Sharing Choices

Out of the total share of 50 per cent, part of it should be in the form of revenue sharing or in the form of grants. Vertical sharing could have two alternative aims: (a) Vertical share equals the total sum of normative fiscal gaps of the states. This may reduce the need for borrowing of the states but widen the fiscal gap of the central government, thereby compelling it for higher borrowings. (b) Vertical transfer is such that it will equalize the sum total of fiscal gap of the states to that of the central government. However, this arrangement might call for allowing the states to go for new borrowings in case of the fiscal gap being a deficit.

Recommendation 8: Horizontal Sharing to Be More Scientific and Objective

The horizontal revenue sharing should be based on objective formulae such as the method described in this book and eliminate the arbitrary selection of the criteria, arbitrary proxying of the criteria and arbitrary assignment of weights in the linear formula. It is advisable that the criteria should be relevant and capable of affecting the fiscal gaps of the states. If a particular criterion is not relevant to the fiscal gap, then to that extent the transfers on that basis are not going to improve the fiscal gap. The criteria can be of three types: capacity criteria, effort criteria and need criteria. The horizontal share determination should have a built-in reward system to encourage better fiscal management. Gross state domestic product (GSDP) and population are the two most important criteria that influence the fiscal gaps at the states' level. The higher the GSDP, higher would be the revenue generation that would reduce the fiscal gap, while higher population would raise the need for more expenditure, thereby widening the fiscal gap. The resultant horizontal share will be higher for the states with large populations and smaller for the states with high GSDP. While this pattern might achieve the equity objective, it will have negative impact on the tax effort and better fiscal management. Therefore, proper care is needed in fine-tuning the horizontal sharing methods.

Recommendation 9: Grants Should Reflect Broader Economic Policies

The remaining quantum of transfers will be by way of grants. Thus, if the total transfers are fixed at 50 per cent of the central government, the total quantum of grants would be the remaining amount left over after the revenue sharing. The grants could be unconditional, conditional, specific-purpose and post-devolution deficit grants. The grant allocation pattern is a policy choice.

Recommendation 10: Incentivize the Grants

Part of the grants can be used to incentivize better fiscal management of the SNG.

Recommendation 11: Capital Grants Should Be Project by Project based on Viability

Capital grants should be more on the basis of project management studies rather than on equity basis. The financing of capital projects will be on the lines of project viability studies.

CONCLUDING REMARKS

Notwithstanding certain weaknesses, the system of intergovernmental fiscal arrangements in India has served well for over 50 years. It has achieved a significant equalization over the years, instituted a workable system of resolving the outstanding issues between the centre and the states and among the states, and adjusted to the changing requirements and thus has contributed to achieving a degree of cohesiveness in a large and diverse country. Thus, it is increasingly being realized that there is no alternative but to reform the fiscal institutions of the federal system and the task needs to be faced upfront by the country. Smooth functioning of a fast globalizing world economy presupposes a stable, secure and predictable environment for economic agents to operate.

Federal Form of Governance

Federal form of governance involves multilayer governance based upon democratic rules and institutions in which the power to govern is shared between national and provincial/state governments. Each level of government enjoys complete independence in some areas and shares powers in other areas. It is well recognized that federal form of governance is best suited for decentralized governance of countries with democratic characteristics, especially appropriate for a society with a vastly diverse economic and cultural background (Oates W., 1999). A federal system is preferred to a unitary system of governance not only for political and administrative reasons but also for economic benefits. Alexis de Tocqueville observed more than a century ago,

> The federal system was created with the intention of combining the different advantages which result from the magnitude and the littleness of nations. (Tocqueville, 1838)

The main advantage of being a large nation is that it can reap the economies of scale. However, governance of a large nation may not be able to satisfy the specific local needs. It is only the small nations that can fulfil the local needs much better. Particularly in a democracy, local needs are better satisfied by provincial governments as they are closer to local populations.

> Federal governance promotes efficiency, both economic and political. Economic efficiency is advanced by the division of governmental functions among different levels depending on their comparative advantage. Assignment of matters that concern the nation, or where there are externalities or large economies of scale to the government at the centre, combined with decentralization of responsibility to provide services that benefit smaller segments of the country or the community to lower level

governments, promotes efficiency in the allocation of resources in the economy. What is more, in a federal polity the economy benefits from the operation of a common market facilitated by free flow of goods, services and factors of production within the country. (Bagchi, 2001, pp. 1–2)

Thus, there are not only political reasons but also powerful economic arguments for preferring a federal system to unitary system of governance. In recent years, it is the economic benefits of federalism that is drawing sovereign nations to join together in economic union even while not surrendering their independence. The European Union is a prime example.

More specifically, the basic advantages of adopting federal form of governance are as follows:

1. *Proximity advantage:* In a federation, every province or state[1] has its own social, political and economic problems. Provincial governments that are in the proximity to the people are in a better position to understand these problems and offer solutions. For example, traffic congestion in Mumbai, India, is a problem that can be best solved by the Maharashtra government keeping local factors in mind, rather than by somebody living in New Delhi.
2. *Ethnic and cultural diversity needs:* Citizens of various provinces may have different aspirations and ethnicity, and follow different cultures. The central government can sometimes overlook these local differences and adopt policies that cater to the needs and tastes of the nation's majority. This is where the regional government steps in. While formulating policies, local needs, tastes and opinions are given due consideration by the state governments that safeguards the aspirations of the minorities too.
3. *Freedom to adopt local specific policies:* In a federation, provincial governments have the freedom to adopt policies which may not be followed nationally or by any other province. For example, same-sex marriages were not recognized by the federal government of

---

[1] In this study, the terms 'province' and 'state' are used as synonyms. In many federal countries, provincial governments are referred as state governments.

the United States until 2015, but were given legal status within the states of Connecticut, Iowa, Vermont and Massachusetts.[2]

4. *Facilitates division of work between different levels of government*: Division of work between the central and the provincial governments leads to optimum utilization of resources. The central government can concentrate more on international affairs and defence of the country, while the provincial government can cater to the local needs such as education and health.

5. *Room for different approaches*: Federalism has room for innovation and experimentation. Two provincial governments can have two different approaches to bring reforms in any area of public domain, be it taxation or education. The comparison of the results of these policies can give a clear idea of which policy is better, and thus can be adopted in the future.

These are some of the advantages of adopting federal form. At the same time, sharing of power between the centre and the states includes some disadvantages too.

1. *Overlapping of work and subsequent confusion*: Sometimes there can be overlapping of work and subsequent confusion regarding who is responsible for what. For example, when cyclone Nilam hit the South Indian region in 2012, there was delay in the rescue work as there was confusion between the state governments and the central government as to who is responsible for which type of disaster management work. This resulted in the loss of many lives.

2. *Expensive*: The federal system of government is very expensive as more people are elected to office, at both the state and the centre, than necessary. Thus, it is often said that only rich countries can afford it. Too many elected representatives with overlapping roles may also lead to corruption.

3. *Unnecessary competition between different states*: Federalism leads to unnecessary competition between different regions. There can be

---

[2] It was only after 26 June 2015, when the US Supreme Court struck down all state bans on same-sex marriages, it was legalized in all the 50 states of the USA.

a rebellion by a regional government against the national government too. Both scenarios pose a threat to the countries' integrity.

4. *Enhance regional inequalities*: Federalism inadvertently promotes regional inequalities. Natural resources, industries, employment opportunities differ from region to region. Hence, earnings and wealth are unevenly distributed. Rich states offer more opportunities and benefits to its citizens than poor states can. Thus, the gap between rich and poor states widens.

5. *Provincial governments can become selfish*: Federalism can make the state governments selfish and concerned only about their own region's progress. They can formulate policies which might be detrimental to other regions. For example, pollution from a province which is promoting industrialization in a big way can affect another region which depends solely on agriculture and can cause crop damage.

Thus, it is understandable that there have been both pros and cons of federalism.

FEDERALISM: ORIGINS AND SPREAD

The origin of the federal form of governance in the modern world can be traced to the American Revolution. When American colonies declared their independence from Britain in 1776, they reacted against the British unitary system in which all political and economic power was concentrated in London. The British control on the colonial governments became a major source of friction that eventually led to the American Revolution, by creating the Articles of Confederation[3] that gave virtually all powers to the states of America. The framers at the constitutional convention tried to balance the perceived domination of the unitary system with the chaos created by the confederal system by outlining a hybrid federal system in the Constitution. Federalism,

---

[3] The Articles of Confederation and Perpetual Union was an agreement among the 13 original states of the USA that served as its first constitution, which eventually evolved into the present federal government by 4 March 1789.

then, became a major building block for preserving freedom while still maintaining order in the new nation.

At present, there are roughly 25 federal countries in the world, together accounting for over 40 per cent of the world population (Form of Federations, 2019). They include some of the largest and most complex democracies—India, the United States, Brazil, Germany, Mexico, Somalia, Nigeria, Russia, Australia, Argentina, Austria, Iraq, Sudan, South Sudan, Bolivarian Republic and so on. Other countries, such as the Philippines, that are contemplating a change in the governing set-up of the nation are also seriously tending towards adopting the federal form.

DIVISION OF POWERS AND FISCAL IMBALANCES

Federal governance involves sharing of revenue and expenditure functions among different layers of government to safeguard the unity in diversity character. Each government entity has responsibilities over the matters that are best addressed at that level of government. By nature, the constituent provinces have relatively large constitutionally assigned spending responsibilities but fewer own-revenue sources while the reverse is true at the federal or central government level. This is so because efficiency requires the federal government to collect revenues and SNGs to take care of more expenditure functions. However, this arrangement invariably leads to fiscal inequity or fiscal imbalances—vertical and horizontal. 'The art of federalism lies in designing institutions with appropriate assignment of powers and functions among different orders of government and rules to regulate their relationship especially in the fiscal arena that can strike the right balance among different objectives and resolve tensions' (Bagchi, 2001). Thus, the main problem with adopting the federal form of government is the possible fiscal inequity or fiscal imbalance that may arise, on the one hand, between the federal government and the constituent provincial governments and among the provincial governments themselves, on the other hand.

Another consequence of the assignments in a federation is the mismatch between the ability to raise revenues and the expenditure needs of different governmental units. Perfect correspondence between revenue capacities and expenditure needs is impossible to achieve even under the most efficient assignments. This is because an efficient tax assignment need not match an efficient expenditure assignment. Such fiscal imbalance may be vertical—between different levels of government, or horizontal—among different jurisdictions within a level. Vertical fiscal imbalance arises because the central government has certain inherent advantages in raising revenues and the state governments, in spending. However, centralizing revenues and decentralizing expenditure could have adverse effects on incentives, accountability and sub-central fiscal autonomy. The prevailing vertical fiscal imbalance essentially represents the trade-off between the gains from efficient assignment of revenues and expenditures (which necessarily results in the imbalances) and losses from delinking revenue and expenditure decisions. Horizontal imbalances occur when the ability to raise revenues or the unit cost of providing public services vary widely among different jurisdictions. This can cause significant differences in the standard of public services provided unless those with lower ability to raise revenue or higher unit cost of public services levy taxes at higher rates. The persistence of horizontal fiscal imbalance can result in unequal spread of physical and social infrastructure and thereby accentuate inter-state inequalities.' (Rao & Sen, 1995, p. 9)

The unabated persistence of the fiscal imbalances might eventually lead to uneven growth and macroeconomic instability. Therefore, revenue and expenditure function asymmetry needs to be balanced. Countries that adopted the federal system differ in dealing with the problem and ways adopted to safeguard the fiscal balances. In countries such as India, this is attempted through a third-party institution, namely, the FC.

Despite these, the imbalances might not be entirely mitigated basically due to methodological errors, unwanted biases, and misplaced priorities. Sometimes, steps taken to remove the imbalances might even worsen the imbalances and regional inequity. Not only that, very often economic reforms and policies adopted might further worsen the federal fiscal imbalances. Therefore, the federal fiscal management needs to be alert and take into account such influences. A well-designed and well-functioning system of federal governance plays a key role in promoting the stability and prosperity of nations as established by the leading federations of the world—the United States,

Canada, Australia and Switzerland. On the other hand, 'unless carefully crafted, federal systems do not endure, as evidenced by the disintegration of many of the federal formations in the last century, such as Soviet Russia, Yugoslavia, Czechoslovakia, Rhodesia, and Nyasaland' (Watts, 1999). The fiscal management agencies and authorities need to adopt dynamic mechanisms to reduce the imbalances and safeguard the macroeconomic stability.

FEDERAL FISCAL TRANSFERS

Countries that adopt the federal form of government essentially seek to reduce the fiscal inequity and make the SNGs to be fiscally independent as much as possible. To some extent, this objective is achieved by dividing and specifying the fiscal powers and responsibilities within the constitution itself in such a way that the fiscal dependence is minimized or reduced. However, experience shows that there may remain some degree of fiscal inequity that needs to be reduced by means of federal fiscal transfers. The federal fiscal transfers take several forms and their adaptation differs among countries in terms of nomenclature and methods to suit their socio-economic needs. (For a detailed description of the country experiences, see Appendix A.)

Among the federal systems in the world, the federal fiscal transfers are managed in three alternative ways: (a) through constitutional means, (b) through negotiations between the different levels of governments and (c) by creating a dedicated institutional system for the purpose. The widely preferred alternative seems to be the third one. It has been the practice to provide institutional mechanisms for periodic fine-tuning of the sharing of the revenue resources of the country among different levels of government. The need arises for two reasons: first, for revising the transfer arrangements to catch up with the changing contours of the economic structure of the country; and second, to maintain equity—vertical between the federal and SNGs and horizontal across the SNGs. These transfers aim not only at reducing the VFIs and HFIs but also to allow restructuring of public finances to restore budgetary balances with a view to achieving macroeconomic stability as also certain socio-economic objectives. Thus, it has become a custom for federal countries to provide for creating autonomous body/bodies to study and recommend such periodic adjustments.

Depending upon the purpose and objective, the transfers can take several forms: tax revenue sharing, tax assignments, grants—general and specific purpose—loans and reliefs. The justifications as also the procedures of disbursement differ. Even with all such institutional arrangements, the federal fiscal management is not without snags and hitches.

INDIA IS A CASE IN POINT

Federal governance is the most suitable for India because of huge diversities in the society—geographical, cultural, economic, religious, ethnic and linguistic. Rooted in the pre-Independence era itself, the federal fiscal system had evolved gradually with suitable institutional set-up (Appendix B). The institutional set-up meant for reducing the fiscal imbalances comprises the constitutional division of powers, the FC, the PC, now the NITI Aayog, and related bodies. The Constitution divides the functions between the federal and state governments and gives broad guidelines. Among these institutions, the FC and the PC, aimed at balanced development, played major roles. Apart from these two, the ministry of finance also influences the transfer system through macroeconomic policies and expenditure allocations.

OBJECTIVES

There are several thorny issues in the federal fiscal management and fiscal sharing mechanism in India, aggravated by other economic policy side effects such as the shift towards liberalization in 1991, the FRBM Act of 2003, the introduction of GST in 2017, the changes in the monetary policies and so on. In short, the economy has come a long way, and there have been major changes in the nature and structure of the economy. The federal fiscal institutional structure, therefore, needs fundamental revamping.

The overall purpose of this book is to derive and suggest suitable alterations in the federal fiscal sharing system in India, taking into account the possible changes in the structure of the economy and the potential revenue generation at different levels of government. The plan of the chapters is as follows:

Chapter 2 provides a theoretical background and starts with a discussion on the broad requirements of a federal fiscal system and methods to be adopted to achieve the fiscal balances and macroeconomic stability in general.

Chapter 3 reviews the evolution of the federal system in India and the experience so far of the operations and working of the federal fiscal institutions, namely, the FC, the PC, the line ministries and so on.

Chapter 4 makes an in-depth critical analysis of the methods and procedures adopted for the federal fiscal transfers and discusses issues that remained unsolved over the years. It also brings out the impact on the federal fiscal transfer system of the restructuring the economy and institutional changes brought in recent years.

Chapter 5 is devoted to providing certain guidelines for the restructuring of the federal fiscal transfer mechanism. It builds up a case for merging the policy advisory bodies and expanding the role of the FC to avoid overlapping approaches and to rationalize the methods. Although considerable work has already been done in this respect, this book consolidates the scattered ideas into one effort.

Chapter 6 describes in detail how the fiscal imbalances, the vertical and the horizontal, can be reduced and how the fiscal transfers can be designed using more rational methods.

Chapter 7 summarizes the discussion and consolidates into certain recommendations for the restructuring of the federal fiscal system in India.

Federal Fiscal System

Broad Requirements

The federal form of governance and the fiscal transfer system vary widely among nations (see Appendix A for a brief summary of selected country experiences). However, there are various choices involved in adopting the federal form of governance.

CHOICES INVOLVED

The adaptation and operationalization of the federal system of governance involve certain basic choices.

1. *Nature and degree of the federal system:* The choice of the number of layers of governments, the degree of centralization, the direction of periodic adjustment transfers—from higher level of government to lower level or from lower level to higher level;
2. *Basic guidelines for resource sharing to be incorporated into the Constitution:* Allocation of taxing and expenditure powers and allocation of tax revenues among the governments;
3. *Extent and nature of periodic transfers:* Whether they should be in the form of revenue transfers or capital transfers; and whether they should be formula-based transfers or non-formula-based transfers such as grants;
4. *Nature of the formula:* If the transfers are to be formula based, then what should be the nature of the formula, what should be the criteria and how should the weights be determined;
5. To what extent the federal fiscal transfer mechanism should consider the socio-economic welfare objectives and equity objectives; and

6. To what extent the federal fiscal transfer mechanism should go hand in hand with the overall macroeconomic management.

THE NATURE OF THE FEDERAL SYSTEM

The foremost step required for adopting the federal form of governance is to determine the number of layers of governance. Globally, the consensus seems to have on three levels of governments: federal, provincial and local. The degree of centralization varies widely.

THE DIVISION OF POWERS

Constitutional division of revenue and expenditure powers between national and SNGs is one of the fundamental requirements for adopting the federal form.

> The division of power, vertically between different levels of government, and horizontally among different jurisdictions within each level, is the starting point for the examination of efficiency in the delivery of public services. ...The mapping of benefits across jurisdictions cannot be perfect; overlapping tax powers can create problems of fiscal disharmony and create incentive for free-riding; nor can there be asymmetry between the assignment of functions and sources of finance at each governmental level. All these problems of fiscal spillovers, disharmony and imbalances have their roots in assignments and, therefore, this issue warrants a careful analysis. (Rao & Singh, 2008, p. 2)

It is a tough task as resources are limited and endowed unevenly across the regions, and constitutional redistribution is not always acceptable. It is important that each of the governments should be provided with sources of raising adequate revenues to discharge the functions entrusted to it. Adequacy of financial independence of SNGs is the backbone of the federal form of governance.

An important consideration for the division of fiscal powers—vertical or horizontal—is the management of 'spillover effects'.[1] As per

---

[1] Government provides public goods and services. By definition, public goods and services have spillover effects, meaning that the benefit or harm of the provision

this theory, public goods and services have spillover effects with different 'spans'—local, provincial, regional, national and international. Ideally, fiscal powers relating to public goods with larger spans of spillover effects should be assigned to higher levels of governments. For example, defence is a public good with spillovers spanning the entire nation, and so it is to be under the central or national government. On the other hand, a park set-up in a locality will have smaller spillovers reaching only the public in that locality and the neighbouring localities. In this case, it is appropriate to assign the maintenance function to a local body. However, where there are overlapping spillovers across certain provinces, there is a need for the higher-level government to concurrently manage the supply of public goods and services. Further, it is suggested in the literature that the assignment of expenditure functions should precede the division of revenue-raising powers so that the latter can be determined by the requirements of different spending agencies.

There are other considerations for allocating the fiscal powers and responsibilities among the three levels of governments. According to Wallace Oates: 'The primary responsibility for macroeconomic stabilization and redistribution of income and wealth should rest with the central government' (Oates, 1972, 1977, p. 3).

> It is difficult for subnational governments with smaller but open economies to pursue independent stabilization policies. They cannot be given the power to vary money supply and the effectiveness of fiscal policy for stabilization at the sub-central levels as the spillover of effective demand spreads to areas outside their jurisdictions. Similarly, potential mobility of economic agents places limits on the ability of sub-national governments to pursue serious redistributive policies. Vigorous redistribution by a sub-national authority can result in driving out the rich from, and inviting the poor into, its jurisdiction, which would be self-defeating. (Rao & Singh, 2008, p. 3)

Globally, the division of functions and responsibilities among the three layers of government is guided by the above theoretical considerations. In practice, however, the pattern varies from one federation

of public goods and services to one locality/state/nation might spread to other localities/states/nations.

to another depending upon the basic preference as to whether to have a centripetal federation or 'cooperative' federation. For example, India follows the centripetal federalism where the central government holds more powers than the states either directly or indirectly. In contrast, the United States is not a centripetal federation. Having been under the tyrannical rule of English kings, the framers of the US Constitution feared centralizing power within a single governmental institution. Therefore, when drafting their Constitution, they gave some powers exclusively to the national government, shared some powers with both the national and state governments and reserved some powers only for state governments.

NEED FOR INTERGOVERNMENTAL FISCAL TRANSFERS

The constitutional division of revenues and expenditures among different levels of government might imply fiscal imbalances that make the intergovernmental transfers inevitable. The inadequacy of resources to meet expenditure functions makes the SNGs dependent on the federal government. The central tax revenues need to be shared between the three levels of governments. In fact, in most developing countries, federal fiscal transfers are the dominant sources of revenues for SNGs. Central transfers finance 85 per cent of subnational expenditures in South Africa, 72 per cent of provincial and 85 per cent of local expenditures in Indonesia, 67–95 per cent of state local expenditures in Nigeria and 70–90 per cent of expenditures in Mexico. The design of these transfers is of critical importance for efficiency and equity of local public services provision and the fiscal health of SNGs.

NATURE OF FISCAL IMBALANCES AND METHODS OF ALLEVIATION

In federal systems, two types of fiscal imbalances can occur: VFI and HFI. When the fiscal imbalance occurs between two levels of government (such as centre and states, or states and local) it is called VFI. When the fiscal imbalance occurs between the governments at the same level, it is called HFI. This imbalance is also known as regional disparity. While HFI requires equalization transfers, VFI is a structural issue and thus needs to be corrected by reassignment of revenue and expenditure responsibilities between the national and SNGs.

In what follows, the theoretical underpinnings, the measurement of the two types of fiscal imbalances, the practices to reduce them will be discussed in detail.

VERTICAL FISCAL IMBALANCES

The difference between the relative revenue and spending responsibilities of the federal and provincial governments is reflective of VFI. It is the gap between own revenues and expenditures of each level of government. It is mostly a structural issue and might arise often by design. Generally, the expenditure responsibilities assigned to the SNGs would require a larger share of resources. The raising of taxes, however, must be largely centralized for efficiency and economic reasons. Thus, a large part of the VFI is by design. Among the established federal countries, Australia seems to have a higher vertical imbalance.[2]

VFI is justified on the basis of the following reasons. First, the central government functions are public goods with larger span of externalities ('spillovers') such that they serve the 'national' interests as opposed to the narrower regional interests. The functions like defence, border security and integrated planned macroeconomic development do require huge resources. Second, the central government needs to meet the equity objectives through the tax policy and expenditure policy. The horizontal fiscal equalization needs greater access to revenue sources. 'A centralized fiscal policy is tantamount to an insurance contract where the higher-level government promises to

[2] 'A chronic feature of Australian federalism, namely, a highly centralised revenue-raising system enabling the Commonwealth Government to raise nearly 80 per cent of the national tax revenue, and a fairly decentralised system of public outlays which are shared almost equally between the Commonwealth and the states. Consequently, financial transfers from the Commonwealth to the states are a major source of financing public outlays of the states, accounting for an average of 44 per cent of the outlays of the states and the Territories during the ten years to 1989–90' (Grewal, 1995).

even out income variations across regions that result from regionally asymmetrical shocks' (Spahn, 1995). Third, certain national taxes such as income tax and manufacturing tax require a uniform administration. Also, the centralized tax administration reduces scope for needless 'tax competition' among the SNGs.

At the same time, there are certain arguments for minimal VFI. First, there is the accountability argument. The fact that the central government collects most of the revenues, and provincial governments collect less but spend more, which requires vertical transfers from the centre to the provinces, may reduce the accountability of the provincial governments. Second, a large VFI makes the central government financially very powerful and the provinces to be weak. Moreover, it is observed that 'when centralized control is exercised through the vehicle of financial transfers instead of direct provision of services, the lines of responsibility for each level of government are blurred' (Grewal, 1975).

Apart from the intended VFI, there could be other undesired components of VFI caused by several factors, some of them are as follows:

1. The nature and extent of actual fiscal autonomy;
2. Conflicting or uncoordinated federal and state priorities (for example, education, agriculture, social welfare, infrastructure expenditures);
3. Shortcomings in the existing revenue-sharing arrangements; and
4. Political conflicts.

More than the tax revenue sharing, tax power sharing could also cause VFI. It depends upon the degree of discretionary change to tax rates or tax bases required for generating additional revenue. This point can be illustrated by contrasting two governments, one of which (say, the central government) raises its revenue from progressive income taxation and the other (say, a state government) from sales tax. In a period of high inflation accompanied by correspondingly high increases in money incomes with little growth in output, the central government would experience high and automatic growth in its tax revenue without having to increase the rate of tax or broaden the tax base while the state's revenue would remain static. The basic idea in correcting the VFI is that 'government at each level can command the financial resources necessary for them to carry out their expenditure responsibilities' (for more detailed discussion on VFI, see Appendix C).

The vertical transfers should be fixed in such a way that the SNGs should be able to meet their assigned expenditure functions. There are two options to reduce the revenue gaps through vertical transfers:

- **Option A** is to completely reduce the fiscal gaps of the SNGs to zero. This may result in a wider fiscal gap at the central government level, which can be met through new borrowings. In this case, the vertical share should be made equivalent to the aggregate of subnational fiscal gaps. There will not be any need for states to go for borrowing.
- **Option B** is to partially fill the fiscal gaps of the federal and state governments keeping them at equal level, and allowing the SNGs, especially the state governments, to go for borrowing. This is a policy issue. In this case, the vertical share should be determined in such a way that the fiscal gaps at the national and subnational levels are equal. In this case, additional fiscal gaps will have to be filled up by borrowings by both the central and state governments individually.

Under option B, a measure of VFI can be developed given the constitutional division of revenue and expenditure responsibilities. The positive difference between the central and state-level fiscal balance is as follows:

$$VFI = (R_c - E_c) - (R_s - E_s) \neq 0$$

where R_c and R_s denote revenues of centre and states respectively, before devolution and transfers and E_c and E_s are respective total expenditures.

As Bird and Tarasov (2002, p. 6) put, if imbalance is the problem, balance is the solution. Therefore, the transfer needed from the centre to states should be such that VFI = 0. Let T be such transfers so that

$$(R_c - E_c) - T = (R_s - E_s) + T.$$

Therefore, the required amount of transfers to the states is

$$T = [(R_c - E_c) - (R_s - E_s)]/2.$$

A part of the VFI is a policy issue over the desired degree of dependence of SNGs on the federal government. As and when the VFI policy changes, the part of the VFI that is consciously built can be corrected to a manageable level by reassignment of revenue and expenditure responsibilities between the two governments. (More details are given in Appendix B.)

Clearly, the policy option A is suitable in the initial stages of federal governance where states by themselves may not be in a position to borrow from the market and have to look up to the centre to help them out. Option B requires less transfers from the centre, gives more independence to the states to borrow to manage their fiscal gaps.

VERTICAL TRANSFER OPTIONS: REVENUE SHARING VERSUS GRANTS

Basically, there are two broad channels of transfers from the federal government to the SNGs: revenue sharing and grants. Once the vertical share is determined, a decision needs to be taken as to how much should be the revenue sharing and how much should be the grants. The issue to be resolved is how to apportion the vertical transfer to be channelled through these two ways.

The merits of revenue sharing are as follows. First, the transfer amount through revenue sharing is in line with the productivity and growth of the central revenue sources (tax and non-tax) unlike the grants which are usually not linked to revenue collections. Therefore, revenue share being a fixed percentage of the revenue collections of the federal government would mean the SNGs can be assured of a reasonably growing amount. Second, transfers through revenue sharing could reduce uncertainty for the SNGs. SNGs can be fairly sure of the amount of revenue they are going to receive and accordingly make suitable spending plans in advance. Third, although the federal government collects the revenues, the bases for the central taxes and non-taxes lie within the states. Therefore, state governments do get a feeling of reclaiming a portion of central collections.

The disadvantages of revenue sharing could be as follows. First, the federal government might be lax in collecting the taxes and non-taxes, being aware that the revenue needs to be shared. Second, transfers in the form of grants give flexibility to determine the form, method of transfers with and without certain conditions. Conditional grants, matching grants and so on give control over the expenditure management of the SNGs.

Tax Sharing: All Taxes versus Tax by Tax

An issue pertaining to revenue sharing that needs attention is whether the sharing should be from all the taxes and non-taxes collected by the federal government or should it be only from selective ones. International experience shows that the revenue sharing from all the revenues collected by the federal government is better than sharing specific tax revenues because experience shows that selective tax-wise sharing biases tax policy over time as federal governments invariably tend to focus more on those taxes and non-taxes which they do not have to share. This issue has been well discussed in the literature. For example, Bird and Smart conclude:

> On the whole, the best way to provide both some degree of stability to local governments and some degree of flexibility to the federal government is to establish a fixed percentage of all central taxes (or current revenues) to be transferred as is (more or less) done, for example, in Colombia and Argentina. Sharing specific national taxes is less desirable than sharing all national taxes because experience shows that it biases tax policy over time as federal governments invariably tend to increase more those taxes which they do not have to share. Sharing all taxes also ensures that the 'pain' as

well as the 'gain' of cyclical variations in central revenue is shared. (Bird & Smart, 2002, p. 900)

Tax Base Sharing

In some countries, the tax base sharing is in vogue. Tax base sharing could occur when the federal and state governments tax the same base with different rates. This has become common especially in the case of value-added tax or GST as in Australia, Canada and India. For example, in Canada, Australia and, more recently, India, the introduction of GST from July 2017 provides for sharing of the GST base between the federal and state governments. With this provision, the current arrangement regarding tax devolution may undergo changes with the introduction of the unified GST.

HORIZONTAL FISCAL IMBALANCES

Horizontal revenue shares are usually determined on the basis of a formula which is a weighted linear combination of selected criteria (suitably quantified). Three kinds of criteria are used for the purpose: (a) those representing need factors; (b) those representing the equity factors; and (c) those representing the fiscal effort and fiscal management factors. Usually, certain proxy variables are selected as representing each of these basic criteria, and the revenue share of the lower tier government is determined as follows:

$$S_i = \sum_{j=1}^{n} w_i X_{ij} \cdots j = 1 \text{ to } n \text{ states,}$$

where S_i is the share of the ith state/SNGs; X_i is the selected criterion variable suitably proxied; and w_i is the appropriate weight.

It is important to analyse factors that cause the fiscal gap. Differences in the fiscal gap can be partly attributable to structural differences among the states leading to differential costs of providing public goods and services, and partly to differences in the effort in raising the revenues. Some of these criteria used by the federations in the world, with brief justifications, are given in Table 2.1. Each of the criteria is to be represented by one or more proxies depending upon the available data and converted to a relative index.

An important drawback of this method is the arbitrariness in identifying the factors, difficulties in choosing the right proxies and quantifying them, and objectively assigning the weights before combining them into a composite index. Utmost caution is needed as the resultant share pattern could be highly sensitive to even small alteration in quantifying the factors.

A more refined procedure could be to express the fiscal gap as a function of all possible factors and estimate the function through regression method on cross-section or panel data as suggested by Sarma (1997). This has been explained in more detail in Appendix D.

The advantage of this method is, first, that it is possible to objectively identify relevant factors or their proxies. For example, if variations in urbanization (measured as a share of the urban population in total) are not relevant for variations in the fiscal gap, its regression coefficient tends to become statistically insignificant. If, on the other hand, it is responsible for variations in the fiscal gap, then the regression coefficient will be statistically significant. The final regression will contain only factors which are significant, implying that those factors are responsible for the size of the fiscal gap. Of course, caution needs to be exercised in properly identifying the fiscal gap, properly identifying the factors, properly specifying and quantifying the proxies and properly estimating the regression. An important advantage of this method is that the weights of the factors emerge as regression coefficients. What is more, when a more refined weighted least-squares method is used, the resultant weights reflect the relative importance of the factors. The estimated fiscal gaps can be used to derive the horizontal shares for each state. The development of the method is given in more detail in Sarma (1997). The regression (more specifically the weighted least-squares regression) can be estimated based on the pooled cross-section and time-series data of the states. The estimated fiscal gaps of the states can indicate the size of the tax shares.

Table 2.1 *Possible Criteria Used in Federal Countries for Horizontal Sharing: With Justification*

Criterion	Type	Justification
1 Area	Need	States with a larger area have to incur higher expenditure in order to deliver a comparable standard of service to its citizens. Higher the area, the higher should be the share.
2 Population	Need	Since population represents the demand for public goods, it is only appropriate to use it as the most important criterion. Also, higher the population, the higher would be the demand for government expenditure, and in the absence of adequate rise in the revenue, wider would be the fiscal gap.
3 Population density	Need	Higher density would mean higher cost of providing public services.
4 Urbanization	Need	Urbanization involves higher costs in terms of roads, utilities, water supply and higher costs of solid waste management. Thus, higher the urbanization, the higher the need for funds.
5 Infrastructure	Need	Infrastructure index represents the development. Distance from the states with highest infrastructural development indicates the need for higher funds.
6 Backwardness/ poverty	Need	Economically backward states require higher share to enable them to catch up with the richer states.
7 Income distance	Equalization	Per capita income represents the economic status of a state, and the relative development is represented by the income distance.
8 Human development index	Equalization	States with lower human development in terms of education and health status would require more funds.
9 Tax effort	Efficiency	Tax effort is represented by the ratio of tax revenue to GSDP, and states with higher tax effort are rewarded by giving higher share.
10 Fiscal discipline	Efficiency	States with better fiscal management are encouraged with higher share.

OPTIONS FOR GRANTS

The other broad channel of federal fiscal transfers is grants. With the transformation to the federal system from the unitary system, with the changes in the tax assignments to the SNGs, and with the provisions to share the tax revenues, one can expect that the needs for grants could be smaller than these were earlier.

International experience shows that although the type and nature of the grants differ depending upon a country's situations, there are certain common features regarding grant systems. For example, virtually all federations have certain equalization grants. In addition, there are grants with conditions that induce the SNGs to meet national objectives. The following types of grants are provided to SNGs in different countries. In some countries, equalization objectives are combined with tax sharing.

General-Purpose Unconditional Bloc Grants

In the case of unconditional grants, no restriction is imposed on the use of funds. It is a lump-sum amount of money provided to the SNGs. In most cases, this grant is provided for equalizing fiscal capacities to ensure that a minimum standard and level of public service is provided to its citizens. Unconditional grants are the best for promoting autonomy of the states and local bodies and inter-jurisdictional redistribution. They are also termed 'bloc grants' which simply augment the recipient's resources.

However, experience with the general-purpose unconditional grants shows that these grants are prone to a phenomenon referred to as the 'flypaper effect'. It implies that grants to SNGs tend to result in more local spending than they would have had the same transfers been made directly to local residents for political and bureaucratic reasons.

Equalization Grants

Adapting the federal system with decentralization of expenditure and revenue raising invariably creates different fiscal capacities across regions, making it impossible to provide comparable levels of public services at comparable rates of taxation. This is so because, to provide a given level of public goods and services, different states require different amounts of expenditure per capita, for the following reasons:

1. Differences in the composition of the population across regions need different types of public services;
2. Differences in the cost of providing a given level of public services, due to different wage costs, transportation costs, population densities and other factors differ across regions;
3. Differences in the regional preferences for public goods and services; and
4. Different tax bases per capita across regions generally requiring different tax rates to generate comparable levels of revenue per capita.

To some extent, the equalization aspect can be taken care by the horizontal tax sharing formula. However, since tax sharing might not eliminate inequity, additional grants can help to further reduce horizontal inequity.

There are two broad types of fiscal equalization: FCE and HEE. FCE is the traditional interpretation, widely used in Canada, Australia, Germany and Switzerland. This model calls for transfers from states with high per capita income and low per capita needs to those of opposite characteristics. The HEE is an alternative view which seeks to apply the rule of horizontal equity (the equal treatment of individuals in equal positions) across the fiscal operation of states and does so on a nationwide basis. The fiscal treatment given by lower level jurisdictions should be the same for individuals in equal positions, independent of the jurisdiction in which they reside. Usually, FCE grants are easier to determine and are more popular. Across the OECD, fiscal equalization transfers average around 2.5 per cent of GDP, 5 per cent of general government spending and 50 per cent of intergovernmental grants (OECD, 2014).

Australia introduced a formal system of horizontal fiscal equalization in 1933 to compensate states/territories, which have a lower capacity to raise revenue. The objective is to achieve full equalization, which means that each of the six states and the Australian Capital Territory and the Northern Territory would have the capacity to provide services and the associated infrastructure at the same standard, if each state/territory made the same effort to raise revenue from its own sources and operated at the same level of efficiency. At present, only GST revenues are distributed to achieve equalization.

Equalization grants seek equalizing fiscal capacity, not fiscal policies, of the states. Nor are these grants expected to result in the same level of services or taxes in all states, nor do they direct that the states must achieve any specified level of service in any area, nor impose actual budget outcomes. The principle is that each state should be given the capacity to provide the average standard of state-level public services, assuming it: (a) operates at an average level of efficiency and (b) makes the average effort to raise revenue from its own sources. The Commonwealth Grants Commission is entrusted with the task of developing state relativities based upon the above principle for use in grant allocation. These relativities are defended in open adversary proceedings by the commission, and a final report is presented to the Commonwealth cabinet for review. The cabinet occasionally revises the recommended relativities based on its own view of relative fiscal needs. Following this review, a final determination is made in the Annual Premiers' Conference.

In Canada, as a federal system of government, there is also a commitment to fiscal equity within the Canadian economic union. Fiscal equity is an extension of the principle of horizontal equity to federal systems of government: individuals in similar economic circumstances should be treated in a like manner by the state government, regardless of the province of residence. If different states are able to provide different levels of net family benefits (NFBs) to their residents, the principle of fiscal equity will be violated. The Parliament and the government of Canada are committed to the principle of making equalization; payments to ensure that provincial governments have sufficient revenues to provide reasonably comparable levels of services at reasonably comparable levels of taxation, so the government of Canada provides the equalization grant to the provinces and territories.

In Nepal, the new Constitution provides for distribution of fiscal equalization grants to the state and local governments, on the basis of two main criteria: expenditure need and revenue capacity (Government of Nepal, 2015, p. Art 60(4) and (5)). Following this provision, the Federal Fiscal Transfers Act specifies that the grant should be provided based on the recommendation of the NNRFC (Government of Nepal, 2017, p. Sections 4 and 5). The main theme of equalization grant is to maintain cost as well as revenue equalization and to minimize the vertical and horizontal imbalances so as to enable the SNGs to provide same level of services to their citizens. To some extent, the formula-based tax sharing can achieve the same objective. Yet, the fiscal equalization grant should aim at further reducing the horizontal imbalances in the administrative and other costs.

Conditional/Specific-Purpose Grants

Conditional grants are specific-purpose grants or categorical grants, wherein the federal government specifies the purpose for which the recipient local body can use the funds.

> In comparison with taxation, intergovernmental grants are likely to create the impression of zero political costs for the recipient government, and thereby result in a loss of accountability and efficiency. If, however, grants are given for specific purposes and carry with them at least some obligations towards the government which gives them, accountability is comparatively enhanced. Thus, on the criterion of accountability, specific-purpose grants should be ranked higher than general revenue grants, which in turn are superior to taxation. (Grewal, 1975)

Conditional grants can be matching or non-matching. In the case of conditional matching grant, the federal government asks local bodies to match certain portion of the expenses on specific programmes as a condition to receive the grant.

A good illustration of a simple but effective output-based grant system is the Canadian Health Transfers programme by the federal government of Canada (Marchildon & Haizhen, 2014). The programme has enabled Canadian states to ensure universal access to high-quality health care to all residents regardless of their income or place of residence. Under this programme, the federal government provides per-capita transfers for health to the states, with the rate of growth of the transfers tied to the rate of growth of GDP. No conditions are imposed on spending, but strong conditions are imposed on access to health care. As part of the agreement to receive transfers from the federal government, the states undertake to abide by several access-related conditions. In Switzerland, the equalization system was introduced in 1938 in the form of conditional grants that varied according to the tax capacity of the cantons.

Matching Grants

Certain grants may incorporate matching provisions—requiring grant recipients to finance a specified percentage of expenditures using their own resources. Matching grants differ from permanent public transfers, such as subsidies for inputs and services or safety nets as well as equalization grant. The matching grant, for instance, will be provided for infrastructure projects based on the feasibility and cost of projects. Factors such as a project's impact, availability of financial, physical and human resources required to implement the project and the project's importance will also be taken into account while extending the matching fund. The matching grant could be open-ended or closed-ended. Open-ended matching grant is a type of grant in which the federal government does not impose a limit on the matching funds. Closed-ended conditional matching grant is such a grant for which the federal government puts a maximum ceiling on the cost to be borne to finance a particular service.

Matching requirement encourages greater scrutiny and local ownership of grant-financed expenditures and is helpful in ensuring that the grantor has some control over the costs of the transfer programme. Matching requirements represent a greater burden for a recipient jurisdiction with limited fiscal capacity. However, matching transfers may distort local priorities and be considered inequitable as richer jurisdictions can raise matching funds more easily. But the latter problem can be offset, if desired, by varying matching rates with jurisdictional wealth and the former may be the desired outcome when the transfer is intended to, for example, internalize spillovers or achieve overriding national policy objectives.

Special Grants

Special-purpose grants are project-based relating to supply of basic services such as health, education and drinking water. States may provide the special grant to the local level as per the same provisions for the same purpose. The province too may provide the special grant to meet the needs. The special- or specific-purpose grant emphasizes the need for enlightening information for conditions to become binding. In Australia, specific-purpose payments (SPPs) are grants the Commonwealth makes to the states, usually subject to conditions as to how the money is spent in areas such as health and education, which the states administer. There are various ways to address this issue. The most common approach is through the provisioning of reporting requirements. A reason for the use of special grant is to promote and consolidate the relation between the federation province and local level and encourage to work commonly with proper coexistence and coordination for national and subnational interests. In Australia too, SPPs aim to promote cooperative arrangements between the Commonwealth and individual states to achieve national standards in particular services, where no individual state could be expected to effectively deliver services or to deliver services in accordance with national objectives (Bennett & Richard, 2007).

Performance-based Grants

Another category of grants that can be useful are the PBGs. PBGs can be used towards providing SNGs with tangible incentives to improve their overall institutional, organizational and functional performance, thus making the grant more effective, efficient and responsive as a strategy for the delivery of public goods and services. By linking the level of funding that SNGs receive in the form of fiscal transfers to their performance, such grants can provide incentives to improve their activities such as revenue collection, planning, budget execution, accountability, financial management and good governance in general.

In countries such as India, PBGs take the form of incentives under the FRBM system. Under this, states are required to keep the fiscal deficit and revenue deficit under certain limits, failing which they attract certain penalty, which is then distributed among those states that manage the deficits within limits. There could be other types of PBGs.

The MCPM Grants

The MCPM is a performance-based system providing incentives to improve local governance, financial management, participation, revenue mobilization, planning, budgeting and service delivery, among others. In Nepal, the government believes that MCPM system has helped promote accountability at the local level and ensure basic local service delivery. The fact that the government of Nepal has included its own funding from the grant system and expanded the original pilot to a nationwide system is a strong indication of major trust in the overall system. Additionally, there is a solid belief that it has enhanced the level of compliance of the local governments with respect to many legal and policy provisions as contained in the MCPM assessment manual. It has also assisted the government to identify capacity gaps of the local governments. Because of this, the multi-donor-funded Local Governance and Community Development Programme has also regarded the MCPM as a major tool for its implementation and has been providing funds to the local governments based on the MCPM results. In Indonesia, MCPM is used to improve the institutional, organizational and functional performance of SNGs in the name of the SNG performance evaluation system. In Ethiopia, it is known as Woreda (City government Benchmarking System).

MCPM grants are based on an objective evaluation of local bodies and a measuring tool to assess their accountability, transparency and responsiveness. This, on the one hand, encourages the local bodies to improve their performance by recognizing their good undertakings and, on the other hand, helps to tie up grants with their capacity that will enable capable local bodies to acquire additional grants. Along with this, it will assess their strengths and weaknesses and improve their performance by minimizing weaknesses. It has been mandatory to fulfil the minimum conditions for measuring performance.

The considered opinion has been that MCPM should be promoted and strengthened as this has proven to be an effective tool to safeguard fiduciary risk of SNG finance. However, the system should continue to focus on public financial management and good governance. There is, of course, a need for sharpening of the system within its existing objectives and limitations. For example, it can be examined if it can also accommodate sectoral or other functional objectives. At the same time, there is a need to see that it does not get overloaded and the system should continue to focus on its core objectives and principles. Hence, it is important to keep the system simple and possible to manage. One aspect of the MCPM that needs attention is to link the system with capacity-building of local bodies. Another concern is regarding the timing of assessment. It is observed that the system has not been able to produce assessment results and subsequent announcement of the grants before the planning session of local bodies starts. The MCPM grants should be continued with these changes, like simplification of assessment process so that it is less time consuming and for the time being (until enhancement of capacity by them in a defined level) applying only MC for village municipalities.

Capital Grants

Federal governments have two reasons to be interested in what state and local governments do in financing infrastructure. First, some local infrastructure projects may involve significant externalities; second, some such projects may constitute essential elements of national development programmes; and third, some of the capital projects may be part of the overall national development plans and therefore need federal government interventions and plan-related grants.

Broad Principles for Designing the Grant Formula

In general, the grant formula has to identify the elements that appropriately reflect the objectives and indicators or proxies for measurement (Table 2.2).

Formula grants are administratively demanding to manage the system. A responsible unit to maintain the database and manage the system is considered necessary. To assess efficiency and effectiveness of the system, or identify issues for revisions, grant systems need to be monitored and tracked continuously.

Table 2.2 *Principles for Grant Formulae*

Grant Objective	Criteria to Be Used
Provide grants for the expenditure needs and regional cost differences	• Population; • Indicators of physical factors influencing costs of service provision, e.g., land area, population density and urbanization; • Measures to reflecting concentration of high cost population, e.g., the percentage of families living below the poverty line, the percentage of people on pensions, and the percentage of school-aged children; • Indicators of infrastructure needs, e.g., miles of paved highways, percentage of households with access to adequate water supply, and infrastructure needs to support economic development.
Equalize local body income or fiscal capacity	• Level of average income or size of tax base; • Amount of money that could be raised if all appropriate tax bases were subjected to normal (average effective) rates.
Provide incentives to increase revenue	• A measure of tax effort and management performance; • Maintenance of a level of revenue mobilization.
Achieve a balance between revenue capacity and expenditure needs	• Defined standards of expenditures for desired levels of service; • Link minimum expenditure requirements with assigned tax revenues; • Interpolation of historical expenditure figures.

The Indian Federal Fiscal System

India with its diverse social, economic and cultural background is an ideal case of adopting the federal form of the government. This fact was well recognized even before Independence, so a system of federal fiscal sharing had been put in place (explained in detail in Appendix B). Yet, the system remains somewhat deficient even after over six decades. Besides the need for overcoming the existing limitations, there is a requirement to modify the federal transfer system to align with the changing contours of the economy, changes in the economic policies and resultant vicissitudes in the overall fiscal mechanism. For example, the tax system is under extensive revision in recent years, such as the implementation of the new Direct Tax Code as well as the introduction of the GST, which calls for many changes in the state-level tax systems. Further, the economic planning process is under complete revision with the replacement of the PC by the NITI Aayog, which led to fundamental changes in the plan transfers. All this might alter the revenue positions of the central, state and local governments. This calls for complete revamping of the federal fiscal arrangements for intergovernmental transfers in India.

Given the general backdrop of the nuances of the federal system in the world, it is easy to understand and assess the Indian federal fiscal system (Figure 3.1). The Indian federation comprises three layers of governance—central, state and local—and is relatively more central-ized and 'centripetal'[1] in nature. The second layer of governance

---

[1] Centripetal federalism is a federal system in which there is a strong federal government and weaker provincial governments and where the powers flow from the centre to the subnational governments. It contrasts with the cooperative

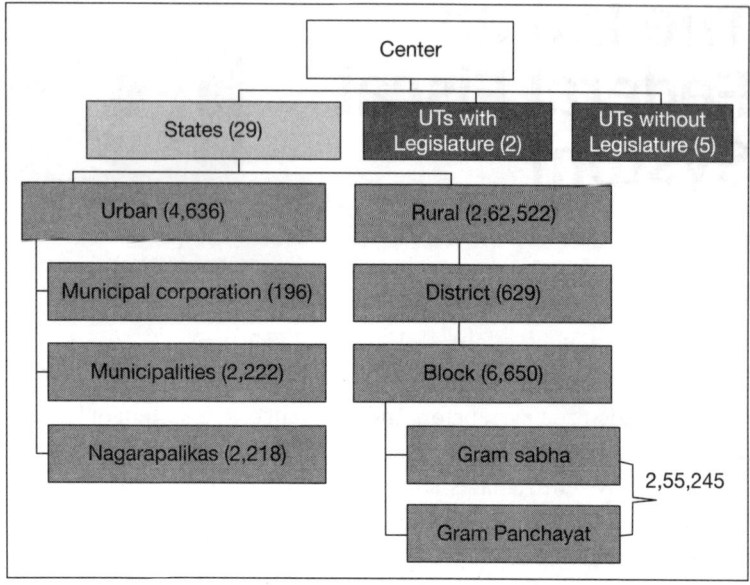

Figure 3.1 *The Federal Governance Structure of India*

originally comprised 14 states in 1956 and gradually became 29 states (until 2017), 2 union territories with legislatures and 5 union territories without legislature.[2] In the third layer, at present, there are

federalism in which national, state and local governments interact cooperatively and collectively to solve common problems, rather than making policies separately.

[2] The States Reorganization Act of 1956 was formed on an ethnic–linguistic basis. Subsequently, several new states have been created out of existing states. For example, Bombay state was split into the linguistic Gujarat and Maharashtra states on 1 May 1960 by means of the Bombay Reorganization Act. The Punjab Reorganization Act of 1956 divided the Punjab into linguistic and religious lines that created Haryana, converting the northern districts of Punjab into Himachal Pradesh. Nagaland was made a state in 1962, Meghalaya and Himachal Pradesh in 1971, and Tripura and Manipur in 1972. Sikkim joined the Indian Union as a state in 1975. Similarly, Mizoram was made a state in 1986, and Goa and Arunachal Pradesh in 1987. However, Goa's northern enclaves of Daman and Diu became separate union territories in 1987. Goa, which comprises one-third of the population, is primarily Christian, but it is not a Christian state. Chhattisgarh was created on 1 November 2000 from eastern Madhya Pradesh; Uttaranchal was renamed Uttarakhand on 9 November 2000, which

about 267,160 local governments, of which 4,636 are urban and the remaining are rural. Among the urban local bodies, 196 are municipal corporations, and the remaining are municipalities and Nagarapalikas. Among the rural bodies, there are 629 at the district level, 6,650 at the block level and 255,245 Gram Sabhas and Gram Panchayats.

CONSTITUTIONAL ARRANGEMENTS

Part XII of the Indian Constitution (Articles 245 to 263) deals with the relations between the union and the states. Article 246 divides the lawmaking powers under three lists:

- *List I or the Union List:* The union Parliament has exclusive powers of legislation with respect to 97 subjects or items in List I.
- *List II or the State List:* The state legislatures have exclusive powers with respect to 66 items enumerated in List II.
- *List III or the Concurrent List:* Both the union and the state legislatures can make laws in respect of the subjects enumerated in the Concurrent List but any union Act can override a state Act in the event of a conflict between the two on a matter in the Concurrent List.

Entries 82 to 92B of List I of the VII Schedule describe the taxation powers of the union government (Table 3.1). Till 2017, the revenue sources of the union government are personal income tax, customs duties, excise duty on petroleum crude, HSD, motor spirit, natural gas, ATF and tobacco and products, corporation tax, tax on value of assets for individuals, companies and on capital value of companies (known as wealth tax), estate duty excluding agricultural land, duties in respect of succession to property other than agricultural land, terminal taxes on goods or passengers carried by railway, sea or air, security transactions tax, stamp duty in respect of financial assets such

created the Hilly regions of northwest Uttar Pradesh; and Jharkhand was created on 15 November 2000 out of the southern districts of Bihar. Uttarakhand is comprised of the Garhwal and Kumaon Divisions, which became the 27th state. In August 2006, the Uttaranchal state assembly and leading movement members renamed the state Uttarakhand. The latest new state Telangana was created in 2015.

Table 3.1 *Taxation Powers of the Central Government as per the Seventh Schedule (Article 246) List I*

82. Taxes on income other than agricultural income.
83. Duties of customs including export duties.
84. Duties of excise on tobacco and other goods manufactured or produced in India except—
(a) alcoholic liquors for human consumption;
(b) opium, Indian hemp and other narcotic drugs and narcotics,
but including medicinal and toilet preparations containing alcohol or any substance included in sub-paragraph (b) of this entry.
85. Corporation tax.
86. Taxes on the capital value of the assets, exclusive of agricultural land, of individuals and companies; taxes on the capital of companies.
87. Estate duty in respect of property other than agricultural land.
88. Duties in respect of succession to property other than agricultural land.
89. Terminal taxes on goods or passengers, carried by railway, sea or air; taxes on railway fares and freights.
90. Taxes other than stamp duties on transactions in stock exchanges and futures markets.
91. Rates of stamp duty in respect of bills of exchange, cheques, promissory notes, bills of lading, letters of credit, policies of insurance, transfer of shares, debentures, proxies and receipts.
92. Taxes on the sale or purchase of newspapers and on advertisements published therein.
92A. Taxes on the sale or purchase of goods other than newspapers, where such sale or purchase takes place in the course of inter-state trade or commerce.
92B. Taxes on the consignments of goods (whether the consignment is to the person making it or to any other person), where such consignment takes place in the course of interstate trade or commerce.

Source: Constitution of India.

as bills of exchange, taxes on the sale or purchase of goods other than newspapers in the course of interstate trade or commerce (central sales tax), and taxes on the consignment of goods in the course of interstate trade or commerce (consignment tax).

Entries 45 to 63 of List II of the VII Schedule specify the taxation powers of the state governments (Table 3.2). Revenue sources of the states include land revenue, agricultural income tax, taxes on

Table 3.2 *Taxation Powers of the State Governments as per the Seventh Schedule (Article 246) List II*

45. Land revenue, including the assessment and collection of revenue, the maintenance of land records, survey for revenue purposes and records of rights, and alienation of revenues.

46. Taxes on agricultural income.

47. Duties in respect of succession to agricultural land.

48. Estate duty in respect of agricultural land.

49. Taxes on lands and buildings.

50. Taxes on mineral rights subject to any limitations imposed by Parliament by law relating to mineral development.

51. Duties of excise on the following goods manufactured or produced in the state and countervailing duties at the same or lower rates on similar goods manufactured or produced elsewhere in India;

   (a) alcoholic liquors for human consumption;

   (b) opium, Indian hemp and other narcotic drugs and narcotics,

   but not including medicinal and toilet preparations containing alcohol or any substance included in sub-paragraph (b) of this entry.

52. Taxes on the entry of goods into a local area for consumption, use or sale therein.

53. Taxes on the consumption or sale of electricity.

54. Taxes on the sale or purchase of goods other than newspapers, subject to the provisions of entry 92A of List I.

55. Taxes on advertisements other than advertisements published in the newspapers and advertisements broadcast by radio or television.

(Continued)

Table 3.2 *(Continued)*

56. Taxes on goods and passengers carried by road or on inland waterways.
57. Taxes on vehicles, whether mechanically propelled or not, suitable for use on roads, including tramcars subject to the provisions of entry 35 of List III.
58. Taxes on animals and boats.
59. Tolls.
60. Taxes on professions, trades, callings and employments.
61. Capitation taxes.
62. Taxes on luxuries, including taxes on entertainments, amusements, betting and gambling.
63. Rates of stamp duty in respect of documents other than those specified in the provisions of List I with regard to rates of stamp duty.

Source: Constitution of India.

land and buildings, taxes on mineral rights subject to any limitations imposed by the Parliament, excise duty and countervailing duties on alcohol and narcotics, taxes on the sale of crude, HSD, motor spirit, natural gas, ATF and alcoholic liquor, taxes on goods and passengers carried by road or on inland waterways, and stamp duty on items other than those in the Union List. Local governments do not have any independent taxing power. However, state governments may assign some taxes to the local governments from the State List. Generally, local governments are provided with property taxes, octroi and taxes on vehicles. Thus, it is clear that more productive taxes are in the hands of the centre. This leads to the fiscal imbalance.

The Constitution also contains several provisions to bridge the gap of finances between the centre and the states. They include various articles in the Constitution, such as Article 268, which facilitates levy of duties by the centre but equips the states to collect and retain the same. Similarly, Articles 269, 270, 275, 282 and 293 specify ways and means of sharing resources between the union and states. The provisions are presented in Table 3.3.

Table 3.3 *Constitutional Provisions for Revenue Sharing between the Centre and States in India*

Article in the Constitution	The Intended Provision
268	Levy of duties by the centre but collected and retained by the states.
269	Taxes and duties levied and collected by the centre but assigned in whole to the states
270, 272	Sharing of the proceeds of all union taxes between the centre and the states. (Effective from April 1, 1996, following the 80th Amendment to the Constitution replacing the earlier provisions relating to mandatory sharing of income tax under Article 270 and permissive sharing of union excise duties under Article 272.)
275	Statutory grants-in-aid of the revenues of states
282	Grants for any public purpose
293	Loans for any public purpose

Source: Constitution of India.

NEED FOR FEDERAL FISCAL TRANSFERS IN INDIA

The constitutional division of tax powers between the central and the state governments could not, however, eliminate the need for further adjustments in the form of intergovernmental fiscal transfers. Like all other federations, the Indian federation also suffers from the problems of fiscal imbalances, both vertical and horizontal. Vertical imbalance occurs because states are assigned more responsibilities and they incur expenditures more than their revenue sources. This is because the states being closer to the local people are able to gauge the needs and concerns of their people more effectively, and hence are more efficient in financing their expenditures. However, the central government is assigned more productive tax powers as it is believed that it is more efficient to collect taxes by a single authority. As a result, the central government collects about 66 per cent of the total revenue raised at all levels of government in the country, while its share in total government

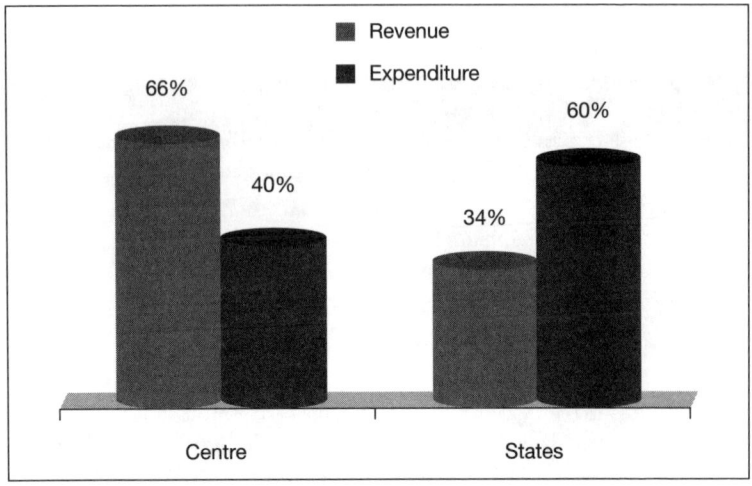

Figure 3.2 *The Extent of Vertical Fiscal Imbalance in India*

spending is only about 40 per cent. The difference between the relative revenue and spending responsibilities of the central and state governments is reflective of significant VFI. Among the established federal countries, only Australia seems to have a higher vertical imbalance[3] than India. The average VFI between the central and state government finances in India is as shown in Figure 3.2.

Horizontal imbalances across states are because of factors such as historical backgrounds, differential endowment of resources and capacity to raise resources. Unlike in most other federations, differences in the developmental levels in Indian states are very sharp. This necessitates resource transfers from the centre to states time to time to minimize the fiscal imbalances.

---

[3] 'A chronic feature of Australian federalism namely, a highly centralised revenue-raising system enabling the Commonwealth Government to raise nearly 80 per cent of the national tax revenue, and a fairly decentralised system of public outlays which are shared almost equally between the Commonwealth and the states. Consequently, financial transfers from the Commonwealth to the states are a major source of financing public outlays of the states, accounting for an average of 44 per cent of the outlays of the states and the Territories during the ten years to 1989–90' (Grewal, 1975).

TYPES OF INTERGOVERNMENTAL TRANSFERS IN INDIA

The two important institutions created in India to guide and recommend the fiscal transfers between the centre, states and local bodies and to minimize fiscal imbalances are the Finance Commission (FC) (a constitutional body) and the Planning Commission (PC) (now replaced with the NITI Aayog). There are certain other channels such as the National Development Council (NDC), the Interstate Council (ISC) and state finance commissions. While the Planning Commission was a permanent body, the Finance Commission was set up with a normal periodicity of five years.

The transfers recommended by these two bodies take several forms: (a) statutory revenue transfers through FC awards (tax revenue shares, tax rentals, assigned taxes, grants-in-aid (GIA)—general-purpose grants, specific-purpose grants and so on); (b) capital transfers by the PC under a set of clearly laid-out rules and for projects assisted by external agencies (grants and loans); and (c) discretionary transfers for CSS and for different non-plan purposes by various union ministries in the form of direct grants under CSS, as also subsidized central loans. With the setting up of the NITI Aayog, from April 2017, the distinction between the plan and non-plan expenditure has been done away with and both are clubbed into one expenditure. The different types of transfers are as in Figure 3.3.

FINANCE COMMISSION

The Indian Constitution provides for constituting the Finance Commission an institutional body to facilitate centre–state transfers. This body came into existence in 1951 under Article 280 of the Constitution, which states:

> (1) The President shall, within two years from the commencement of this Constitution and thereafter at the expiration of every fifth year or at such earlier time as the President considers necessary, by order constitute a Finance Commission which shall consist of a Chairman and four other members to be appointed by the President. (Government of India, 2015a)

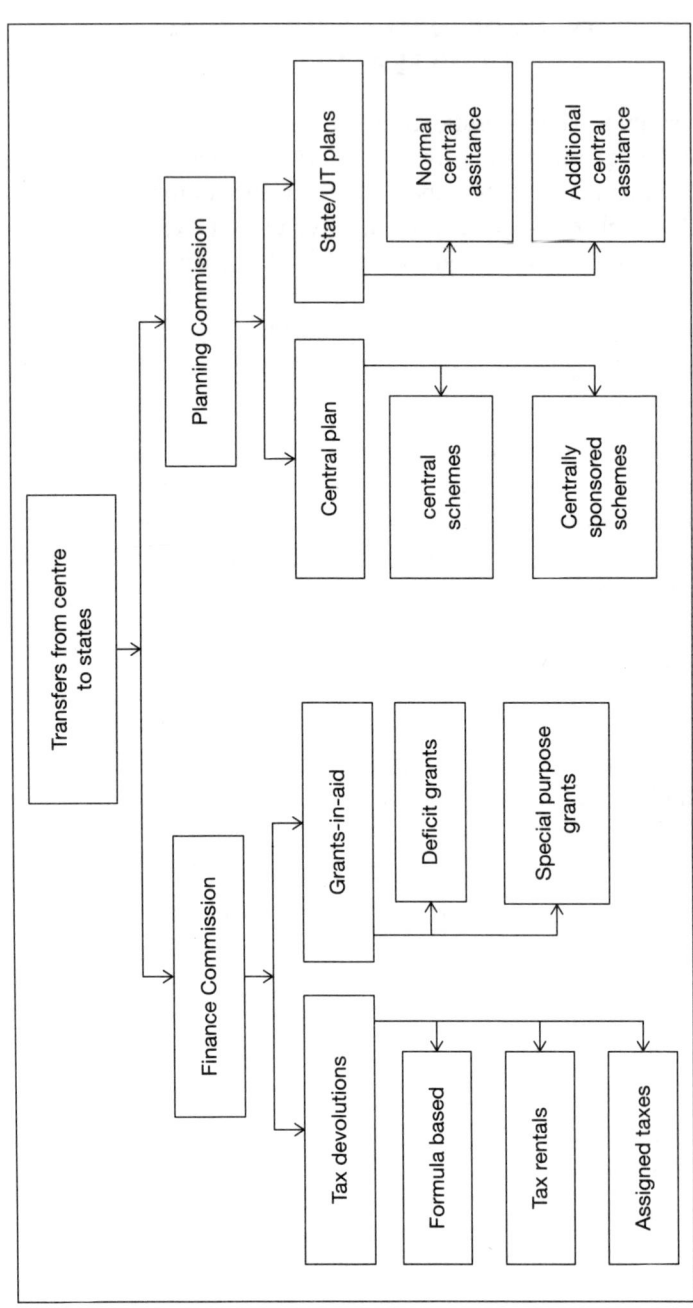

Figure 3.3 *Types of Transfers from Central to State Governments in India*

Accordingly, the FC shall comprise a chairman and four other members, and their main task is to make recommendations to the President regarding the distribution of the net proceeds of taxes between the union and states and the allocation of the same among the states themselves. It is also under the ambit of the FC to define the financial relations between the union and the states.

Since the institution of the first FC,[4] many changes have occurred in the Indian macroeconomic scenario, leading to major changes in the FC's recommendations over the years. Until today, 14 FCs have submitted their reports (Table 3.4). Recently, the fifteenth FC has been constituted.

Table 3.4 Finance Commissions Appointed in India So Far

Finance Commission	Year of Establishment	Chairman	Operational Duration
First	1951	K. C. Neogy	1952–1957
Second	1956	K. Santhanam	1957–1962
Third	1960	A. K. Chanda	1962–1966
Fourth	1964	P. V. Rajamannarr	1966–1969
Fifth	1968	Mahaveer Tyagi	1969–1974
Sixth	1972	K. Brahmananda Reddy	1974–1979
Seventh	1977	J. M. Shellet	1979–1984
Eighth	1983	Y. B. Chavan	1984–1989
Ninth	1987	N. K. P. Salve	1989–1995
Tenth	1992	K. C. Pant	1995–2000
Eleventh	1998	A. M. Khusro	2000–2005
Twelfth	2003	C. Rangarajan	2005–2010
Thirteenth	2007	Vijay Kelkar	2010–2015
Fourteenth	2012	Y. Venugopal Reddy	2015–2020
Fifteenth	2017	N. K. Singh	2020–2025

[4] While referring the different FCs in this book, we shall abbreviate by the number followed by FC. For example, the First Finance Commission will be abbreviated as 1FC, Second Finance Commission as 2FC and so on.

FC Transfers: Evolution

Fiscal transfers recommended by successive FCs have undergone many changes over time. Prior to the enactment of the Constitution (80th Amendment) Act, 2000, the sharing of the union tax revenues with the states was in accordance with the provisions of Articles 270 and 272, as they stood then. While Article 270 provided for the 'compulsory' sharing of the net proceeds of the income tax (excluding corporation tax), Article 272 permitted for sharing of the net proceeds of union duties of excise (excluding duties of excise on medicinal and toilet preparations), if Parliament by law so provided. Consequently, the principles adopted for revenue sharing differed between the two taxes significantly.

Thus, central transfers consisted of:

1. Taxes levied by the centre but collected and retained by the states (Article 268; mainly stamp duties);
2. Taxes levied and collected by the centre but assigned in whole to the states (Article 269; interstate sales tax);
3. Compulsory share of the proceeds of the non-corporate income tax (Article 270);
4. Optional share in the proceeds of union excise duties (Article 272); and
5. Statutory GIA of revenues of states (Article 275).

Vertical Sharing

Thus, prior to the 80th Amendment of the Constitution, only two central taxes were sharable: non-corporate income tax and union excise duties. In addition, there was a tax rental arrangement between centre and states with respect to additional excise duties in lieu of sales tax on three commodities. A brief review of sharing of the two taxes is given below.

Income Tax

By the time the 1FC was constituted, the share of states in the 'net proceeds' of income tax had already been fixed at 50 per cent (see

Appendix C). The 1FC raised the share to 55 per cent owing to increase in the number of states. The second, third and fourth FCs raised the share gradually to 60, 66.67 and 75 per cent, respectively, to compensate for the non-inclusion of corporate income tax and surcharge. The 5FC did not raise the share, but recommended inclusion of advance tax collections and arrears thereof in determining the proceeds of income tax during a financial year. The 6FC raised it to 80 per cent, as the arrears of advance collections were not available anymore. The 7FC further increased the share to 85 per cent in response to the grievance of the states that the centre had raised the union surcharge as a revenue measure rather than for meeting any specific purpose, thus depriving the states of a share in the increased revenue. While the 8th and 9th FCs did not alter the position, the 10FC felt that the authority that levies and administers a tax should have a significant and tangible interest in its yield and accordingly revised the share of the states in the proceeds of income tax downward to 77.5 per cent, but increased the share in the net proceeds of the union excise duties to protect the level of overall devolution to the states.

Union Excise Duties

At the time of the 1FC, there were 12 important commodities subjected to union excise duties in 1951–1952. The 1FC felt that it was advisable to share the excise revenue from a select number of commodities of common consumption that yielded sizeable revenue for distribution. Accordingly, the Commission recommended sharing of the excise on three commodities—tobacco (including tobacco products), matches and vegetable products and the share was fixed at 40 per cent. The 2FC increased the number of commodities for sharing the excise duty revenue to eight but reduced the share to 25 per cent. While the coverage of commodities was expanded by the 3FC and 4FC, the share was reduced to 20 per cent. The 5FC and 6FC, while keeping the share at 20 per cent, extended the sharable excise duties to special and auxiliary duties as well. The 7FC doubled the share with a view to reducing the elements of GIA. The 8FC increased the share by adding additional 5 per cent, which was to be distributed among the deficit states. The 9FC, in its second report, retained the share at

45 per cent for distribution among the deficit states. The 10FC further raised the share of the states to be 47.5 per cent with 7.5 per cent distributed among the deficit states.

80th Amendment

The 80th Amendment of the Constitution altered the pattern of sharing of union taxes in a fundamental way. The genesis of this change was a recommendation of the 10FC. The 10FC in its alternative scheme of tax devolution suggested that instead of sharing of individual taxes, the states may have a share in the total net proceeds of all central taxes excluding surcharges and cesses. In determining the share of the states in the total net proceeds of the central tax revenues, the Commission distinguished between shares in income tax, basic excise duties and grants in lieu of tax on railway passenger fares as a proportion of central tax revenues (S1), on the one hand, and the share of additional excise duties in lieu of sales tax in respect of items covered by tax rental arrangement on the other (S2). The Commission observed that the average value of S1 had been 24.32, 22.22 and 24.3 per cent during the five-year-periods 1979–1984, 1984–1989 and 1990–1995 respectively, and that of S2 at 2.96, 3.22 and 2.95 per cent. Having regard to these values, the commission recommended that the share of states in the gross receipts of central taxes should be 26 per cent, and until the tax rental arrangement is terminated, a further share of three per cent in the gross tax receipts of the centre to compensate for the additional excise duties in lieu of sale tax.

After the 80th Amendment, the FC is required to recommend a share of all taxes or duties referred to in Article 270. There is considerable merit in the change, as it gives greater freedom and flexibility to the centre in pursuing the tax reforms in an integrated manner and enables the states to share the aggregate buoyancy of central taxes. Under this amendment, Article 272 was dropped, and Article 270 was substantially changed. The new Article 270 provides for sharing of all the taxes and duties referred to in the Union List, except the taxes and duties referred to in Articles 268 and 269, respectively, surcharges on taxes and duties referred to in Article 271 and any cess levied for specific purposes.

The main principles of vertical sharing as in the new Article 270[5] are summarized as follows:

1. All central taxes and duties, except those referred to Articles 268 and 269 respectively and surcharges and cesses, are to be shared between the centre and the states.
2. Only states in which these taxes and duties are 'leviable in that year' are entitled to get a share in these taxes and duties.
3. A percentage of 'net proceeds' of these taxes and duties as may be prescribed by the President on the basis of the recommendations of the FC is to be shared by the states.
4. The percentage of 'net proceeds' of these taxes and duties which is assigned to the states in any financial year shall not form part of the Consolidated Fund of India. (Prior to the amendment, proceeds attributable to the union territories and taxes payable in respect of union emoluments were to be excluded from the sharable net proceeds.)
5. The share to be given to each state is only in respect of taxes and duties which are leviable in that state in the relevant year.
6. The new amendment also does not require the FC to separately suggest changes in the principles governing the distribution of additional excise duties in lieu of sales tax on textiles, tobacco

---

[5] '(1) All taxes and duties referred to in the Union List, except
   (a) the duties and taxes referred to in Articles 268 and 269, respectively,
   (b) surcharge on taxes and duties referred to in Article 271 and any cess levied for specific purposes under any law made by Parliament shall be levied and collected by the Government of India and shall be distributed between the Union and the states in the manner provided in clause (2).
 (2) Such percentage, as may be prescribed, of the net proceeds of any such tax or duty in any financial year shall not form part of the Consolidated Fund of India, but shall be assigned to the states within which that tax or duty is leviable in that year, and shall be distributed among those states in such manner and from such time as may be prescribed in the manner provided in clause (3).
 (3) In this Article, "prescribed" means—
   (i)   until a Finance Commission has been constituted, prescribed by the President by order, and
   (ii) after a Finance Commission has been constituted, prescribed by the President by order after considering the recommendations of the Finance Commission.'

and sugar, and the grant in lieu of the repealed railway passenger fare tax.

The 11FC was the first to take these changes into account, while recommending the share of the states in the divisible pool. The 11FC, while considering the issue of vertical devolution of the central tax revenues, reviewed the past trends in the aggregate share of states in the net proceeds of all union taxes and duties, excluding surcharge and cesses during the last two decades. It was observed that the share of the states in all union taxes and duties (worked out on the basis of share of all states in the union excise duties and income tax recommended by successive FCs) fluctuated between 26.17 per cent (in 1988–1989) and 31.79 per cent (in 1993–1994). The year-to-year fluctuations had been significant even within the devolution period covered by the same FC, largely due to fluctuations in the rates of growth of income tax and union excise duties, the only taxes shared with the states before the 80th amendment to the Constitution.

After completing the assessment of the central resources and state finances for the period, from 2000–2001 to 2004–2005, the 11FC recommended that the share of the states be fixed at 28 per cent of the net proceeds of all taxes and duties referred to in the Union List, except the taxes and duties referred to in Articles 268 and 269, and the surcharges and cesses, for each of the five years starting from 2000–2001 and ending in 2004–2005. The 11FC further noted that as a consequence of the amendment, which inter alia deleted Article 272, additional excise duties levied under the Additional Excise Duties (Goods of Special Importance) Act, 1957, had become part of the revenue receipts of the central government and were sharable with the states. This brought the total tax devolution recommended by the 11FC to 29.5 per cent of the net proceeds of all sharable central taxes and duties.

Thus, an important improvement has been the combining of all the central taxes for revenue sharing as recommended by the 10FC and implemented through the Constitutional 80th Amendment. Yet, several central revenue sources such as cesses and service tax proceeds are left out of the sharable pool. The 11FC, for example, notes that

The share to be given to each state is only in respect of taxes and duties which are leviable in that state in the relevant year.... The union Ministry of Finance has informed us that at present all taxes except the expenditure tax and service tax are leviable in every state of the country. Expenditure tax and service tax are not leviable only in the state of Jammu & Kashmir. We have kept this position in view while determining the inter se share of the states in the distribution of central taxes. (Eleventh Finance Commission, 2000)

The 12FC and 13FC followed suit (Table 3.5).

Table 3.5 *Trends in the Vertical Tax Share Recommended by the Past Finance Commissions*

	Income Tax	Union Excise Duties (Basic)		
Commission	States' Share (%)	States' Share (%)	Number of Articles Covered	Remarks
1	2	3	4	5
First	55	40	3	
Second	60	25	8	
Third	66.7	20	35	
Fourth	75	20	All	
Fifth	75	20	All	Including special excise duties
Sixth	80	20	All	Including auxiliary duties
Seventh	85	40	All	
Eighth	85	45	All	5% for deficit states
Ninth	85	45	All	Including share for deficit states
Tenth	77.5	47.5	All	7.5% for deficit states
Eleventh	29.5	29.5	All taxes	
Twelfth	30	30	All taxes	
Thirteenth	32	32	All taxes	
Fourteenth	42	42	All taxes	

Source: Vithal and Sastry (2001) and the reports of the FCs.

88th Amendment

Another constitutional amendment that is of relevance to centre–state fiscal relations in India is the 88th Amendment enacted in January 2004 through the Constitution (88th Amendment) Act, 2003, relating to service tax. This amendment provides for a specific entry in the Constitution to authorize levy of service tax.[6] The central government has been imposing and collecting this tax as a residual item under entry 97 in the Union List, and the net proceeds thereof are distributed between the centre and the states as per Article 270 of the recommendations of the FC. According to this amendment, taxes on services are levied by the central government, and the net proceeds of such taxes are to be collected and appropriated by the centre and the states in accordance with such principles of collection and appropriation as may be formulated by Parliament, by law. Further, in the Seventh Schedule to the Constitution, an item, 'Taxes on services,' is to be inserted in the Union List under entry 92C, thereby assigning the power to tax services clearly to the central government. A new Article, 268A, has been inserted, whereby service tax is to be taken out of the divisible pool of central taxes and consequently out of the jurisdiction of the FC.

Horizontal Sharing

Clause (3)(a) of Article 280 of the Constitution stipulates the FC to make recommendations to the President as to not only the vertical sharing of the net proceeds of taxes which are to be, or may be, divided

---

[6] To enable Parliament to formulate by law principles for determining the modalities of levying the service tax by the central government and collection of the proceeds thereof by the central government and the states, the amendment vide Constitution (92nd amendment) Act, 2003, has been made. Consequently, new Article 268A has been inserted for service tax levy by the union government, collected and appropriated by the union government. In the Seventh Schedule to the Constitution, in List I (union list) after entry 92B, entry 92C has been inserted for taxes on services. Clause (1) of Article 270 has been amended to include 'Article 268A'.

between them but also their allocation among the states.[7] The following are the important milestones in the evolution of the criteria used for horizontal sharing.

Differential Criteria for the Two Sharable Taxes

The basic approach of the past FCs regarding the horizontal sharing of the income tax and union excise duties has always been to specify the key criteria and assign weights for distribution of the sharable tax revenue among the states. There was a reason why the FCs up to the 10FC adopted different principles for the two taxes. The reason was that the FCs felt that these two sharable taxes had different roles to play in the total scheme of devolution. Income tax provided a certain basic resource to the states by virtue of the historical background of the states' participation in the proceeds of this tax. The union excise duties were considered to be an additional way of supplementing the resources of the states to the extent that the share of income tax was not considered adequate.

> In determining the extent to which the resources of the states as a whole, or of any individual state, were to be augmented, the needs and financial status of the state had to be considered. It is in this context that the Commissions started considering, in the case of excise duties, several factors which in their view were indicative of the level of development, and therefore of the need, of a particular state. They did not adopt this approach in the case of the proceeds of income tax because they felt that there was an element of entitlement here. To the extent there was an element of need in this also, they felt that population was an adequate measure of both entitlement and need for this limited purpose. (Vithal & Sastry, 2001)

[7] Article 280.

(3) It shall be the duty of the Commission to make recommendations to the President as to
   (a) the distribution between the Union and the states of the net proceeds of taxes which are to be, or may be, divided between them under this Chapter and the allocation between the states of the respective shares of such proceeds;
   (b) the principles which should govern the grants-in-aid of the revenues of the states out of the Consolidated Fund of India; ....' (Constitution of India, Part XII)

The 8FC felt that since 10 per cent of the proceeds of income tax were to be distributed on the basis of contribution, the common formula for distribution could be applied only to the remaining 90 per cent. The 9FC followed this procedure of using a common formula for the distribution of the proceeds of union excise duties and 90 per cent of the proceeds of income tax. Thus, in its first report, the weight for population was expressed as 25 per cent of 90 per cent of the proceeds, and in the second report, it was shown as 22.5 per cent of the total proceeds, since 25 per cent of 90 equals 22.5 per cent of 100. The factor of contribution in the case of income tax prevented these two commissions from adopting the same formula for the distribution of the entire divisible pool, including the states' share of both income tax and union excise duties. It was only when the 10FC finally dropped the factor of contribution in the case of income tax that it became possible to adopt the same formula fully for both. However, by this time, the FCs had started allocating a certain percentage of union excise duties for deficit states. Therefore, in a strict sense, the formula was again different for the two taxes.

It was only in the alternative model suggested by the 10FC the common formula was used, which came into practice through the Constitution 80th Amendment Act, 2000, and followed by the 11FC.

The Criteria Used

The criteria used by successive FCs for determining the horizontal shares of the states have been different at different times. The criteria not only differed for different FCs, but also the same FC prescribed different sets of criteria for different tax revenue. The selection, justification, proxying and the quantification differ from FC to FC. Broadly, the criteria represent the capacity factors:

1. Contribution
2. Population 1971
3. Demographic change
4. Income distance
5. Inverse per capita income
6. Backwardness

7. Poverty
8. Area adjusted
9. Forest cover
10. Infrastructure distance
11. Revenue equalization
12. Non-plan deficit
13. Tax effort
14. Fiscal self-reliance

There has been considerable discussion and deliberation on the use of some of the criteria.

The contribution criterion

A significant milestone in the evolution of the criteria for horizontal sharing has been the declining importance of the contribution factor. The contribution factor continued to be an essential factor for determining the horizontal shares of the tax devolution until the 10FC.

For a long time, states felt that tax devolution is a matter of right and entitlement. It is interesting to note that during the time of the 1FC, the states were of the view that the basis of population was unscientific and suggested that the contribution of each state should be the main factor in the allocation income tax.

The then Bombay state government, for example, argued that the bulk of the income tax collection was contributed by the industrially advanced states. Besides, these states argued that the existence of big industries and the presence of a large and concentrated population of industrial labour created special problems for these states such as the law and order. They pointed out that these states had to provide for the welfare and amenities of industrial labour and could claim a fair share of the revenue from income tax on these considerations. Accordingly, they suggested that 25 per cent of the share should be allocated on the basis of collection, 25 per cent on the basis of industrial labour and 10 per cent on the basis of other considerations such as need, backwardness and so on. The West Bengal government even went further to the extent of claiming that 'each state should get back out of the net proceeds attributable to it the percentage share assigned to the states as a whole...' Further, they argued that the money raised in one state could not be made available to another state. Using the language of Article 270, they argued that

> the sharing of income tax was conditioned by the leviability of the tax and that the manner of distribution contemplated by the Article merely required the President, after retaining the central share, to place the balance in the hands of the governments in whose respective territories the taxes had been levied or to whom they were attributable, as the case might be, to be disposed of under the control of their respective legislatures. It was not a case of the centre expending or disposing of the money on any principle of merit but simply the separation of a common pool of money so as to place in the hands of each the share to which it was entitled.

However, the 1FC did not agree with this extreme view of the states that contribution factor should be the sole determinant of the income tax share among the states.

The 2FC felt that although there might be a case for weight being given to collection in the restricted field of personal income tax, 'taking all factors into account, collection should be completely abandoned in favor of population as the basis of distribution.' However, to prevent a sudden break in the continuity, it proposed that the distribution of the states' share should be 10 per cent on the basis of collections and 90 per cent on the basis of population. 'This should make it easy to complete, in due course, the process of eliminating the factor of collection altogether and distributing the entire amount of the states' share on the basis of population.' It took nearly half a century before this view of the 2FC—that the factor of collection should be altogether eliminated—was recommended by the 10FC.

The 3FC again increased the weight for contribution from 10 to 20 per cent on the ground that even the 2FC had recognized that 'there might be a case for weight being given to collection in the restricted field of personal income tax'. It also quoted the 1FC on the view that there was 'a core of incomes, particularly in the range of personal and small business incomes, which could be treated as of local origin'. As the corporate tax was excluded from the divisible pool, the 3FC felt that 'a higher percentage than before of the total yield of income tax now represented tax derived from incomes of local origin'. Therefore, it chose to increase the weight for contribution from 10 to 20 per cent. The 4FC also endorsed this view.

The 5FC went back to 10 per cent weight for collections, but this was linked with moving away from collection to assessment as representing the factor of contribution. Its argument for doing so was that it was difficult, in the absence of suitable statistics, to form a direct estimate of the contribution to the income tax pool made by incomes of local origin in each state. The criterion of collection hitherto adopted as a measure of contribution has been recognized to be inadequate and unsatisfactory. Moreover, the figures of collections may include large overpayments or underpayments, which are adjusted only on assessments. Hence, the Commission opined that instead of figures of collections, the statistics of assessments in different states would provide a more reliable basis to measure the factor of contribution. Accordingly, it recommended that 90 per cent of the states' share of the divisible pool of income tax should be distributed among them on the basis of population and the remaining 10 per cent on the basis of figures of assessments after allowing for reductions on account of appellate orders, references, revisions, rectifications and so on. This weight of 10 per cent for contribution on the basis of figures for assessment continued to be adopted by the subsequent commissions till the 10FC. The 10FC dropped the contribution factor altogether on the grounds that economic interdependence among the states makes the case for locally originating incomes to be weak.[8]

---

[8] '5.33 ... The country as a whole represents a common economic space and market, and growing interdependence in economic activities has considerably weakened the case for locally originating incomes in the non-agricultural sector. We are, therefore, persuaded that there is no need to retain contribution as a criterion of distribution. Besides, the only factor that now stands in the way of a common formula for distribution of the two taxes is this component of "contribution" in the case of income tax. Accordingly, we have not used "contribution" as a factor in determining the respective share of states in the distributable amount of the net proceeds of income tax. To the extent, however, "contribution" is interpreted as "collection", it is the effort of the states in collecting their own taxes that is relevant rather than a tax levied and collected by the Centre. We have recognized this while recommending later that tax effort of the states, which

The use of 'contribution' factor also emanates from the need to motivate states to federate. Otherwise richer states that are in a position to contribute more to the central taxes but are required to accept lower shares of transfers would find it difficult to get motivated to remain in the federation. However, this argument is not acceptable as there are several indirect benefits of staying in the federation. For example, the saving of the expenditures on defence and law and order, and the possible enhancement in the revenue productivity due to wider markets enjoyed by the entrepreneurs in these states with little or no interstate trade barriers. Moreover, this argument relating to motivation to remain in the federation might hold for those federations which are formed by independent sovereign countries. But the states in India are more in the nature of administrative divisions. Thus, there is little case for considering 'contribution' as a criterion for federal transfers in India. It only complicates the process and will not serve any useful purpose.

Population as criterion

Population is the most important criterion adopted by the various commissions. Implicit in the use of this criterion is the assumption that higher the population, higher would be the demand for government expenditure and, in the absence of adequate rise in the revenue, wider would be the fiscal gap (expenditure – revenue). This is because the main purpose of the federal transfers is to help the states to bridge the fiscal gaps inherent in the federal system, and to help the states to meet the demand for provision of public goods in their jurisdictions. Since population represents the demand for public goods, it is only appropriate to use it as a relevant criterion.

While the weight assigned to it varied between income tax and union excise duties and from FC to FC, population is used as a tax-sharing criterion in all the formulae adopted by all the commissions. The strength of this criterion has been the perception that it is objective. Any substitute for population is not altogether

necessarily includes collection effort, be a factor with a weight of 10 percent in the distribution of the divisible pool.' (Government of India, 1995) free from what was perceived, by one state or the other, to be statistical bias.[9]

One issue pertaining to the population criterion that could not be resolved so far has been as to which census figures of population to be used. The 1FC used population figures according to the census of 1951. The 2FC also used the same figures. The 3FC and 4FC as well as the 5FC presumably used the 1961 census figures available to them, though no specific mention was made of any particular census in their reports. The 6FC might have used the 1971 figures that were the latest available at that time. It was only in case of the 7FC the ToR clearly mentioned that the Commission shall adopt the population figures of 1971 which, in any case, would have been the latest census figures available. At the time of the 8FC, however, the Commission was specifically asked to adopt the population figures of the 1971 census, although the 1981 census figures would have been available to this Commission.

However, in para 7 of the ToR: 'In making its recommendations on the various matters aforesaid, the Commission shall adopt the population figures of 1971 in all cases where population is regarded as a factor for determination of devolution of taxes and duties and grants-in-aid' (Government of India, 1984). The Commission, while following this directive, noted that this was in accordance with a policy statement made by the government of India.

---

[9] 'It is for this reason that, even in the case of the Gadgil Formula for the distribution of central assistance for state Plans, it has been difficult to obtain a consensus to reduce the weight of sixty percent given for population. Population has the advantage of being an undisputed factor without any statistical bias. Further, it is broadly true that the most populous states are also the most backward, for example, Uttar Pradesh and Bihar. The fact that some prosperous states like Maharashtra are also populous vitiates the validity of population as an index of need. However, it can be argued that even such states are prosperous only because of one or two metropolitan centres and that they too have areas which are as backward as those in other states. On the other hand, there are states which are either sparsely populated like Rajasthan or have a small population like Orissa but which are admittedly backward. When we are looking for a criterion which would represent entitlement and need, these very drawbacks of population as a factor, might appear to be advantages.' (Vithal & Sastry, 2002)

In a federal system, the sharing of central resources with the states is a matter of considerable importance. In all cases where population is a factor as in the allocation of central assistance to state plans, devolution of taxes and duties, and grants-in-aid, the population figures of 1971 will continue to be followed till the year 2001. (Government of India, 1982)

Subsequently, all commissions followed this directive in their ToR and did not make an issue of it. However, the 9FC, in its second report, raised the issue whether the constraint in the ToR applied only where population was a factor for the determination of devolution of taxes and duties, and GIA. It argued that the distribution of additional duties of excise fell under a different category:

5.18 As far as population is concerned, we are making a departure from our first report. Earlier we had adopted the 1971 population for calculating the shares of the states. We have reconsidered at length whether for calculating the shares of the states in the net proceeds of Additional Duties of Excise, the 1971 or the 1981 census figures of population should be used. Paragraph 6 of the terms of reference, no doubt, lays down that this Commission should adopt the population of 1971 in all cases where population is regarded as a factor for determination of devolution of taxes and duties and grants-in-aid. But the question is whether distribution of Additional Duties of Excise is really devolution or grant. (Government of India, 1990b)

The 10FC also agreed with this view and used 1991 census figures for the distribution of additional excise duties. The next three FCs followed suit.

The 14FC had a different term of reference with regard to the population.

Contrary to the earlier requirement that the Commission shall generally take the base of population figures as of 1971, in all cases where population is a factor, our ToR indicates that we may also take into account the demographic changes that have taken place since 1971, which are best captured by the census figures of 2011.

Taking cue from that the 14FC considered another factor called the 'demographic change' as a criterion for horizontal share determination. 'Our ToR mandates us to take the population figures of 1971 when framing our recommendations, but, at the same time, allows us to consider subsequent demographic changes' (Government of India, 2015b). The 14FC felt that there is a case for using the latest census data on population. Yet, it also realized that the use of latest population data would penalize states that have taken effective population control measures.

> On the basis of the exercises conducted, we concluded that a weight to the 2011 population would capture the demographic changes since 1971, both in terms of migration and age structure. We, therefore, assigned a 10 per cent weight to the 2011 population (see Annex 8.2). (Government of India, 2015b)

The 15th FC's suggestion to use population figures from 2011 census instead of 1971 census for sharing tax revenue among states has triggered strong opposition from South India. The practice of past population figures was justified by some as disincentivizing states from letting their population proliferate. Especially, states such as Bihar and Chhattisgarh with higher rates of population growth may become relative winners compared to their southern and eastern counterparts under the 15th FC, if the latest census data of 2011 are considered for allocation of resources, against 1971 census data used earlier. Among major states, Bihar with an annual population growth of 25.1 per cent, Chhattisgarh with 22.6 per cent and Jharkhand with 22.3 per cent have the highest decadal (2000–2011) population growth rates, according to the 2011 census. On the other hand, states such as Andhra Pradesh with 11.1 per cent, West Bengal with 13.9 per cent, Odisha 14 per cent and Punjab with 13.7% have the lowest decadal population growth rates.

Per capita income

After population, per capita income has been the factor used, in one form or the other, by most commissions. The validity of population as an indicator of economic and financial needs arises out of the fact that each citizen is a unit of public needs and consumption that the state government has to meet. These needs are affected by the income distribution among the population. The 5FC used per capita income as a factor for the first time, and it took this as a criterion that would represent both the potential for raising resources and relative backwardness in economic and social development. The Commission recommended that 13.34 per cent (two-thirds of 20 per cent allocated for the criteria other than population) should be distributed among states

> whose per capita income is below the average per capita income of all states in proportion to the shortfall of the state's per capita income from all states' average, multiplied by the population of the state. For this purpose, Nagaland, for which the requisite per capita income statistics are not available, should be equated with Assam. (Government of India, 1990a)

The 6FC followed this distance method for all states with no cut-off point for eligibility. In this, the distance of per capita income of each state from the per capita income of the state which has the highest per capita income is measured. This value is then multiplied by the population of each state. In this method, the distance in the case of the state with the highest per capita income would be zero, but the commissions have adopted a method by which this state is also given a share on the basis of a notional distance between the per capita income of that state and that of the next highest-income state. The sixth, eighth, ninth and tenth commissions used this method.

Another method is based on income-adjusted total population (IATP). As mentioned earlier, it is the inverse of per capita income of a state/multiplied by its population. The share of a state is determined by the percentage of IATP of the state to the aggregate IATP of all states. The seventh and eighth commissions, and the ninth commission in its first report, used this method.

In all the cases, the commissions have taken the average state domestic product (SDP) for three years since the SDP of any particular year might be affected by chance factors such as a fall in agricultural production due to adverse seasonal conditions. The average for three years was expected to even out such year-to-year variations.

Indices of backwardness

The 3FC suggested the percentage of Scheduled Castes and Tribes and backward classes in the population, as a factor to be taken into account in determining the share to be allocated to the states. The 4FC took the following factors into account but did not indicate how the share was worked out: (a) per capita gross value of agricultural production; (b) per capita value added by manufacture; (c) percentage of workers (as defined in the census) to the total population; (d) percentage of enrolment in classes I to V, to the population in the age group 6–11; (e) population per hospital bed; (f) percentage of rural population to total population and (g) percentage of the population of Scheduled Castes and Tribes to total population. The 5FC took the following six factors: (a) scheduled population; (b) number of factory workers per lakh of population; (c) net irrigated area per cultivator; (d) length of railways and surfaced roads per 100 sq. km; (e) shortfall in the number of school-going children as compared to those of school-going age and (f) number of hospital beds per 1,000 population. Economic backwardness for fiscal transfers was introduced as an important criterion by the 8FC in the case of income tax. The 9FC worked out a composite index of backwardness combining two indices, that is, population of scheduled castes and scheduled tribes and the number of agricultural labourers in different states. The 10FC evolved an index of infrastructure consisting of five subsectors for economic infrastructure, that is, agriculture, banking, electricity, transport and communications; and two for social infrastructure consisting of education and health.

To the extent, the level of development of a state depends on the level of initial endowments and historical factors that are not in its control, perhaps, assisting them to equalize the provision of public goods and services would be a laudable objective. But the inherent danger in such a transfer system is that it tends to reward economic retardation rather than encouraging developmental efforts.

Poverty ratio

This criterion was used by the 7FC and 9FC only. The 7FC used this for the first time, stating:

37. In the light of these considerations, we have decided that the shares of the states in the divisible pool of excise should be determined giving equal weight to the population factor, the inverse of the state Domestic Product, the percentage of the poor in each state measured by a method which Prof

Raj Krishna has evolved for us, and a formula of revenue equalisation which we have worked out ... (Government of India, 1990c).

The Commission explained in detail the methodology used by it for estimating the state-wise poverty ratios. The 9FC next adopted this criterion with a reduced weight of 12.5 per cent for the year 1989–1990.

Revenue deficit as a criterion

We have seen, from the 8FC onwards, that the revenue deficit of a state has been used as a criterion for distributing a certain percentage of the net proceeds of union excise duties. The 4FC had taken the opposite view:

> ... we do not think that it is proper to bring in the element of grant into the distribution scheme of divisible taxes. In our view such non-plan revenue deficits as are left in certain states, after taking into account the share of central taxes on the basis of general and uniform principles applicable to all states, should be covered by explicit grants under Article 275 rather than by adjustments in the formulae for distribution of taxes. (Report of the Fourth Finance Commission, para 57)

The 5FC also felt that as a broad measure of the needs of different states, due regard should be given to certain selected criteria 'rather than the relative financial weakness or budgetary deficits of the states'. The 7FC felt that the role of an FC 'should not be negative, of filling in the revenue gaps only, but positive'. By 'positive', it meant that 'as many of the poorer states as possible' should be left with 'surpluses on revenue account'.

Therefore, up to the 8FC, the general view was that revenue deficits should be dealt with under Article 275 GIA rather than by any adjustments in the formulae for distribution of taxes among the states. The 8FC, however, took the view that 'this pattern of distribution between the amount received as shares of taxes and as grants needs to be corrected, so that dependence on an inelastic source of revenue like the grant-in-aid is minimized'. For this purpose, they felt that 'a progressive and simple formula of distribution among the states' would not be sufficient and that, therefore, 'it should also make a special provision to deal with the revenue deficits of the states'. The revenue deficit at the end of the process of devolution can be dealt with in its totality by GIA under Article 275. If larger resources are required for covering such revenue deficits, it does not make any difference to the total process whether a further amount is transferred to the states as additional GIA or additional devolution of the proceeds of any particular tax. The only advantage in the latter course would be that it would give to the transferred amount an elasticity which GIA do not have. It is this aspect that the 8FC took into account in increasing the percentage of the net proceeds of union excise duties to be devolved to the states and earmarking it for deficit states.

As we have mentioned earlier, in the second report of the 9FC, this particular portion of the devolved amount was more completely integrated into the formula for distribution by including it as one criterion in the formula, rather than showing it as a separate percentage amount specifically intended for states with revenue deficits.

The later FCs have used tax effort and fiscal discipline as factors representing the fiscal management efficacy.

Grants-in-Aid

Under Article 275 of the Constitution, FCs are mandated to recommend the principles as well as the quantum of GIA to those states which need assistance and that different sums may be fixed for different states. Thus, one of the prerequisites for grants is the assessment of the needs of the states. The 1FC had laid down five broad principles for determining the eligibility of a state for grants. The first was that the budget of a state was the starting point for examination of a need. The second was the efforts made by states to realize the potential, and the third was that the grants should help in equalizing the standards of basic services across states. Fourth, any special burden or obligations of national concern, though within the state's sphere, should also be considered. Fifth, grants might be given to further any beneficent service of national interest to less advanced states. By and large, these principles have guided the grants recommended by all the FCs.

Grants recommended by the FCs are predominantly in the nature of general-purpose grants meeting the difference between the assessed expenditure on the non-plan revenue account of each state and the projected revenue including the share of a state in central taxes. These are often referred to as 'gap-filling grants'. The issues relating to non-plan deficit grants are discussed in detail in a separate section. Up to the 5FC, grants were recommended only for covering the non-plan revenue deficits of states after tax devolution with only a few exceptions. The 1FC recommended grants for the expansion of primary education. The 3FC recommended grants to cover 75 per cent of the revenue component of state plans. The Government of India did not agree with this recommendation on the ground that since central assistance was specifically sanctioned for the third five-year plan (FYP), there was no need for grants for plan purposes.

The position began to change with the 6FC when that it was asked to consider the requirements of states which were backward in standards of general administration with a view to bringing them to the levels obtaining in the more advanced states. It took the view that an FC was basically concerned with expenditure on revenue account and therefore recommended upgradation grants for meeting the revenue expenditure deficiencies of certain states in areas such as general administration, administration of justice, jails, police, primary education, medical and public health and welfare of scheduled castes, scheduled tribes and other backward classes. The 7FC was asked to consider upgradation of standards in non-developmental sectors and services. The commission restricted the scope of grants to administration of taxes, treasury and accounts administration, judicial administration, general administration, police and jails. Like the 7FC, 8FC and 10FC were asked to consider non-developmental sectors. However, both these commissions recommended grants for developmental sectors such as education and health. As the ToR of the 9FC did not specifically refer to the requirements of upgradation, it did not recommend any grants in its report for the period 1990–1995. The commissions also recommended a mechanism to monitor the utilization of upgradation grants. The 11FC and 12FC did not recommend any upgradation grant.

As indicated earlier, the 6FC considered grants for meeting revenue expenditure alone. The 7FC took the view that there was no restriction imposed by Article 275 in making grants for capital expenditure. It took into account the requirements on capital account while recommending grants under upgradation and special problems. Even so, the scope of the FC grants remained GIA of the revenues to enable states to meet capital expenditure. These grants were by no means capital resource devolution.

Over the years, the scope of grants to states was extended further to cover special problems. The 8FC felt that one of the objectives of the GIA was to support states in their efforts to solve special problems facing them. Accordingly, it recommended grants for special problems in 10 states. The 9FC, too, recommended special problem grants for the year 1989–1990 but did not recommend any such grant for the period 1990–1995 on the ground that such problems were meant to be dealt with by the plan itself. The 10FC, 11FC and 12FC also recommended grants for solving special problems.

Following the 73rd and 74th amendments to the Constitution, the FCs were charged with the additional responsibility of recommending measures to augment the Consolidated Fund of a state to supplement the resources of local bodies. This has resulted in further expansion in the scope of FC grants. The 10FC was the first cCommission to have recommended grants for rural and urban local bodies, though its ToR were not amended consequent to the constitutional amendment. All the subsequent commissions had recommended grants to rural and urban local bodies. Grants to local bodies constituted 17.5 per cent of the total grants recommended by the 10FC.

The 12FC further extended the scope of grants to achieve equalization of expenditure across different states. While full equalization of expenditure would require a steep step up in the grants, the Commission restricted itself to partial equalization of services in two sectors: education and health. The Commission recommended grants under education to eight states and those under health to seven states, where the levels of revenue expenditure were lower relative to the average expenditure. The Commission adopted a new approach by recommending grants for the maintenance of roads and bridges and public buildings. These grants are in addition to the normal expenditure that the states would be incurring on the maintenance of these assets.

Thus, over the years, there has been considerable extension in the scope of GIA. Now the FC grants cover, in addition to meeting the non-plan revenue deficits, requirements of states on account of special problems, and partial equalization of certain basic services. They even cover the capital expenditure needs of states in these sectors. As a result, the share of the gap grants in total grants had come down to about 40 per cent during the period covered by the 12FC.

PLANNING COMMISSION

Let us now examine the plan transfers and find out how it has worked from the point of view of equity in interstate distribution.

Background

The offer of financial assistance from the centre to the states for implementing planned development has been an extremely important matter right from the beginning of the Indian planning process. Historically, central assistance to the states for financing development schemes had been in vogue even before the advent of the FYPs in the form of post-war development grants to the then provincial governments. After 1950–1951, the transfer of resources for development purposes under the plans came to be made under Article 282 of the Constitution. The broad channels of transfers to state by the PC are shown in Figure 3.4.

As development planning gained emphasis, the PC became a major dispenser of funds to the states.[10] Prior to the fourth FYP, the allocation

---

[10] The Planning Commission functioned as follows. It worked out FYP investments for each sector of the economy and each state. With this as background, the states worked out their respective annual plans for each year, based on the estimated resource availability, which included the balance from current revenue, contributions of public enterprises, additional resource mobilization, plan grants and loans, market borrowings and other miscellaneous capital receipts.

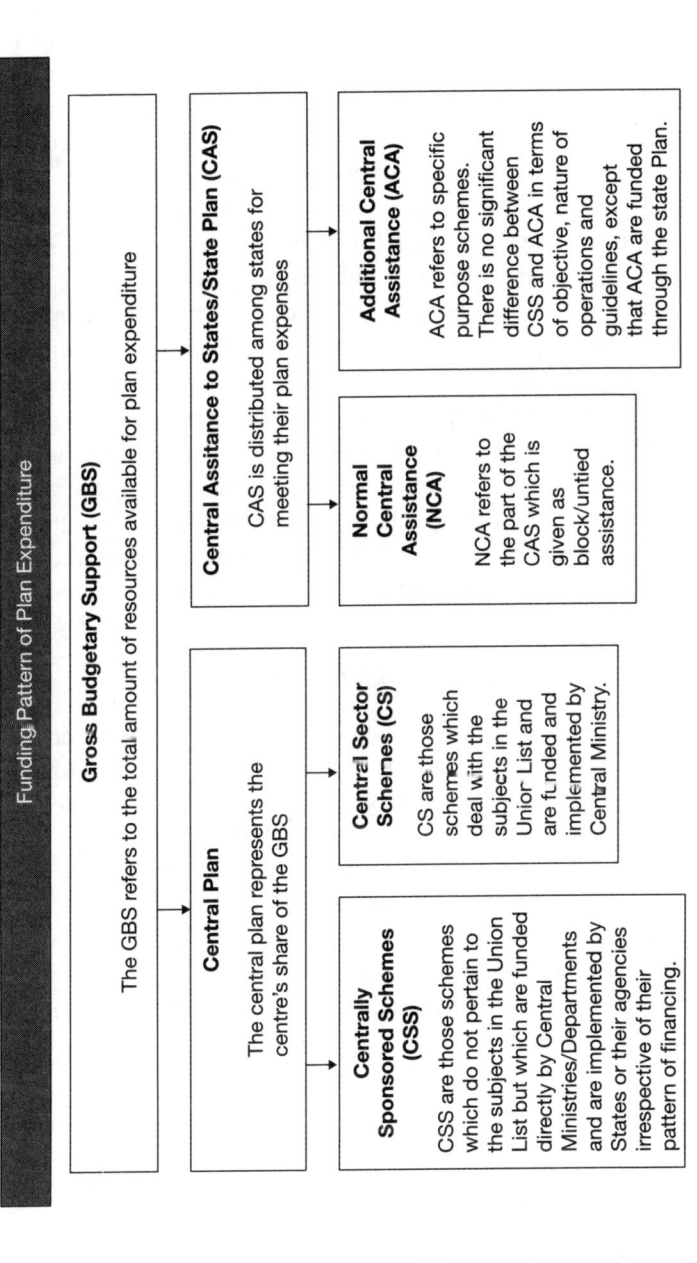

Figure 3.4 *Main Channels of Funding the Plan Expenditure to the States*

of central assistance to the state plans was based on a schematic pattern, and there was no definite formula for allocation. The first FYP had provision of only a marginal central assistance which did not play an important part. Due to this, in the second FYP, substantial importance was given to it. And in the third FYP, the states had laid more stress on planning and had become critical. In fact, they were given a choice set of various schemes with various proportions of grants and loans attached. This led to an obvious result. The states with larger resources and power could choose schemes with a greater share of grants in them. On the other hand, poor states had to finance almost all their plans by the loans given by the central government. Consequently, there were huge variations in the averages of grants and loans received by the states. A developed state which had resources received 40 per cent as grants; an underdeveloped state which had no resources received 12 per cent as grants while the average was 22 per cent. The commissions did not use a distinct criterion for allocation of resources. As a result, states were dissatisfied when they realized that the larger states were getting a bigger share in the pie.

The Gadgil Formula

In view of the general demand for an objective and transparent formula for allocation of central assistance for state plans, a formula known as the Gadgil formula was evolved in 1969, which was adopted for distribution of plan assistance during the fourth and fifth FYPs on the basis of a consensus formula decided by the NDC.[11] The arrangement as approved by the NDC was as follows:

1. The requirements of special-category states such as Assam, Jammu and Kashmir and Nagaland should first be met out of the total pool of central assistance.

The state plans were then approved by the Planning Commission. Thus, in the final analysis, given the amount of central transfers to the states as determined by the formula, at the margin it was mainly the own resource position of the states that determined their plan sizes.

[11] The NDC is chaired by the prime minister, and its members include all cabinet ministers at the centre, chief ministers of the states and members of the PC.

2. The balance of the central assistance should be distributed among the remaining 14 states on the basis of the following criteria:
   a. 60 per cent on the basis of population;
   b. 10 per cent on the basis of per capita state income, assistance under this criterion going only to those states whose per capita incomes are below the national average;
   c. 10 per cent on the basis of tax effort, determined on the basis of individual state's per capita tax receipts as percentage of the state's per capita income;
   d. 10 per cent on the basis of spillover into the fourth plan of major continuing irrigation and power projects;
   e. 10 per cent for special problems of individual states.

The reasons for the given weights were as discussed further.

Population

In a country such as India, population acts as an apt measure to represent the requirements of the people because a major portion of the population lives below the poverty line. This proposition was also supported by the empirical data, which showed a negative correlation between population of states and their per capita income.

Tax Effort

This is an important factor to measure the potential of the state as far as its own resources are concerned. This relative measure incentivizes the states to undertake measures to increase their own potential through various tax measures.

State Per Capita Income

A problem regarding unequal development among the states was faced in the earlier plans because of larger states with their large plans were able to get a larger share of resources from the centre. This led to increased inequalities amongst the states. Therefore, to make the distribution fairer, smaller states with a lesser than national per capita average income were given extra share in the resources.

Special Problems

This factor was introduced so as to provide enough resources to states to overcome problems such as droughts, famines and so on. In the absence of this share, such states would have suffered huge losses because of these problems and the implementation of their plans could have been hindered. This was a discretionary element in the formula which required proper scrutiny of the states' situation by the FC.

According to the recent formula, 30 per cent of the funds available for distribution are kept apart for the special-category states. Assistance to them is given on the basis of plan projects formulated by them, and 90 per cent of the transfer is given as grants, with the remainder as loans. The 70 per cent of the funds available to the major states is distributed with 60 per cent weight assigned to population, 25 per cent to per capita SDP, 7.5 per cent to fiscal management and the remaining 7.5 per cent to special problems of states. Of the 25 per cent weight assigned to per capita SDP, the major portion of the funds, 20 per cent is allocated only to the states with less than average per capita SDP on the basis of the 'inverse' formula; the remaining 5 per cent of the funds are assigned to all the states according to the 'distance' formula. For the major states, assistance is given by way of grants and loans in the ratio of 30:70. The transfers given to the states for plan purposes are not related to the required size or composition of plan investments. Also, in 1968, the PC induced the state governments to come to an agreement. The system of varying proportions of grants and loans from scheme to scheme was abolished. Central assistance to states was now given uniformly in blocks. Each state received 70 per cent loans and 30 per cent grants. There was no special manoeuvrability and therefore no special advantage on the part of the bigger states.

This type of settlement also faced problems because of the artificial division between the non-plan and plan expenditures. The former type of expenditure was to be looked after by the FC awards and the latter by the PC. The loan part which was given to the state had gotten accumulated, and for some of the states, the loan obligation and repayments became bigger than the assistance they received. In 1969, after the draft the fourth FYP was presented, the PC officially discussed with the states the impact of the FC awards on their finances. Great variations in the provision of these awards were witnessed amongst the states. Some states had a substantial surplus and other states could not even meet their budgetary responsibilities.

Another problem was of the ways and means advances. To overcome the temporary difficulties faced by the state governments, the Reserve Bank of India provided this facility so that the states could balance their balance sheet and remain solvent. This was the extra debt that was to be cleared quickly. After the droughts and famines hit India, states had huge overdrafts year after year. Therefore, it was recommended by the PC that resources must first be set aside for meeting the deficits of the states and then help in enabling states to put the new resources into their plans. This was an effort towards bringing non-plan and plan expenditures together. This has partially helped in solving the problem of artificial division of expenditures into plan and non-plan expenditures.

The other problem was that the total division of resources did not lead to equality in the development in the states. The larger states with their own resources could have a larger plan and the states with less of own resources at their disposal could only have smaller plans. This led to unequal patterns of development in the country. This problem was partly solved by providing 10 per cent of the total resources to states with lesser per capita income than the national average in the formula. This solution led to two other problems:

1. The states at the margin suffered a loss due to this, as the states, even marginally upper than the national average, could not avail of its rightful share.
2. Even after giving no central assistance to certain states, their per capita plan expenditure was larger than those states which entirely depended on central assistance for the finance of their plans. And it was inevitable for the government not to give any central assistance to these states.

The Gadgil formula, though well intentioned, did not achieve much success in reducing interstate disparities. For instance, Andhra Pradesh and Tamil Nadu, which came under the low-income category at the time, received below-average plan assistance, and Bihar and Uttar Pradesh just managed to get plan assistance equal to all the states' average. Therefore, there was an increasing clamour for modification of the formula, especially from the economically backward states.

The Gadgil–Mukherjee Formula

This formula was modified in 1980, and the modified formula became the basis for allocation during the sixth and seventh FYPs. The modified formula was again revised in 1990 and formed the basis for allocation of central assistance for 1991–1992 only. The NDC meeting held on 11 October 1990 discussed and approved a new revised formula, which is popularly known as the Gadgil–Mukherjee formula after the name of then deputy chairman of the PC Dr Pranab Mukherjee.

The new revised formula as approved by NDC gives weightages as follows: population (55 per cent), per capita income (25 per cent), fiscal management (5 per cent) and special problems (15 per cent). Under the new revised formula, population was given maximum weightage by considering it as the most important factor for the allocation of central assistance, but in comparison with old Gadgil formula, the weightage has been reduced by 5 per cent. The share of per capita income has increased from 20 to 25 per cent. Out of 25 per cent, 20 per cent will continue to be allocated on the principle of the deviation method (the per capita state domestic product is calculated by taking an average of per capita state domestic product whose actual data are available, for the latest three years) to those states whose per capita income is below the average national per capita income and the rest 5 per cent will be allocated to all states on the principle of the distance method (the distance of per capita income of each state from the state which has the highest per capita income) is calculated, then these values are multiplied with the respective value of the population of each state. This was done to meet the objections such as less developed states were allocated less and given low weightage. In addition, the states whose per capita income was slightly higher than the average national per capita income were deprived of share under this particular criterion.

Fiscal management, as a new criterion, has been introduced with a 5 per cent weightage by discarding the earlier tax effort criterion, which was given a 10 per cent weightage in the old Gadgil formula. Fiscal management criterion is to be assessed on the basis of a state's actual resource mobilization for its plan in comparison with the target agreed upon the PC. Therefore, this criterion is considered to be more comprehensive for fiscal efficiency than the tax effort criterion. Fiscal management was given only 5 per cent weightage due to the danger arising from the manner in which it is defined. It can develop an unhealthy competition among the states to show their resources less at the time of preparing initial resource estimates. The remaining 5 per cent weightage of tax effort has been given to the special problems criterion due to which its weightage increased from 10 to 15 per cent. The NDC has defined special problems under seven heads: coastal areas, flood- and drought-prone areas, desert problems, special environmental issues, exceptionally sparse and densely populated areas, problem of slums in urban areas and special financial difficulties for achieving minimum reasonable plan size.

By comparing the new revised Gadgil formula with the old Gadgil formula as a whole, only 85 per cent of the total central assistance has been distributed on the basis of four well-defined criteria, whereas these criteria were given 90 per cent weightage in the old Gadgil formula.

Revised Gadgil Formula in 2000

At the advent of the 21st century, the formula was reviewed, and the component of 'performance' by the respective states was adopted. The allocation accruing to the states under this head was 7.5 per cent. Within this, 2.5 per cent of the allocation was based on tax efforts of the states, 2 per cent for fiscal management at the state level and 1 per cent for undertaking population control measures. Special attention was also paid to the sluggish improvements in female literacy, and 1 per cent allocation was set aside taking female literacy into account. Timely completion of externally funded projects and land reforms undertaken accounted for the remainder of the 7.5 per cent.

CENTRALLY SPONSORED SCHEMES

CSS refer to specific-purpose schemes which are funded by the central government and implemented by states or other local agencies. These schemes were originally instituted to redress development concerns of national importance. For this purpose, through the conduit of CSS, schematic support is provided by the central government for subjects that constitutionally fall within the domain of states. The Government of India is involved in a large number of programmes in sectors/areas such as education, health, labour, skill development and so on that are in the State List through operation of CSS and provision of central assistance to state governments. These programmes essentially arose from the above national objectives and cut across state boundaries. CSS are operationalized by central ministries based on scheme-specific guidelines and are implemented by state governments or their designated agencies. These schemes had a national character and dealt with areas/concerns such as family planning, agricultural workers, research and training and so on. Since its inception, the number of schemes covered under the CSS category has multiplied.

In the initial plan years, the number of CSS was very large (190 at the end of the fifth plan, which increased to 360 at the end of the ninth plan). The total number of CSS has reduced gradually over time. Further, generally the pattern has been reduction in the number of schemes at the end of the plan after a review and subsequent increase in new schemes during the course of the plan. For example, in the 11th plan, the number of schemes declined from 155 (2005–2006) to 99 (2007–2008) at the beginning of the eleventh plan and subsequently increased to 147 (2011–2012). Transfer of funds to the states is taking place through CSS, additional central assistance (ACA) and normal central schemes. Of the total CSS provision of ₹660,506.40 crore during the eleventh plan, the nine flagship CSS alone constituted ₹524,465.99 crore, that is, 79.4 per cent.

Despite the initial intention to limit the number of CSS to matters of national policy, there was proliferation of CSS across successive plan periods (1997–2012). While the total number of schemes has declined from the 9th FYP, when there was a total of 360 CSS, to 147 during the 11th FYP, the share of CSS in the total gross budgetary support (GBS) has steadily been increasing. At the end of 11th plan, the percentage share of the CSS in the total GBS was 42 per cent, an increase of 11 percentage points from its share at the end of the 9th plan. A significant proportion of the allocations for CSS are accounted for by the central government's nine flagship schemes, which alone constituted 79.4 per cent of the total CSS provision.

THE NITI AAYOG

The Government of India, in keeping with its reform agenda, constituted the NITI Aayog in 2015 to replace the PC, to better serve the needs and aspirations of the people of the country. The NITI Aayog is expected to act as an important platform for bringing the states to act together in national interest and thereby foster 'cooperative federalism'. Let us examine the approach and scope of the former PC and the new NITI Aayog.

The PC followed a top-down approach for developing India. It meant that someone at the top decided what was suitable for people and provided monetary resources to the state governments accordingly. Under this approach, the states with fewer monetary resources had to depend upon the centre, although they had equal responsibility for the development. From this perspective, this was quite an undemocratic approach because the PC being a non-constitutional and unelected body was deciding how India was going to develop. Even in the central government, various departments had to convince the PC for departmental allocations. Further, with all these powers, there was no mechanism to assess the performance of schemes designed and implemented by the PC.

The NITI Aayog will not involve itself in planning and resource allocation and will rather function as an in-house think tank and guide the centre and states in designing better development programmes and schemes. It will not wield any decision-making power. It will focus on designing strategic and long-term policies and programmes for the Government of India. The members of the NITI Aayog include the chief ministers of all the 29 states and the seven union territories. It will have powers to allocate resources to states as per their needs and also provide relevant technical inputs. Unlike the PC's FYPs, the NITI will design a 15-year strategy for development. It is expected that the intergovernmental transfer system will be streamlined accordingly.

MAGNITUDE OF INTERGOVERNMENTAL TRANSFERS IN INDIA

The vertical fiscal transfers from centre to states recommended by successive FCs are shown in Figure 3.5. It is clear that the perceived VFI between the central and state governments in India has gradually increased close to 50 per cent of the central government tax revenues. The FCs recommended vertical transfers form only a part (albeit the major part) of the total transfers. The other transfers are due to institutions such as the PC, central sponsoring and so on.

At this stage, it may be useful to examine the historical trends in the transfers from the centre to states through major channels in India.

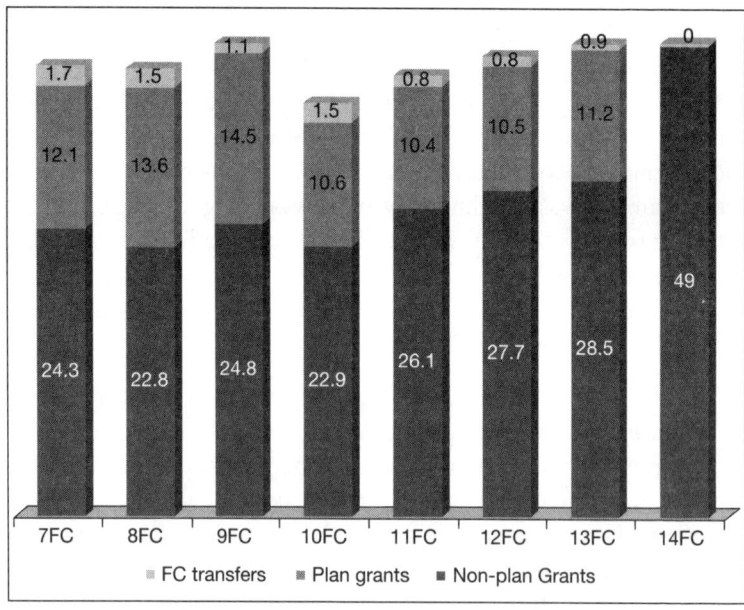

Figure 3.5 *Transfers Recommended by Different Institutions*

Table 3.6 Transfers from Centre to States as a percentage of Revenue Receipts of the Centre: 1970–1971 to 2015–2016

₹ crore

Year	Receipts of the Central Government				Resources transferred to the States						Ratios	
Finance Commission / Year	Revenue receipts including State share of taxes	Capital receipts (excluding repayment of loans)	Budgetary deficit/draw down of cash balances of Central government	Total receipts of Central government	Share of States in Central taxes	Grants from the Centre to the States and Uts	Loans (gross) from Centre to States and Uts	Repayment of loans by States and Uts	Gross transfers to States	Net transfers to States	Transfers to States as ratio to Central revenues	Tax devolution ratio
1	2	3	4	5	6	7	8	9	10	11	12	13
5th (1969–74) 1970–71	4,097	1,124	285	3,506	755	612	1,028	658	2,395	1,737	31.55	18.43
1971–72	4,972	1,207	519	6,698	944	891	1,209	854	3,044	2,190	32.70	18.99
1972–73	5,645	1,240	869	7,754	1,067	947	1,541	655	3,555	2,900	37.40	18.90
1973–74	6,247	1,504	328	8,079	1,174	952	1,576	969	3,702	2,733	33.83	18.79
6th (1974–79) 1974–75	7,782	1,583	721	10,086	1,224	1,060	1,093	507	3,377	2,870	28.46	15.73
1975–76	9,674	2,662	366	12,702	1,599	1,289	1,296	746	4,184	3,438	27.07	16.53
1976–77	10,429	3,671	131	14,231	1,690	1,622	1,481	656	4,793	4,137	29.07	16.20
1977–78	11,590	2,747	933	15,270	1,798	1,961	1,956	881	5,715	4,834	31.66	15.51
1978–79	13,197	4,203	951	18,351	1,957	2,635	2,769	892	7,361	6,469	35.25	14.83

(Continued)

Table 3.6 (Continued)

₹ crore

Finance Commission	Year	Receipts of the Central Government					Resources transferred to the States						Ratios	
		Revenue receipts including State share of taxes	Capital receipts (excluding repayment of loans)	Budgetary deficit/ draw down of cash balances of Central government	Total receipts of Central government	Share of States in Central taxes	Grants from the Centre to the States and Uts	Loans (gross) from Centre to States and Uts	Repayment of loans by States and Uts	Gross transfers to States	Net transfers to States	Transfers to States as ratio to Central revenues	Tax devolution ratio
	1	2	3	4	5	6	7	8	9	10	11	12	13
7th (1979–84)	1979–80	14,746	3,959	2,433	21,138	3,406	2,411	2,762	844	8,579	7,735	36.59	23.10
	1980–81	16,621	6,309	2,577	25,507	3,792	2,796	3,146	917	9,734	8,817	34.57	22.81
	1981–82	19,848	7,276	1,392	28,516	4,274	2,855	3,460	1,264	10,589	9,325	32.70	21.53
	1982–83	22,730	9,111	1,655	33,496	4,639	3,635	4,298	1,444	12,572	11,128	33.22	20.41
	1983–84	25,739	12,116	1,417	39,272	5,246	4,402	5,059	1,941	14,707	12,766	32.51	20.38
8th (1984–89)	1984–85	30,161	14,041	3,745	47,947	5,777	5,220	6,177	2,454	17,174	14,720	30.70	19.15
	1985–86	36,698	17,441	4,937	59,076	7,491	7,067	8,473	2,739	23,031	20,292	34.35	20.41
	1986–87	42,730	19,215	8,261	70,206	8,476	7,744	7,895	2,909	24,115	21,206	30.21	19.84
	1987–88	48,001	22,458	5,816	76,275	9,598	9,210	9,414	3,563	28,222	24,659	32.33	20.00
	1988–89	55,721	26,365	5,642	87,728	10,669	10,076	10,046	3,316	30,791	27,475	31.32	19.15

Plan	Year											
9th (1989–95)	1989–90	67,198	26,630	10,592	1,04,420	13,232	8,713	11,311	3,356	33,256	29,900	28.63	19.69
	1990–91	71,408	34,542	11,347	1,17,297	14,535	13,293	14,522	4,653	42,350	37,697	32.14	20.35
	1991–92	85,460	35,018	6,855	1,27,333	17,197	15,805	13,199	3,781	46,201	42,420	33.31	20.12
	1992–93	97,092	36,088	12,312	1,45,492	20,522	17,943	13,335	4,639	51,800	47,161	32.41	21.14
	1993–94	1,00,840	54,946	10,960	1,66,746	22,241	20,956	15,263	5,192	58,460	53,268	31.95	22.06
	1994–95	1,19,221	62,362	961	1,82,544	24,840	20,297	18,807	4,494	63,944	59,450	32.57	20.84
10th (1995–2001)	1995–96	1,43,062	54,428	9,807	2,07,297	29,285	21,577	19,627	4,790	70,489	65,699	31.69	20.47
	1996–97	1,65,532	54,004	13,154	2,32,690	35,061	23,545	24,031	6,459	82,637	76,178	32.74	21.18
	1997–98	1,90,223	7,828	66,288	2,64,339	43,548	30,452	14,729	7,125	88,729	81,604	30.87	22.89
	1998–99	2,01,503	1,01,536	–144	3,02,895	39,145	25,844	15,935	9,475	80,924	71,449	23.59	19.43
	1999–2000	2,42,527	1,21,944	–13,817	3,50,654	43,481	29,837	21,462	9,791	94,780	84,989	24.24	17.93
11th (2000–05)	2000–01	2,56,602	1,13,359	6,911	3,76,872	51,945	37,684	20,490	11,691	1,10,119	98,428	26.12	20.24
	2001–02	2,73,332	82,078	62,923	4,18,333	53,528	42,489	24,528	14,002	1,20,545	1,06,543	25.47	19.58
	2002–03	3,06,340	1,24,918	10,095	4,41,353	56,841	43,167	28,231	30,303	1,28,239	97,936	22.19	18.55
	2003–04	3,53,612	99,852	4,796	4,58,260	67,366	48,430	25,449	61,179	1,41,245	80,066	17.47	19.05
	2004–05	3,99,417	1,61,676	63,819	6,24,912	80,159	53,873	24,806	59,737	1,58,838	99,101	15.86	20.07
12th (2005–10)	2005–06	4,59,361	83,760	–64,850	4,78,271	95,887	73,677	5,654	8,799	1,75,218	1,66,419	34.80	20.87
	2006–07	5,69,012	1,04,913	–25,930	6,47,995	1,22,330	90,185	4,970	15,338	2,17,485	2,02,147	31.20	21.50
	2007–08	7,19,316	1,60,586	–310	8,79,592	1,53,600	1,08,377	6,706	8,290	2,68,683	2,60,393	29.60	21.35
	2008–09	7,23,037	1,85,584	–1,52,193	7,56,428	1,61,979	1,24,090	7,115	2,711	2,93,184	2,90,473	38.40	22.40
	2009–10	7,70,151	4,57,873	11,155	12,39,179	1,67,992	1,40,955	7,907	8,664	3,16,853	3,08,189	24.87	21.81

(Continued)

Table 3.6 (Continued)

₹ crore

Finance Commission	Year	Receipts of the Central Government				Resources transferred to the States						Ratios	
		Revenue receipts including State share of taxes	Capital receipts (excluding repayment of loans)	Budgetary deficit/draw down of cash balances of Central government	Total receipts of Central government	Share of States in Central taxes	Grants from the Centre to the States and Uts	Loans (gross) from Centre to States and Uts	Repayment of loans by States and Uts	Gross transfers to States	Net transfers to States	Transfers to States as ratio to Central revenues	Tax devolution ratio
	1	2	3	4	5	6	7	8	9	10	11	12	13
13th (2010–15)	2010–11	10,44,013	3,89,900	–14,189	14,19,724	2,23,203	1,57,181	10,299	9,327	3,90,683	3,81,356	26.86	21.38
	2011–12	10,46,933	4,24,514	–1,11,156	13,60,292	2,59,412	1,77,426	10,088	10,754	4,46,926	4,36,172	32.06	24.78
	2012–13	12,06,682	5,17,765	–2,338	17,22,109	2,94,357	1,77,708	14,059	9,511	4,86,124	4,76,613	27.68	24.39
	2013–14	13,76,568	5,43,785	11,437	19,31,790	3,22,880	1,94,119	11,090	10,119	5,28,089	5,17,969	26.81	23.46
	2014–15(R.E.)	15,11,624	5,13,079	–35,499	19,89,204	3,42,928	3,23,923	12,121	9,135	6,78,972	6,69,837	33.67	22.69
14th (2015–20)	2015–16(B.E.)	17,14,503	5,83,080	–42,104	22,55,479	5,29,648	2,97,572	12,679	9,372	8,39,899	8,30,527	36.82	30.89

Source: Government of India, Indian Public Finance Statistics, 2015–16 (Table 6.4)

Notes: 1. Figures in brackets represent the ratios after adding the loans given to the States for clearing their overdrafts/deficits with the R.B.I. to the total receipts of the Central Government as well as to the gross transfer to the States.

2. Article 270 of the constitution, was retrospectively amended with effect from 1st April, 1996. Under the provision of the Constitution (80th Amendment) Act, 2000, prescribed share of States in the net proceeds of Central taxes and duties does not form part of the Consolidated Fund of India.

Over the four decades or so, from 1970–1971 to 2015–2016 (period covered up to the 14th FC), the actual transfers (revenue and capital) from the central government to states rose from 32 to 36 per cent, that is, more or less remained constant. The aggregate share of states in the net proceeds of all union taxes and duties, excluding surcharge, cesses and the cost of collection during the last two decades has fluctuated between 26 and 30 per cent (Table 3.6). The year-to-year fluctuations in terms of the percentage of all union taxes and duties may have largely been due to fluctuations in the rates of growth of income tax and union excise duties, which were the only taxes shared with the states before the 80th amendment to the Constitution, apart from the grants given in lieu of passenger tax, and the collections from additional excise duty in lieu of sales tax on these commodities.

Major Issues of the Federal Fiscal Transfer System

4

The federal fiscal system being a crucial aspect of the Indian economy needs fundamental revamping. This is required not only because of the major changes in the structure of the economy but also because of the persistence of certain shortcomings in the existing federal fiscal mechanism. Over time, to some extent, the principles and methods adopted have undergone substantial changes and rightly so in keeping with the changing economic structure and policy environment. However, there is a necessity to bring more fundamental changes in the approach to make it more objective and scientific.

ISSUES WITH THE PRESENT TRANSFER METHODS

In India, there have been multiple agencies involved in determining and administering the intergovernmental transfers: FC, PC, NDC, ISC as well as central ministries. The transfers are of varied types: tax power sharing, tax base sharing, tax devolutions, tax assignments, general-purpose grants, conditional grants, specific-purpose grants and so on. The formula-based central assistance to states and the associated political pressures impede unified developmental efforts. Therefore, there is a need to integrate the institutional structure for an efficient intergovernmental transfer mechanism.

Multiple Agencies with Overlapping Advisory Functions

Today, apart from the FC, there are many agencies, councils, commissions, committees and so on that are involved in the design and monitoring of the economic policies. For example, the PMEAC advises the prime minister on a host of economic issues such as inflation, microfinance, industrial output and so on. It is supported in its functions by a team of officials and administrators. There is no fixed definition on the exact number of members and staff of the PMEAC. For administrative, logistic, planning and budgeting purposes, the NITI Aayog serves as the nodal agency. The PMEAC, for example, recommended initiating the process of fiscal consolidation given that the international financial crisis has started to ease and the government had to re-initiate its commitment to the Fiscal Responsibility and Budget Management Act. The policy advices given by these agencies have profound effect on the federal fiscal balances. For example, the GST, petrol pricing, direct tax reforms and other macroeconomic policies have a direct bearing on the federal fiscal balances. There seems to be considerable overlapping of the functions of such bodies with the FCs. In most instances, the FC through the ToR is also entrusted to look into each of these matters and make recommendations. When PC was in existence and making independent transfer polices for capital expenditure requirements of the states, there arose significant lack of coordination between the two bodies. This was partly averted by inducting one member of the PC into the FC. Nevertheless, there is a need to merge all the advisory bodies into the FC and expand its scope of operations.

The Permanency Issue

An aspect that has received persistent attention is whether the FC should be made to be a permanent organ of the government administration and how, then, its role can be enhanced. This issue has been debated over the years since the 2FC itself. However, the issue was somewhat misunderstood as a step towards the transfer of an increasing amount of funds from the centre to the states. This issue has been examined by many scholars (Sarma & Bhaskar, 2012). The setting up of the FC at five-year intervals has been leading to a variety of immature acts. For example, as observed by Sarkar (1969):

> The Uttar Pradesh government, for instance, hustled its pay commission to conclude its work, issued a government order on the pay body's report

and sent copies of the order and of the report by a chartered plane—to New Delhi, only to meet the deadline for submission of Statements set by the Fourth Finance Commission. The West Bengal government raised the dearness allowance of its staff by Rs.9 crores on March 27, 1969, to show the amount as committed expenditure for the last financial year which was to expire in another three days.

Besides,

> Many state governments are also known to submit one set of financial statements to the Finance Commission and another for the Planning Commission. In the former, they normally try to show an inflated figure of deficits in non-plan revenue account, the obvious intention being to reinforce their demand for a larger share of divisible taxes and grants in aid. In statements for the planning body, they quite often draw a much more elastic estimate of their resources to justify their demand for a big state plan ... Every effort is made at present to shake off even the faintest suggestion of continuity between successive Commissions. (Sarkar, 1969)

Actually, even the 1FC suggested the setting up of a small organization preferably in the secretariat of the president for conducting continuous study of the finances of the state governments, working of state undertakings and so on. This was indeed accepted by the government, but all that was done was to set up a small cell in the finance ministry. The 2FC also suggested that a nucleus staff with experience of the work of the FC should be retained within the finance ministry and its services be made available to future commissions. The 3FC also stressed the importance and necessity of arranging the compilation of reliable statistics. The cell, maintained in the finance ministry, consists of only some ministerial staff. No data except the central and state budgets are kept. So, the 4FC suggested that the cell should be strengthened by the addition of personnel with suitable research experience who would be able to continue to collect and analyse the relevant material.

Such permanent bodies are in fact in existence in some countries with federal constitutions. The Australian Federal Grants Commission, which bears some similarity to our FCs in terms of its functions, is a permanent institution. In the United States, two permanent agencies look after interstate and federal–state financial issues. While the council of state governments (CSG) deals mostly with the issues arising between states, the advisory committee of intergovernmental relations (ACIR) performs somewhat extended functions. In fact, the World Bank has, for long, voiced that making FC a permanent body (as in Australia for example) would improve coordination and data collection. However, there are arguments against a permanent FC. For example, one argument is that it will induce states to show perennial deficits in their revenue accounts. Not only will they refrain from taking measures to make up the deficits, but they will manipulate the figures in such a way that the deficits continue. But it has been pointed out that when there is a permanent body, keeping vigil on the states' performances round the year, the states in turn would have less scope for putting pressure on the Commission to secure higher allotments. And the centre can always make them feel that they cannot live by deficits alone. Thus, it is time to think of establishing a permanent structure for the purpose.

Vertical Federal Fiscal Sharing: Major Issues

Intergovernmental transfers are needed not only to correct the inherent fiscal mismatch between the revenue sources and expenditure needs of the federating units, but also to reduce the possible inequalities with respect to their revenue capacities and unit costs of providing public goods and services. In India, the issue of devising an appropriate transfer mechanism aimed at reducing the fiscal imbalances—vertically between the central government and provincial governments, and horizontally among different provincial jurisdictions—remains contentious.

Along with the revamping and strengthening of the institutional structure, it is important to apply scientific and rational methods for determining the transfers. The vertical sharing formula in India, for example, inadvertently follows an incremental approach. FC after FC the objective appears to increase the share of the states, albeit marginally. Unfortunately, the determination of the vertical transfer has mostly been intuitive, and there is no evidence of any scientific derivation of the share.

Horizontal Fiscal Sharing: Issues

Although significant efforts are made by the FC to bring about some amount of objectivity and integrate the system of tax devolution and enlarge the divisible pool to include all union taxes, with regard to the horizontal revenue sharing however, not much attention seems to have been paid. One aspect that remains a source of controversy is the near-subjective identification of the criteria determining the horizontal shares, and arbitrary assignment of weights to them.

In the past, successive FCs in India used several criteria for determining the horizontal shares of the tax devolution transfers. The basic criteria used so far by are (a) population, (b) transformations of income such as 'distance' and 'inverse' ('income-adjusted population' as sometimes referred to), (c) developmental indicators such as poverty, backwardness and infrastructure, (d) contribution, (e) tax effort and (f) fiscal self-reliance.

As observed by the 10FC, the criteria for determining the inter se shares of states have tended to converge since the 7FC. Yet, the selection of a particular set of factors and the weights assigned to them for determining the shares largely remained subjective and continue to be 'a gamble on the personal views of five persons, or a majority of them' (Dissent Note to the Report of the Fourth Finance Commission as quoted by Guhan 1995). As Rao and Sen (1995) observe, 'The tax devolution is recommended mainly on the basis of general economic indicators and not fiscal disadvantage per se...' (p. 142).

Even if one is in broad agreement with the selected criteria for horizontal transfers, the assignment of weights to these factors still poses a problem. The weights assigned by the FCs do not seem to flow from any comprehensive theoretical framework. If there exists a scientific basis for deriving these numbers, none of the FCs has cared to explain it. As the magnitudes of transfer shares are highly sensitive to the assigned weights, even the slightest modification in them is likely to result in significantly different patterns of shares. Thus, there is a need to reduce the discretionary elements in the assignment of weights.

As regards the horizontal sharing, the approach adopted so far reflects some inherent confusion: whether and to what extent states' efficiency should be rewarded, to what extent equity should be built, to what extent the state-specific factors and circumstances should be taken into account while assessing the fiscal management of the states and so on.

For example, as Sarma (1997) pointed out:

> In several cases the transfers are subject to a great deal of experimentation and frequent modification. Often, the lack of agreement on the criteria has led to dominance of political considerations rather than economic rationale. … the debate shows that an objective transfer mechanism has eluded the policy-makers so far. Although significant efforts have been made by the last two Finance Commissions (10th and 11th FCs) to integrate the system of tax devolution and enlarge the divisible pool to include all union taxes, with regard to the horizontal revenue sharing however, not much attention has been paid.

Sarma (1997) then proceeded to develop a method of objectively identifying the criteria and deriving of weights for deciding the horizontal revenue shares within a fiscal behavioural framework. The selection of a particular set of factors and the weights assigned to them for determining the shares largely remained subjective and continues to be 'a gamble on the personal views of five persons, or a majority of them'.[1] As Rao and Sen (1995) observe, 'The tax devolution is recommended mainly on the basis of general economic indicators and not fiscal disadvantage per se …' (p. 142).

Looking at the evolution and development of the tax-sharing process through successive FCs, it can be observed that the criteria for determining the inter se shares of states have tended to converge since the 7FC.[2] The convergence process was aptly summed up by the 11FC

[1] Dissent Note to the Report of the Fourth Finance Commission as quoted by Guhan (1995).

[2] Typically, the formula used by the past FCs for determining the tax devolution shares of states is a linear combination of the selected quantified factors. For example, the 11FC used area, population of 1971, per capita income distance from the highest (average of the top three states), infrastructure distance (average

as follows: 'Up to the Seventh Finance Commission, the formulae used for determining the income tax shares were clearly distinct from those for the union excise duties. Since then, a process of convergence between the two sets of formulae is distinctly noticeable.'

Inclusion of Surcharges and Cesses, Cost of Collection and Non-tax Revenues

An important improvement has been the combining of all the central taxes for revenue sharing as recommended by the 10th FC and implemented through the Constitutional 80th Amendment. Yet, several central revenue sources such as the cesses and service tax proceeds are left out of the sharable pool. More importantly, it is necessary to apply the objective method for determining the vertical share.

It has been argued that the power to levy surcharges, instead of meeting any emergent requirements of a specific nature, is used as a normal source of revenue. Article 271 gives the power to levy surcharge on all union taxes and not merely on income tax and the taxes specified in Article 269, as was the position before the 80th

of the top three states), tax effort (T/Y) and fiscal discipline index. The equation used was of the form:

$$G = 0.1 \times P_{1971} + 0.075 \times A + 0.625 \times (Ky - Y/P) \times P_{1971} + 0.075 \times (Ki - I) \times P_{1971}$$
$$+ 0.05 \times (T/Y) \times (P/Y)0.5 \times P_{1971} + 0.075 \times Fe/Fb \times P_{1971},$$

where G = total tax devolution; P_{1971} = population according to 1971 census; A = of the geographical area; Y = GSDP; P = current population; Ky = highest per capita income (average of the top three states); I = infrastructure index; Ki = highest infrastructure index; T = tax revenue; Fe = ratio of own revenue to total expenditure relative to all-state average ratio in the last three years; Fb = ratio of own revenue to total expenditure relative to all-state average ratio in the base three years. (All variables expressed as shares in respective totals.)

It can be observed that all the criteria except area are multiplied by the 1971 population, which clearly means that the variation in the tax devolution share with population is taken for granted. Equity is sought among the states not with respect to the total transfers but with respect to the per capita transfers. In other words, the above equation can actually be viewed as

$$G/P_{1971} = 0.1 + 0.075 \times A/P_{1971} + 0.625 \times (Ky - Y/P) + 0.075 \times (Ki - I)$$
$$+ 0.05 \times (T/Y) \times (P/Y)0.5 + 0.075 \times Fe/Fb.$$

Amendment to the Constitution. Surcharge levied on any tax is not sharable, and therefore, to the extent that power to levy surcharge is used as a revenue-raising measure, it affects the states. The concept of net proceeds, instead of gross proceeds of union taxes, does not provide any incentive to the union to reduce the collection cost. The cost of collection of the union taxes, which was only 0.67 per cent of the gross tax revenue in 1980–1981, has gone up to 1.06 per cent of the gross tax revenue.

Also, over the years, the non-tax revenue of the union has increased significantly. In 1980–1981, non-tax revenue was only 24 per cent of the total revenue receipts of the union, which grew to almost 30 per cent in 1999–2000. The non-tax revenue is non-sharable. Hence, the union government is now better equipped, financially, to meet with its expenses and therefore there is a scope for higher devolution of union taxes to the states.

Taxation of Services

Although there is no explicit mention of services in the Seventh Schedule, taking cue from entry 97, which allows the central government to levy taxes on the residual items, the central government has been levying taxes on services under this entry. The selective taxation started with three services (telecommunications, non-life insurance and stockbrokers) in 1994 and was progressively extended to 26 services by 2000–2001. In the 2001–2002 budget, the tax was extended to 14 more services. Out of these, telecommunication, non-life insurance, brokerage, advertising and courier contribute to over 90 per cent of the revenue from service tax.

There has been considerable discussion on sharing of the power to levy the tax on services between the centre and states. To begin with, the constitutional scheme assigning the power to levy sales tax on goods and not services is not in keeping with the modern methods of production and distribution and led to multiple taxation and other distortions. The most important consideration warranting a discussion on sharing of power to tax services is the need to convert the central excise with state-level VAT. In the absence of sharing of powers of service taxation, the state VAT will only be partial as it would not be possible to extend credit to input tax on services.

Two alternative models are suggested for sharing of tax powers with the states. One model is to clearly distinguish between services having nationwide ramifications and those with regional spread and assign the latter to the states. This can lead to several harmonization complications.

The alternate approach to sharing tax powers with the states is to give concurrent power to levy tax on all services to the centre as well as states. This will enable the states as well as the centre to include all tradable services in the tax base and provide credit on all input as well as output taxes paid on services forming inputs in the production/trading of other goods and services. This would require the amendment of the Constitution to place taxation of services in the Concurrent List.

IMPACT OF RESTRUCTURING THE ECONOMY

Three of the important milestones in the economic reforms that can have deep impact on the federal fiscal relations and therefore call for revamping of the relevant institutions are taken up for analysis in this study, namely (a) economic liberalization in 1991, (b) abolition of the PC and setting up of the NITI Aayog in 2014 and (c) the introduction of GST in 2015.

Over the last two decades, the Indian economy has been experiencing significant growth along with structural transformation necessitating vital economic reforms not only for sustaining the economic growth but also to bring about necessary changes in the policy environment to cope up with the structural changes in the economy. The federal fiscal system being a crucial aspect of the Indian economy also needs fundamental revamping. The analysis of federal fiscal arrangements in India assumes particular importance in the wake of the economic liberalization process initiated since 1991. With the reassessment of the role of the state, a review of federal fiscal arrangements has in fact become necessary. Among other factors, the intergovernmental fiscal arrangements in India and institutional framework to conduct and monitor them have evolved to suit the requirements of the public sector-dominated, heavy industry-based, import-substituting development planning strategy adopted in the four and a half decades since Independence. As the planning agency passes on the allocational role to the market, and as the economy is opened up to face international competition, intergovernmental fiscal arrangements and the institutional framework to conduct them will have to adapt to the new role of the state' (Rao & Sen, 1995, p. 4). To some extent, realizing this fact, the FC is being increasingly entrusted with many other tasks, including that of the overall macroeconomic and fiscal management of the country. Instead of such cosmetic changes as in the ToR, it is time for fundamental institutional changes in the form and working of the FC. It is, therefore, imperative that some thought should be given to this aspect and sufficiently debated.

The changeover to a more liberalized and open economy in 1991 involved designing and sequencing of the reforms and redefining the governmental role. In the new situation, the governments at the central, state and local levels need to shift their focus from direct participation in production and distribution activities to strengthening the regulatory mechanism. It, in turn, has necessitated relatively more active participation of the subnational governments in the regulatory set-up than during the earlier era. This is because the market regulation is more effective when implemented at decentralized levels. At the same time, the SNGs will have to continue to provide quasi-public goods.

The structure of intergovernmental relationship and the various institutions to conduct and monitor them have evolved over the years in the framework of a planned economy. Of course, unlike the comprehensive central planning followed in socialist economies, Indian planning did give a substantial role to the private sector as well as sub-central levels of government. Nevertheless, to direct resource allocation to the desired activities and regions, it was necessary to secure the resources required by the public sector investments, and centralization of economic power was inevitable. With the opening up of the economy, a greater role is assigned to the market in resource allocation, and substantial restructuring of intergovernmental fiscal relationships becomes necessary in order to provide public services to cater to diverse preferences.

IMPACT OF CLOSING THE PC IN FAVOUR OF THE NITI AAYOG

In May 2014, the Government of India abolished the PC. The main idea for this step appears to be to strengthen the role of the states in the process of economic development. No doubt, the states' representation in NITI Aayog is stronger than in PC, but there is a need to make the capital transfers to the states with more flexibility and control of the states, and with increased accountability. The transfer and allocation mechanisms need improvement also in terms of transparency, monitoring and evaluation.

In the Indian federal system, fiscal transfers are essentially of three types: from current revenues as determined by the FC, capital transfers for financing investment by the erstwhile PC and transfers under CSS.

As regards the CSS and projects, it is suggested rightly that the centre takes full responsibility for financing investment and operational costs of projects that have spillover across states, regardless of the authority that implements them (centre or state):

> This is so because under the current system of centrally sponsored schemes, under which the centre provides partial funding for the project's investment cost and for its operational cost for a limited period has had the unfortunate effect that projects get started and completed, but once completed are not fully utilized because states have not provided the needed costs of operating them once it became their exclusive responsibility to provide them. The centre assuming full financial responsibility will avoid this waste. (Singh, 2015, p. 53)

It is suggested that

> (ii) The NITI Aayog serve as a fund for public investment (FPI) for both the centre and states. Its shareholders would be the state and central governments. The Fund, much like a multilateral development bank, would appraise the projects proposed for their economic and social returns as well as feasibility and soundness of proposed financing (from the centre or state's

own resources, borrowing from domestic and foreign sources and capital transfers from the centre, if relevant. (Singh, 2015, p. 53)

Now, the money for central schemes, though vastly pruned, is released by the finance ministry, which does not have the wherewithal to do it. The finance ministry is now the nodal agency, with the distinction between plan and non-plan expenditure done away with. Also, the states will have to directly deal with the central ministry concerned for centrally sponsored projects, which were earlier routed through the PC. The 14th FC also ensured that states received 10 per cent more untied money from the centre.

THE IMPACT OF GST

An important milestone in the Indian economy is the introduction of GST. India has been making efforts towards transforming its indirect tax system into a full-fledged VAT system in line with the worldwide trends. However, being a federal country where the constituent states enjoy independent fiscal powers, countrywide tax system reform involves coordinated and harmonized changes across the country to minimize the likely distortions in the centre–state and interstate economic relations. After considering different options, it was decided to have a concurrent VAT system, wherein both the central and state governments would simultaneously levy the VAT. Accordingly, a variant of full value-added taxation was launched in the name of GST on 1 July 2017.

GST is levied within a state both by the state government (SGST) and by the central government (CGST). Both would be levied on the same value excluding any prior tax. In case of transactions across the states or union territories, the two GSTs are combined into one and called the integrated GST (IGST). The following taxes are subsumed under GST:

Central taxes

1. Central excise duty
2. Duties of excise (medicinal and toilet preparations)

3. Additional duties of excise (goods of special importance, textiles and textile products)
4. Additional duties of customs (commonly known as countervailing duty)
5. Special additional duty of customs (SAD)
6. Service tax
7. Central surcharges and cesses on supply of goods and services

State taxes

1. State VAT
2. Central sales tax
3. Luxury tax
4. Entry tax (all forms)
5. Entertainment and amusement tax (except when levied by the local bodies)
6. Taxes on advertisements
7. Purchase tax
8. Taxes on lotteries, betting, and gambling

Impact on the Federal Fiscal Balance

The introduction of GST required the states to surrender their power to tax sales, which has been their most important revenue source. This would compel them to depend more on federal fiscal tax-sharing arrangements. Prior to the implementation of VAT, the states on average derived about 70 per cent of their tax revenue from their own sources, and the rest 30 per cent came from the centre through tax devolution by the FC. Under the GST option, their dependence on the centre for meeting their current expenditure will be likely to go up from less than 40 per cent to about 65 per cent. The centre is already collecting 62 per cent of the total tax revenue; GST is expected to increase this amount to 83 per cent, leaving the states with bare resources.

Although the loss in revenue of the states due to introduction of GST is promised to be compensated by the centre (as provided for in the GST Bill) for some time, yet, it does not make good a state's loss of the political right to fix its own tax rates. The states will have no power to decide what rates to impose on which goods, including luxuries and necessities. State governments will be left with no alternate ways to fund deficits and overdrafts, which they could do under the existing fiscal policy. Furthermore, the excess of powers given to the centre would hamper the democratic and federal set-up, leaving the state governments, usually made up of various political ideologies, completely at the mercy of the centre. Moreover, the restrictions imposed by a uniform tax regime could adversely impact states that may be more committed to welfare expenditures.

Thus, with the tax powers of states severely limited, fiscal decentralization, which is advocated on efficiency grounds (that is, for permitting the citizens to determine the quantum and content of public services at the local levels according to their preference pattern), would be seriously undermined. Further, if the revenue is collected by the states but pooled and distributed through a revenue-sharing formula, there would be little incentive for the states to take the responsibility for administering it unless the distribution is made largely based on collection. The state governments will be left with negligible control over funds for the working of their states and will be dependent on the centre for means to fund disasters and welfare programmes.

Establishing the GST Council is not viable and practical because the council will be a centrally run institution, and the centre will have a lot of stakes in the decisions of this body. All of this, inadvertently, diminishes the powers of the states, seriously threatening the federal structure that India has sustained for so long.

The Indian model of having a GST is at two levels: one levied by the centre (CGST) and the other by the states (SGST). But the problem under dual GST relates to vertical tax externality. This happens when both the levels of the government, centre and states, levy tax on the same base. The tax policy decisions of one level of government will affect the tax base of the other. For instance, if the central government increases the tax rate levied on a commodity, the tax liability of taxpayers will rise. In turn, the consumer will reduce the demand for the commodity, which will reduce the total tax amount payable to both the levels of government. This will lead to a reduction in the tax base, adversely affecting the tax revenue of the states as well as the central government. While the Bill will help in expanding the tax net, curbing tax evasion and increasing revenues from taxation, it will also negatively impact the state governments' financial autonomy and planning. Also, if the concerns of the states are not taken seriously, GST will end up profiting big corporate houses.

Indicators suggest that of all the countries which have introduced a uniform tax structure, no country with a federal structure has been able to successfully implement the system while retaining the centre–state balance.

In the light of the introduction of GST and the possible increase in the states' dependence on the centre, the sharing responsibility of the FC increases. This would call for reviewing the sharing formulae, making it less arbitrary and more acceptable.

The above economic reforms and the restructuring measures call for changes in the federal fiscal sharing system. Even under the existing system, there exist several thorny issues that need basic changes in the working of the FC.

Guidelines for Restructuring

This chapter suggests strengthening of the federal fiscal management by reviewing the constitutional provisions, revamping the institutional structure as well as reforming the system and the methods of inter-governmental transfers. The trends in the approaches by successive FCs clearly indicate a gradual transition from a centripetal type of federalism towards cooperative federalism where the SNGs have more say in the economic management. It might be useful to restructure and rationalize the institutional structure and mechanism. Singh and Srinivasan (2013) also proposed that the centre–state transfers through the FC, PC (now its successor, NITI Aayog) and the ministries have to be looked at in a unified framework.

BROAD INSTITUTIONAL STRUCTURE AND ORGANIZATION

We have observed that over the last five decades, there has been steady widening of the FC's mandate and the change in the ToR. Gone are the times when the basic function of the FC was to merely recommend vertical and horizontal sharing of revenues between the centre and the constituent states. Of late, the FC has been entrusted with several tasks including recommending for better macroeconomic and fiscal management. Besides the macroeconomic management, other issues include calamity relief to states, need for ensuring reasonable returns on investments in power, transport and industrial enterprises (Government of India, 1988).

Therefore, instead of having multiple agencies for economic policies that directly or indirectly influence the federal fiscal sharing with the risk of little or zero coordination, it is advisable to have a single permanent agency, empowered to take care of the macroeconomic policies, fiscal policy reviews, fiscal monitoring, achieving federal fiscal balance. The institution of FC should be shaped up and needs to be strengthened for the purpose.

The first and foremost task in this respect would be to make the FC set-up permanent. To begin with, although the chairman and members might be for a limited period, the Commission's secretariat and administration should be functioning all the time. Its functions can be expanded to include not only to focus on current revenue sharing, but also to take care of aspects of fiscal and economic management such as the capital expenditure planning, public debt management, fiscal monitoring, and overall macroeconomic management. It would be advisable to expand the membership of the FC to have more members, say at least 10 members, and more experts, somewhat like the erstwhile PC. The permanent FC can be expected to be the country's macroeconomic manager, as an apex instrument body to monitor the economy of the country as well as the states and local bodies, and as the think tank for the design of the important economic policies. A permanent commission can take up these matters with the states and make them implement reforms such as tax reforms and GST. Even the GST Council can be part of the FC.

In short, the institutional structure for the financial management of the country would comprise of the three basic organizations: the Ministry of Finance, the FC and the NDC. The Ministry of Finance gives broad guidelines for the macro fiscal policy; the FC formulates the detailed recommendations based on meticulous research. These recommendations will be studied, discussed and agreed upon by the NDC by way of states' cooperation. Thereafter, the Ministry will implement the final recommendations. The FC basically acts as a think tank for the government and provides the research support to the fiscal policies of the government. It also takes into account the states' views and builds the consensus among the states so that the policies will have the cooperation of the state governments.

Second, there will be a change in the hierarchy and reporting. At present, when the FC submits its reports, they are deliberated in the Parliament before implementation. There is hardly any scope for reflecting the states' views in the report. The FC customarily collects the states' views and makes its own recommendations that need not always be based on the states' consensus. In the new set-up, there will be sufficient scope for ascertaining the consent of the states on the FC proposals before submitting the recommendations. The NDC[1] can be the ideal forum and, therefore, the NDC can be designated as the nodal agency for the FC. This way, the cooperative federalism can be sustained. This is particularly preferable as the NDC is composed of state government representatives. The FC being a neutral body can help generate a sense of confidence in the states that any injustice done to them need not be endured for five long years. FC recommendations will be first submitted for discussion to the NDC before they are tabled in the Parliament. In this way, there is little chance of states being unhappy about the FC recommendations.

Third, the various economic management institutions such as the NITI Aayog and the PMEAC can be merged with the FC to avoid conflicting views. The FC will have different wings or sections looking after different aspects of the economy such as planning and infrastructure development wing, local bodies wing, tax design wing, state finances wing, union finances wing, social development wing, apart from the revenue-sharing wing and grants wing. As all these are interlinked, it is all the more reason to make them function within the FC. In short, the FC will be the main think tank for the economic policies of the country.

[1] The NDC is the apex body for decision creating and deliberations on development matters in India, presided over by the prime minister. Set up on 6 August 1952 to strengthen and mobilize the effort and resources of the nation in support of the plan, to promote common economic policies in all vital spheres, and to ensure the balanced and rapid development of all parts of the country. The council comprises the prime minister, union cabinet ministers, chief ministers of all states or their substitutes, representatives of the union territories and the members of the NITI Aayog. The NDC can be used for discussing the FC recommendations and achieve consensus.

REVAMPING THE FINANCE COMMISSION

As discussed in the previous section, the revamped permanent FC will have tasks such as

1. Macroeconomic planning;
2. Monitoring the finances of central and state governments;
3. Determining federal fiscal transfers using objective methods;
4. Devising integrated capital development plans for the country;
5. Designing rational tax reform;
6. Recommending strategies for good public debt management;
7. Recommending steps for social development; and
8. Recommending better management of environment.

Macroeconomic and Fiscal Planning

Fiscal health of the nation as a whole, irrespective of whether it is the centre, the state or local bodies, should be of primary concern. The FC has to take cognizance of the prevailing fiscal and macroeconomic situation, particularly the need to sustain the growth momentum, while bringing about fiscal consolidation. The overall macroeconomic planning can be taken up by the expanded and independent FC. As the macroeconomic planner, the FC will devise policies for growth and macroeconomic stability, suggest ways of controlling fiscal deficit and debt management, as also design the fiscal frameworks for economic reforms. Indeed, the 13FC has explicitly recognized the need 'to respond transformationally, rather than incrementally, to national and global imperatives that are causing fundamental changes to the national development agenda' (Government of India, 2009, p. 255). It emphasized the need for a 'fiscal framework equipped to meet the challenges of the future and to enable India to make the most of its demographic dividend'.

Government finances and macroeconomic performance should not be viewed in isolation but rather as interdependent and integrally linked. Any restructuring plan has to aim at eliminating revenue deficit and bring down fiscal deficit to levels consistent with macroeconomic stability. Determining the right size of fiscal deficit and the debt in relation to GDP is important for prudent fiscal management. The adoption of a fiscal correction and restructuring plan by the states can be facilitated and induced to some extent by built-in incentives and rewards provided for within the scheme of transfers.

In fact, the issue of macro fiscal management has been explicitly figuring in the ToR of the FC since 1968. For example, from the 5FC onwards, the FC was required to link the GIA to the better fiscal management 'as also for economy consistent with efficiency which may be effected by the states in their administrative maintenance, developmental and other expenditure' (Government of India, 1970). Indeed, the 5FC went into conceptualize the fiscal management.

> Fiscal management is a multi-dimensional concept ... Briefly stated, in assessing sound fiscal management one should have regard both to the manner in which the state has endeavoured to raise the resources needed for meeting its commitments and also the manner in which it has deployed the resources so raised so as to get the best possible results for the expenditure incurred. A review of fiscal management in this broad sense will call for a comprehensive and critical survey of the fiscal policies and administration of state governments over a period of time. (Government of India, 1970)

Since the 11FC, it has become customary that the FC is asked to 'suggest a plan by which the governments, collectively and severally, may bring about a restructuring of the public finances restoring budgetary balance, achieving macroeconomic stability and debt reduction along with equitable growth' (Twelfth Finance Commission, 2005). The ToR of the 11FC onwards included reference to budgetary balance and macroeconomic stability. The plan for restructuring is required to also address the objectives of debt reduction and equitable growth.

> The requirement implies that revenue sharing between the centre and the states cannot be decided in isolation but must be anchored to a macro framework defined by parameters of fiscal adjustment in the desired directions along with incentives to induce prudent and efficient fiscal management. Also, restructuring calls for spelling out directions of reform over a wide front spanning fiscal policy, budgetary practices and design of intergovernmental transfers but also the monetary, legal and administrative systems within which budgets operate, in order to facilitate the implementation of the restructuring Plan. (Vithal & Sarma, 2002)

The basic objectives of fiscal restructuring would be not only balancing the receipts and expenditure on revenue account of all the states and the centre but also generating surpluses for capital investment and reducing fiscal deficit; raising the tax–GDP ratio for the centre and tax–GSDP ratios for the states; and in the context of debt reduction, that corrective measures in regard to states' debt may be suggested, consistent with macroeconomic stability and debt sustainability. Therefore, an important task of the FC should be to develop an integrated framework for restructuring public finances to address these interrelated objectives. Fiscal restructuring aimed at macroeconomic stabilization requires a broad analytical framework. The impact of the size and composition of government expenditure on growth, inflation, interest rate and the external account has to be considered in a framework that takes into account relevant interrelationships and feedbacks. The structure of public finances relates, apart from other features, to the size and composition of expenditure.

Macroeconomic management aims at keeping the economy to its long-term growth with stabilization while keeping the inflation rate within acceptable limits. It is desirable to design public finances to remove the structural constraints such as supply bottlenecks and bring potential output closer to full employment levels. In this context, the structure of government expenditure, particularly the share of capital expenditure and its allocation, becomes important. In regards to the second issue, in achieving stabilization, the management of aggregate government demand in response to the cyclical movements of potential output along its growth path becomes relevant.

FC as a Fiscal Monitoring Agent

An important task of the FC will be to make continuous assessment and forecasting of the central and state revenues and expenditures. It involves making projections of resources and assessing the capacity of the centre and needs for each individual state. In making the assessment of central resources and corresponding needs, expenditure on civil administration, defence, internal and border security, debt servicing and other committed expenditures and liabilities need to be taken into account.

The approach to assessment of states' revenue and expenditure should consider the need for a normative basis. This is necessary to have an objective macroeconomic restructuring plan. These assessments should take into account the additional taxation efforts of the central government and each state government as against 'targets' and 'potential' in order to improve the tax–GDP and tax–GSDP ratios. The forecasting should have a built-in mechanism to take into account the yearly critical events like the award of a pay commission or the onset of a recession. In other federations, alternative mechanisms have been evolved to cope with the problem of information lag. For example, in Canada, the transfers for any one year remain 'open' for four years, and as new data come in, entitlements are reworked on principles that have already been determined. In Australia, there is a five-yearly cycle of 'Review' whereby the Commonwealth Grants Commission formulates the methodology of determining the 'relativities', but the calculation is done on an annual basis using latest available data, which are called 'Updates'.

CAPITAL AND DEVELOPMENT PLANNING

Until recently, the PC was taking the responsibility of capital and infrastructure development of the economy and accordingly making allocations across the country. However, the initial objective of allocating funds for overall development was diluted in favour of regional equity and related formulae. There is a need to revive the objectives more towards balanced development. For this purpose, adoption of the project design and implementation methods on the lines of those employed by the international funding agencies such as the World Bank, Asian Development Bank and so on is required.

In this regard, as suggested by Singh and Srinivasan (2013), it is better that the centre take full responsibility for financing investment and operational costs of projects that have spillover across states, regardless of the authority that implements them (centre or state).

The current system of centrally sponsored schemes, under which the centre provides partial funding for the project's investment cost and for its operational cost for a limited period, has had the unfortunate effect that projects get started and completed, but once completed are not fully utilized because states have not provided the needed costs of operating them once it became their exclusive responsibility to provide them. The centre assuming full financial responsibility will avoid this waste (Singh & Srinivasan, 2013).

Second, let the NITI Aayog or similar agency serve as an FPI for both the centre and states. Its shareholders would be the state and central governments. The fund, much like a multilateral development bank, would appraise the projects proposed for their economic and social returns as well as feasibility and soundness of proposed financing (from the centre or states' own resources, borrowing from domestic and foreign sources and capital transfers from the centre, if relevant).

FC TO INCULCATE FISCAL ACCOUNTABILITY

To the extent that India's fundamental governance problem is one of accountability, one can argue that India's centralized traditional accountability mechanisms, relying as they do on hierarchical political and bureaucratic control and monitoring, have been ineffective. A more robust federal structure, extending political accountability more effectively at the subnational level, is important to consider as a way of increasing the efficiency of governance. At the same time, the MPF perspective emphasizes the importance of having the right restrictions on the sphere of action of SNGs vis-à-vis the market. The objective will be to encourage prudent fiscal management. For this purpose, the incentivization of grant allocations, as also penalties for inefficient budget management, needs to be put in place.

Fiscal Rules and Monitoring

Recent experience in fiscal consolidation suggests that institutional reforms, well-defined rules and transparency facilitate fiscal reforms. Institutional reforms should aim at achieving and maintaining fiscal consolidation while leaving enough scope for coping with business cycles through automatic stabilizers as well as discretionary action. Three main ingredients of such reforms relate to formal deficit and debt rules, specification of expenditure rules and fiscal transparency. The Maastricht Treaty rule of 3 per cent of GDP as the fiscal deficit target and 60 per cent as the desired debt–GDP ratio are well known. In the United Kingdom, a 'golden rule' of limiting borrowing only to finance capital expenditure has been followed since 1997 as a sustainable investment rule. In other countries, such as the United States, Finland, the Netherlands and Sweden, procedural requirements have been used to support expenditure limits. Fiscal transparency has been emphasized in countries such as New Zealand, Australia, and the United Kingdom. Fiscal transparency implies being open to public regarding the structure and functions of government. Transparency requires that any policy change must be introduced with a clear statement of relevance and objectives. Strategies of fiscal consolidation require a longer term focus and the need to promote growth. In this context, the central government's initiative in enacting the FRBMA is a welcome step. Some state governments have also brought about fiscal responsibility legislations. In our view, other states would do well to emulate this example.

FC as a Monitoring Agent

The FC should be entrusted with the responsibility of monitoring the economic adjustments recommended by it. The past practice of such commissions has been to consider their duty done once they submitted their report. The 12FC broke with this passive tradition and urged the setting up of a high-level monitoring mechanism in every state headed by the chief secretary and comprising the finance secretary and secretaries/heads of departments as members to lay down at the beginning of each year financial and physical targets with definite time frames to achieve specific milestones for ensuring proper utilization of the grants. The Commission also stipulated that the committee should meet at least once in every quarter to review the progress and issue directions for mid-course corrections.

It is not enough to keep a watch over the mode of utilization of grants by states. The entire mind-set of the parties and alliances ruling the states needs to be attuned to the spirit of mutually cooperative and supportive fiscal federalism. States should check their tendency to squander away thousands of crores of rupees of precious resources on freebies and seek to plug the gap by unconscionably heavy borrowings in the hope of being bailed out by the centre. The states must realize that they bear an equal, if not greater, responsibility to augment their revenues and avoid infructuous expenditure. The axe should mercilessly fall on unjustifiably high expenditures incurred by the state governments and their agencies on salaries and perks of employees without establishing correlation with norms of performance.

The 12FC could only be said to have let off the centre lightly, without insisting on any monitoring and review mechanism and without binding the government to any parameter of revenue mobilization or expenditure control. This is strange because, actually, it is the centre that should be called upon to set an example in whatever it preaches to state governments. Far from living up to that obligation, it has been giving an impression of adopting a business-as-usual attitude.

PUBLIC DEBT MANAGEMENT

Debt relief often underwrites lack of fiscal discipline of the past. It could be unfair and could give significantly adverse signals if the benefit of relief is largest for the state, which was the most profligate in the past. In the literature relating to fiscal federalism, considerable attention has been given to the deleterious effects of a soft budget constraint, which refers to the relative ease with which states can borrow. This also has implications for the assessment of interest payments. If any amount of interest payments liability can be considered as legitimate claim for determining transfers, all normative assessments of current expenditures would be rendered redundant. All that a state would need to do is to borrow more in the current period and generate 26 12FC larger claims for the future. It is imperative that interest payments be assessed normatively and a hard budget constraint be imposed. We have considered the issue of debt relief in the light of these considerations. In the context of the question of debt relief, account needs to be taken of the fact that the nominal interest rates have fallen. There are also grounds to believe that the margins that the central government may have charged on its own lending to the states may have been unduly high in the past. It is clear that any debt relief will have to be linked to a desired path of fiscal adjustment including targets for revenue and fiscal deficits. The PC may also need to ensure that the size of a state plan is consistent with a sustainable level of debt, as the state plans are almost fully financed by borrowing in one form or another.

All said and done, the FC can only make recommendations and proposals. The modalities of implementation of these recommendations will rest with the Ministry of Finance or other concerned ministries after proper parliamentary approval.

While arriving at the recommendations, the FC will be in constant touch with other available experts, elicit their views, organize seminars and so on

FC AS FISCAL DATA MANAGER

The 11FC had earmarked more than ₹10,000 crore for creation and computerization of databases at the district, state and central levels on the finances of local bodies and accounts of village- and intermediate-level panchayats and the Comptroller and Auditor General (CAG) was made responsible for prescribing the necessary formats for the compilation of data. Again, a shadow has fallen between intention and execution.

The 12FC emphasized the need for statistical agencies to design and implement a plan to produce more timely data on GSDP. The 12FC clearly brought out the difficulties of working without reliable data.

We have been constrained to use the latest available estimates of GSDP which are for years less recent than we would have liked. This is an issue that requires most urgent attention in order to eliminate time lags in the availability of data and to bring to a close the cumbersome process of generating comparable GSDP data. There should, in our view, be no hesitation on the part of all agencies concerned, whether at the central, state or district level, to put aside any perceived questions of mandate or primacy and collectively agree to a blueprint and methodology for delivering comparable GSDP data on a regular and timely basis. It is equally important that the central Statistical Organization (CSO) assume greater responsibility for producing GSDP at market prices, and for generating estimates of income accruing to states inclusive of net inward remittances. It is important to recognise that data is vital for the business process underpinning effective policy making, monitoring and devolution, and that the availability of quality data is a factor that will determine whether future policy making is able to rise to the challenges posed by a rapidly changing social and economic environment. (Twelfth Finance Commission, 2005)

Scientific and Rational Methods for Vertical and Horizontal Sharing

The FC will design a scheme of transfers that could serve the objectives of both equity and efficiency and result in fiscal transfers that are predictable and stable. These transfers, in the form of tax devolution and grants, are meant to correct both the vertical and horizontal imbalances. This raises the question as to the division of the transfers into tax devolution and grants. If the transfers through tax devolution are too low compared with those of grants, many states would emerge in assessed deficit and would be entitled for grants. States that emerge with pre-devolution surplus would be eligible for lower amounts of grants. Therefore, the tax devolution should be calibrated to ensure that at least the requirement of minimum vertical transfers is met. Some of the past FCs have recommended the vertical share in such a way that most states emerge in assessed revenue deficits. There is also the consideration that the share of tax devolution is very nearly downward rigid in the sense that states generally prefer higher share in the central revenues.

It is suggested that the tax devolution should include the surcharges/cesses. The surcharges and cesses should also be treated as normal source of central tax revenue and included in the divisible pool, at least after a time limit. Various commissions have observed that surcharges/cesses should not be levied by the centre except to meet emergent requirements only for limited periods but still the centre raises revenue through this measure for longer periods. In fact, some economists such as Guhan (1995) suggested that the divisible pool should include non-tax revenues as well.

A minimum guaranteed devolution of central taxes from the centre to the states should be fixed, to restore predictability in devolution of share of central taxes to the states and provide necessary stability in fiscal management of the states.

The methods used to determine the tax devolution share employed by the successive FCs vary widely over the years, and the variations in the methods cannot be explained rationally. Many a time the fixation of the vertical and horizontal shares smack *ad hoc* thinking on the part of the commission. Since the amounts involved are large, a small alteration in the method can change the outcome significantly and not always in the desired ways.

VFI MEASUREMENT

The vertical sharing objectives need to be clearly defined and the share will be determined accordingly. Similarly, the horizontal sharing should come away from the present arbitrary selection of criteria, proxying, quantification and weights and needs to follow a rational objective methodology.

For example, the measurement of VFI should preserve the basic idea that 'government at each level can command the financial resources necessary for them to carry out their expenditure responsibilities'. Given the constitutional division of revenue and expenditure responsibilities, a measure of vertical transfers T can be derived defined as

$$T = [(R_c - E_c) - (R_s - E_s)]/2,$$

where R_c and R_s denote revenues of centre and states before devolution and transfers and E_c and E_s are the respective total expenditures.[1] As Bird (2002) puts it, if imbalance is the problem, balance is the solution.

---

[1] The detailed derivation of T is explained in Appendix D.

Therefore, the transfer needed from the centre to states should be such that VFI=0.

The optimal transfers as a percentage of gross central revenues as against the actual transfers are as shown in Table 6.1. It can be observed that until 1996–1997, the gap between the optimal and actual was modest while in the post-1996 period, the gap has become wider.

Table 6.1 *Vertical Federal Fiscal Transfers: Optimal and Actual (as a Percentage of Centre's Gross Revenue Receipts)*

	Optimal Transfers $T = [(R_c - E_c) - (R_s - E_s)]/2$	Actual Transfers	Difference (Optimal–Actual)
1980–1981	27.40	29.20	−1.80
1981–1982	28.40	26.70	1.70
1982–1983	27.10	26.50	0.60
1983–1984	27.30	26.00	1.30
1984–1985	25.00	25.40	−0.40
1985–1986	23.00	27.50	−4.50
1986–1987	21.90	26.70	−4.80
1987–1988	25.10	27.20	−2.10
1988–1989	24.60	25.70	−1.10
1989–1990	20.80	23.90	−3.10
1990–1991	23.30	26.70	−3.40
1991–1992	27.50	27.90	−0.40
1992–1993	27.50	29.40	−1.90
1993–1994	27.70	28.20	−0.50
1994–1995	27.10	25.30	1.80
1995–1996	30.30	26.30	4.00
1996–1997	27.20	27.20	0.00
1997–1998	26.40	37.40	−11.00
1998–1999	30.80	22.40	8.40

(Continued)

Table 6.1 (Continued)

	Optimal Transfers $T = [(R_c - E_c) - (R_s - E_s)]/2$	Actual Transfers	Difference (Optimal – Actual)
1999–2000	32.80	21.10	11.70
2000–2001	31.70	25.10	6.60
2001–2002	35.30	25.10	10.20
2002–2003	34.10	24.20	9.90
2003–2004	35.95	19.05	16.90
2004–2005	36.67	20.07	16.60
2005–2006	30.47	20.87	9.60
2006–2007	39.60	21.50	18.10
2007–2008	40.85	21.35	19.50
2008–2009	34.20	22.40	11.80
2009–2010	35.81	21.81	14.00
2010–2011	31.38	21.38	10.00
2011–2012	33.78	24.78	9.00
2012–2013	42.79	24.39	18.40
2013–2014	45.16	23.46	21.70
2014–2015	39.29	22.69	16.60
2015–2016	37.89	30.89	7.00

Source: Indian Public Finance Statistics, various issues.

Notes: R_c, R_s denote pre-transfer revenues, and E_c, E_s denote pre-transfer expenditures of centre and states, respectively.

This measure needs to be interpreted with care. For example, some revenue sources such as central sales tax and stamp duties are partly under the control of the central government in that the power to change the rate structure lies with it, although the revenues are collected and retained by the states. Similarly, certain expenditures are conditioned by central government through either plan process or other national requirements. To that extent, the states are not entirely free to manipulate their pre-transfer fiscal gaps. In other words, a part of the VFI is inherent in the fiscal structure. On the whole, it can be concluded that the actual transfers are fall short of the optimal required transfers, most of the time which underlines the need to build rationality in determining the vertical share for the states.

HORIZONTAL SHARING

As regards the horizontal sharing, the approach adopted so far reflects some inherent confusion: whether and to what states' efficiency should be rewarded, to what extent equity should be built, to what extent the state-specific factors and circumstances should be taken into account while assessing the fiscal management of the states and so on.

For example, as has been pointed out in Sarma (1997):

> In several cases the transfers are subject to a great deal of experimentation and frequent modification. Often, the lack of agreement on the criteria has led to dominance of political considerations rather than economic rationale. … the debate shows that an objective transfer mechanism has eluded the policy-makers so far. Although significant efforts have been made by the last two Finance Commissions (10th and 11FCs) to integrate the system of tax devolution and enlarge the divisible pool to include all union taxes, with regard to the horizontal revenue sharing however, not much attention has been paid.

Sarma (1997) then proceeded to develop a method of objectively identifying the criteria and deriving of weights for deciding the horizontal revenue shares within a fiscal behavioural framework.

The first and foremost task towards determining the process of horizontal sharing of federal transfers is to be clear and firm about the objectives of such transfers. The vast literature on federal fiscal transfer practices suggests that the basic economic motivations of the federating units for coming together are to attain greater fiscal efficiency, scale economy and equity. The method to be used for fiscal transfers should also support these motivations. This is made amply clear by Rangarajan (chairman, 12FC) in his speeches during the visits of the commission to states:

> The considerations that should go in determining the distribution of revenue among states have been examined in great length by earlier Finance Commissions. Equity issues have dominated such discussions. The effort

has been to identify variables which reflect the equity concerns. In designing a suitable scheme of fiscal transfers, three considerations seem relevant—needs, cost disability and fiscal efficiency. Needs refer to expenditures required to be made but not met by state's own resources. Cost disabilities refer to such characteristics of a state that necessitate more than average per capita cost in service provision due to factors that are largely beyond its control like large areas with low density of population, hilly terrains, poor infrastructure, proneness to floods and droughts. Fiscal efficiency encompasses parameters like maintaining revenue account balance, robust revenue effort, economies of expenditure linked to efficient provision of services and the quality of governance.

A sound transfer system has to establish a balance between equity and efficiency, a system where fiscal disadvantage is taken care of but fiscal imprudence is effectively discouraged. Needless to say, fiscal responsibility must be shared by both the centre and the states. With the two channels of tax-devolution and grants, it should be possible for the Finance Commission to achieve the goals of equity and efficiency through a proper mix.[2]

It is only fair that the criteria and the weights for horizontal distribution should be related to the basic economic motivations of the federating units for coming together. To be more specific, federal fiscal efficiency requires offsetting of the inequity among the federating units (hereafter referred to as states) with respect to the NMBF. The NMBF of each federating unit can be understood as the difference between the marginal fiscal benefit and marginal fiscal costs of federation (Breton, 1965; Gramlich, 1987; Rao & Chelliah, 1991). The fiscal costs to a state for agreeing to be in the federation are in terms of tax powers and revenue forgone, while the fiscal benefits are the gains in terms of increases in the government revenues (owing to possible rise in the tax base due to lower trade barriers across the states and so on), and increased supply and/or lower unit costs, of providing the public goods.

Operationalization of this principle requires, as a first step, measurement and comparison of the NMBF of each state which, in a way, is likely to be reflected in its own revenue—total expenditure gap (hereafter referred as 'fiscal gap'). Before offsetting the inequity in the

---

[2] Speech by Dr Rangarajan, chairman 12FC, on the occasion of visit of the 12FC to Rajasthan.

fiscal gap among the states, it is necessary to identify the 'true' fiscal gap of each state because it could be affected by temporary random factors. It is necessary to remove or scale down such effects. Fiscal gap of a state depends upon a number of factors. Some are common for all the states and some are specific for each state. For example, it is well known that the amount of tax revenue raised by a state government depends on its proxy base, namely, the gross domestic product (GSDP). Since this is true for all states, GSDP can be taken as a factor common for all states explaining the variations in the tax revenue. Similarly, variations in government expenditure across states can be partly explained by variations in the size of population. Thus, population can be taken as a common factor for all states for the purpose of explaining the variations in the government expenditure. Thus, the first step in identifying the justifiable fiscal gap is to list out the common factors.

As a matter of fact, it is the common factors influencing the fiscal gap that can help us in identifying the criteria and designing of weights for inter se distribution of fiscal transfers. For example, if X is an important factor influencing the fiscal gap with say ω weight (derived from its coefficient), it would mean that transfers linked to the criteria X with its weight can enable the states to reduce their respective fiscal gaps in an equitable measure. In contrast, if instead, some other criterion Y that is not so relevant for the fiscal gap is used for the inter se distribution, it is difficult to expect equitable mitigation of the fiscal gap. This underlines the need to specify only those factors which have significant influence on the fiscal gap behaviour of the states, as criteria for horizontal sharing.

Second, not all factors influencing the fiscal performance of states are common. There are certain factors that are specific for a state. For example, some states have a peculiar geographical structure that has a bearing on the revenue collection and cost of providing public goods and services. Some states are prone to frequent natural calamities such as floods while some others are subject to draughts. Similarly, some face the problem of refugees from the neighbouring states that can be a burden on its finances. There must be a way of recognizing and capturing the impact of such state-specific factors.

To be clearer, let the fiscal gap $G_{it}=R_{it}-E_{it}$ of the ith state in tth year represent the shortfall of own revenue (R_{it}) to meet its expenditure needs (E_{it}). Let the revenue of ith state at time t be

$$R_{it}=f\,\{K_{it},\,F_i,\,u_{it}\},\qquad\qquad(1)$$

where K are common factors representing revenue capacity, F are state-specific factors influencing the revenue raising and u are random factors.

Similarly, let the expenditure of the ith state be

$$E_{it}=f\,\{N_{it},\,C_{it},\,D_i,\,v_{it}\},\qquad\qquad(2)$$

where N are common factors representing expenditure needs, C are factors representing unit cost, D_i are state-specific factors influencing the government spending, and v are random factors.

The fiscal gap is

$$G_{it}=f\,\{K_{it},\,N_{it},\,C_{it},\,Z_i,\,e_{it}\},\qquad\qquad(3)$$

where Z_i is the combined effect of the state-specific factors on the revenue and expenditure, and e_{it} is the combined effect of the random factors.

The true fiscal gap that can be compared across the states would be

$$G_{it}^*=G_{it}-e_{it}=f\,\{K_{it},\,N_{it},\,C_{it},\,Z_i\}.\qquad\qquad(4)$$

The FC transfers aimed at offsetting the inequity among the states with respect to fiscal gap should bear a one-to-one relation to the true fiscal gap. The main task, therefore, would be to identify the factors responsible for variation in the fiscal gap across the states, use them as criteria for determining the horizontal shares. The weights for the criteria should be determined according to the degree of their relevance. While doing so, the effect of the random factors will be purged out and also quantify the effect of the state-specific factors on the fiscal gap so that norms can be derived.

The best way to achieve this would be to estimate the relevance of the factors using econometric methods, particularly the panel data techniques. An appropriate specification of the panel model depends on the assumptions regarding the nature of the state-specific factors. A few assumptions in this respect could be as follows. First, the influence of the common as well as state-specific factors differs from state to state. Second, the influence of common factors is uniform across the states but that of state-specific factors differs.

If the influence of state-specific factors on the fiscal gap is relatively stable or regular, then the appropriate specification would be a 'fixed-effects' (FE) model. On the other hand, if the influence of the state-specific factors is unstable and irregular, then perhaps the 'random effects' model would be more appropriate. It is also possible to use a model combining both the types of the effects, which, under certain plausible assumptions, can also be used to separate the effect of the controllable state-specific factors from that of the uncontrollable factors.

The estimated fiscal gap function renders considerable flexibility in selecting the common factors responsible for the variation in the fiscal gaps of the states. For a given set of factors, the function automatically determines the weight of each factor in relation to its degree of relevance to offset the fiscal gap. For example, if population is a factor responsible for the growing revenue gap, the function will automatically assign the weight needed depending upon the degree of importance of population on the fiscal gap.

Determining the Norms

The true fiscal gap thus derived (after purging of the random and adjusted for efficiency components) can be a good proxy for the NMBF of a state. Once the fiscal gaps are made comparable across the states, the next step would be to derive 'normative' or 'justifiable' fiscal gaps.

The 'norms' are necessarily in relative terms. Given the fiscal gap model, norms can be worked out from the estimated parameters of the model in different ways by varying the assumptions regarding the variability of the behaviour across the states. For example, depending upon the degree of freedom allowed, the coefficients of some or all the factors of the model can be allowed to vary across the states or restricted to be uniform across the states.

The estimated gap function can also be used to build in other policy norms. For example, if population figures are to be kept constant, say, at the 1971 level, then the relevant shares can be derived by plugging the 1971 population figures into the gap function.

$$G^n_{it} = f\{K_{it}, N_{i1971}, C_{it}, Z_i\} \tag{5}$$

Similarly, if the FEs are indicative of the fiscal efficiency levels, then some restrictions can be imposed on them. (The details of the method are illustrated in Appendix E.)

The Adjustment for Using Past Population

While estimating the model, an important determinant of the fiscal gap is the population. It basically represents the expenditure needs of a state. However, it has been mandatory for the FCs to use the 1971 population figures instead of the current period figures.[3] The idea is to keep the pattern of population size across the states to be the same as in 1971. Since the expenditure function is specified to be sensitive to the size of the population, we escalated the 1971 population of each state uniformly using the escalation factor, namely, the all-India population growth. Accordingly, in deriving the fiscal gaps and transfer shares, we could preserve the 1971 size distribution of population across the states.

Advantages of the Model

The model has several advantages over the conventional intuitive formula-based determination of the horizontal shares. The main

[3] 'In making its recommendations on the various matters aforesaid, the Commission shall adopt the population figures of 1971 in all cases where population is regarded as a factor for determination of devolution of taxes and duties and grants-in-aid' (Terms of Reference of Finance Commission).

advantage is that the transfer shares are determined on the basis of rational fiscal behavioural framework keeping in view the basic motivations of the federating units for coming together.

Second, the criteria and the weights for horizontal distribution of transfers in this model are derived from those factors that are responsible for variations in the basic NMBF and not imposed from outside, as has been the case so far. The NMBF (proxied by the own revenue–expenditure gap) is subdivided into three components: (a) a component that varies with factors common to all the states, (b) a component that varies with state-specific factors and (c) a component that varies with random factors. After removing the effect of random factors, the remaining two components of the fiscal gap are made comparable by restricting the parameters of common factors to be uniform for all the states. The common factors are akin to the criteria, and their estimated uniform parameters are similar to the weights. In this way, whatever criteria emerge from the model are related to their respective NMBF, and the weights are in accordance with the degree of their relevance to the NMBF.

Third, while determining the shares, state-specific factors such as cost disabilities due to geographic and climatic conditions that influence the fiscal behaviour are fully taken into account in the form of state-specific 'FEs'. These factors are not easy to identify and not amenable for prescribing as quantifiable criteria. The model does away with the need to identify the state-specific factors, although their effect is fully taken into account.

Fourth, although it was well recognized in the past that the three considerations—needs, cost disability and fiscal efficiency—should form the basis in designing a suitable scheme of fiscal transfers, an objective way of striking a balance between them eluded the FCs so far. As a result, past FCs are led to devise exotic criteria such as the income–distance criteria, the inverse income criteria, the fiscal performance criteria, the tax effort criteria, poverty criteria and so on. Their form and their relevance are not easy to digest. In contrast, our model and estimation procedures automatically allow striking an optimal balance between the equity and efficiency objectives of the transfers.

Possible Further Improvements

Within the framework, several alternative model specifications are possible. For example, the variables to be used as the determinants of the fiscal gap are largely based on intuitive reasoning and therefore are subject to change. However, once a few major factors are specified, the inclusion of other factors and their specific transformations depend not only on their association with the dependent variable but also on their covariance with the major factors. For example, if one is intuitively sure of the major role of population as a determinant of the fiscal need, the other factors such as income, poverty will qualify for inclusion only if they represent the other dimensions of influence. Other possible variants of the model can be specification in linear or non-linear form, inclusion of the state-specific factors as fixed or random, inclusion or non-inclusion of the time-trend variable and in alternative ways, and so on. Some of these choices can be resolved on the basis of statistical tests involving extensive econometric work.

Conclusions and Recommend- ations 7

The art of federalism lies in designing institutions with appropriate assignment of powers and functions among different orders of government and rules to regulate their relationship, especially in the fiscal arena that can strike the right balance among different objectives and resolve tensions. According to many, the Indian federal system, though decentralized, is quasi-federal at best and does not allow enough room for the states to function freely. The restricted decentralization has been the problem of the Indian economy and a major factor responsible for its stunted growth. In China, on the other hand, growth has been propelled greatly by the 'market preserving federalism' practised there, allowing autonomy to provinces in running their economies. This book recommends revamping of the federal fiscal institutional system in India. The following are the summarized recommendations.

Recommendation 1: Permanent Finance Commission

Make the FC permanent. The setting up of the FC at five-year intervals has been leading to a variety of immature acts.

Recommendation 2: Converge the Relevant Bodies into the Finance Commission

Merge all the bodies concerned with economic and fiscal policy design such as the PMEAC and NITI Aayog, with the FC. This will reduce possible duplication, conflicts and coordination problems.

Recommendation 3: Extended ToR and Expanded Membership

The FC will have expanded membership and expanded ToR. It will also take care of macroeconomic planning and management. There has already been substantial diversification in the ToR given to the FC. The additional ToR include the tax design, macroeconomic stabilization, fiscal monitoring, public debt management and dealing with natural calamities and so on.

Recommendation 4: Involve the NDC for States' Cooperation

Before submitting the quinquennial report to the President as required and deliberated in the Parliament, the FC will present it to the NDC with proper representation from the states and make it acceptable. This will reduce the possible dissent from the states, and it will make the system closer to cooperative federalism.

Recommendation 5: Federal Fiscal Sharing Should Be from All Revenues of the Centre

Federal fiscal sharing should be from all the revenues of the central government and not just the tax revenues alone. This will include not only taxes but also surcharges and cesses, as also the non-tax revenues of the central government. This will eliminate the room for allegations of biases in raising the revenues by the centre.

Recommendation 6: Transfer Share (Revenue Share + grants) to Be Consensus Based

The total transfers (tax devolution + grants) from the centre to the states can be fixed on the basis of consensus. For example, 50 per cent of the centre's total revenues.

Recommendation 7: Vertical Sharing Choices

Out of the total share of 50 per cent, revenue sharing and grants should be partly divided. Vertical sharing could have two alternative aims: (a) vertical share equals the total sum of normative fiscal gaps of the states. This may reduce the need for borrowing of the states, but widen the fiscal gap of the central government, thereby compelling it for higher borrowings; and (b) vertical transfer is such that it will equalize the sum total of fiscal gap of the states to that of the central government. However, this arrangement might call for allowing the states to go for new borrowings in case of fiscal gap being a deficit.

Recommendation 8: Horizontal Sharing to Be More Scientific and Objective

Horizontal revenue sharing should be based on objective formulae such as the method described in this report and eliminate the arbitrary selection of the criteria, arbitrary proxying of the criteria and arbitrary assignment of weights in the linear formula. It is advisable that the criteria should be relevant and capable of affecting the fiscal gaps of the states. If a particular criterion is not relevant to the fiscal gap, then to that extent the transfers on that basis are not going to improve the fiscal gap. The criteria can be of three types: the capacity criteria, the effort criteria and the need criteria. Horizontal share determination should have a built-in reward system to encourage better fiscal management. GSDP and population are the two most important criteria that influence the fiscal gaps at the states' level. Higher the GSDP, the higher would be the revenue generation that would reduce the fiscal gap, while higher population would raise the need for more expenditure, thereby widening the fiscal gap. The resultant horizontal share will be higher for the states with large populations and smaller for the states with high GSDP. While this pattern might achieve the equity objective, it will have negative impact on the tax effort and better fiscal management. Therefore, proper care is needed in fine-tuning the horizontal sharing methods.

Recommendation 9: Grants Should Reflect Broader Economic Policies

The remaining quantum of transfers will be by way of grants. Thus, if the total transfers are fixed at 50 per cent of the central government, the total quantum of grants would be the remaining amount left over after revenue sharing. Grants could be unconditional, conditional, specific-purpose and post-devolution deficit grants. The grant allocation pattern is a policy choice.

Recommendation 10: Incentivize the Grants

Part of the grants can be used to incentivize better fiscal management of the SNGs.

Recommendation 11: Capital Grants Should Be Project by Project Based on Viability

Capital grants should be more on the basis of project management studies rather than on equity basis. The financing of capital projects will be on the lines of project viability studies.

CONCLUSIONS

A well-designed and well-functioning system of federal governance, by virtue of its manifold benefits, plays a key role in promoting the stability and prosperity of nations as the heights attained in development by the leading federations of the world—the United States, Canada, Australia and Switzerland—demonstrate. On the other hand, unless carefully crafted, federal systems do not endure as evidenced by the disintegration of many of the federal formations that came into being in the last century (Soviet Russia, Yugoslavia, Czechslovakia, Rhodesi and Nyasaland).

It is increasingly being realized that there is no alternative but to reform the fiscal institutions of the federal system. Smooth functioning of a fast globalizing world economy requires a stable, secure and predictable economic environment. Federalism in India, as everywhere else, has to face the overwhelming challenges of the new millennium. That underlines the fact that no federal system can suit all countries for all times. Maintaining an appropriate balance in the relationship between the centre and the constituent units in a federation has not been easy. The federal structure needs to be perpetually altered to cope with the changing environment and emerging challenges. For the federal structure to be stable and flexible, attention of both experts and the wider public is imperative all the time.

In a longer term context, there is a need to emphasize stability in federal relations in general and in the system of transfers in particular. Growing disparities in fiscal capacities and levels of services upset this stability, as widening disparities require larger and more progressive transfers. States also need to give greater attention to policies aimed at accelerating growth and reducing intra-state regional inequalities. It is only when interstate and intra-state disparities are reduced that the federal fiscal system would become stable. A coordinated effort is required to reduce inequalities, which would also make the system more stable.

APPENDIX A: FISCAL FEDERAL MANAGEMENT— COUNTRY EXPERIENCES

Intergovernmental fiscal transfers finance about 60 per cent of subnational expenditures in developing countries.

> Intergovernmental fiscal transfers are a dominant feature of subnational finance in most countries. They are used to ensure that revenues roughly match the expenditure needs of various orders (levels) of subnational governments. They are also used to advance national, regional and local area objectives such as fairness and equity and creating a common economic union. The structure of these transfers creates incentives for national, regional and local governments that have a bearing on fiscal management, macroeconomic stability, distributional equity, allocative efficiency and public services delivery. (Shah, 2006, p. 1)

Although there exist certain common practices among the federal systems in the world, it is important to note, at the outset, that the circumstances and objectives that shaped the fiscal transfers differ from country to country, and their transfer mechanisms have evolved over time to suit their specific requirements.

GENERAL FEATURES

For example, Australia comprises three levels of government: central (the Australian or 'Commonwealth' government); state (six states—New South Wales, Queensland, Victoria, Tasmania, Western Australia and South Australia, and two territories—the Northern Territory (NT) and the Australian Capital Region (ACT) with state-type powers); and local (562 local governments). The Commonwealth and the state-level governments independently exercise expenditure powers within their own areas of policy. The local governments play a minor role by international standards, with their responsibilities mainly confined to local public works (Koutsogeorgopoulou & Tuske, 2015; Searle, 2001, p. 3).

The aim of this political confederation was twofold: defence and a more intensive economic cooperation and exchange on the Australian continent.

> As to government revenue, the states had expected their financial independence to be preserved under the Constitution. However, legal constraints as well as historical events have led to centralization of revenue functions and an ever-increasing financial dependence of the states on the central government. (Shah, 2014, p. 49)

The Canadian federal system is one of the most decentralized ones and has three levels of government: federal, provincial or territorial, and municipal. A unique feature of Canada is that the provinces have responsibility for social programmes such as health care, education and welfare. Together, the provinces collect more revenue than the federal government. However, the federal government using its spending powers such as the Canada Health Act can initiate national policies in provincial areas.

The German federal system can be termed as cooperative federal system. It comprises 16 federal states which are collectively referred to as Bundesländer. Each state has its own state constitution and is largely autonomous in regard to its internal organization. Two of the states are city-states consisting of just one city: Berlin and Hamburg (Wurzel, 1999).

Fiscal federalism in Switzerland can be characterized in terms of overall fiscal restraint and minimizing the centralization of fiscal power. It is regarded as 'bottom-up' federalism.

> Since the first Constitution of 12th September 1848, Switzerland has been, in institutional terms, a relatively complex system of three layers of government: (1) the communes, at the local level, (2) the Cantons, at the intermediate level, and (3) the Confederation, at the national level—which are interconnected by many vertical and horizontal relationships. (Dafflon & Tóth, 2005, p. 2)

> Swiss federalism is unique on two accounts: the first is its substantial fragmentation, with 26 federated states, or cantons, and 2,255 local communities for a total population of only eight million people; the second is the relatively low degree of centralization, the federal government accounting for roughly 30% of spending and tax revenues, whereas 70% is under the responsibility of the federated states and the local communities. (Bessard, 2013, p. 43)

The cantons have a high degree of independence. Each canton has its own constitution, own parliament, government and courts. However, there are considerable differences between the individual cantons, most particularly in terms of population and geographical area. The cantons comprise a total of 2,485 municipalities.

CONSTITUTIONAL DISTRIBUTION OF POWERS: COUNTRY PRACTICES

Among the federal systems in the world, irrespective of the degree of centralization, certain common patterns can be observed. Broadly, the pattern of division of functions among different layers of governments prevailing in most federations is as follows. Subjects such as defence, foreign affairs, money and banking, countrywide communications and responsibility for macro-management of the economy are assigned to the central or federal government, while matters of primarily regional or local concern such as public order, education, public health and sanitation, water supply, irrigation and canals, and industries other than those declared by parliament to be of strategic interest are entrusted to the states. In addition, some expenditure functions are concurrent between the central and state governments. The local governments are responsible for local infrastructure management and share the responsibilities with the provinces in providing certain services. As for revenues, the federal governments retain the income taxes, customs and other taxes where countrywide uniformity in the rate structure is required or where the tax bases spill over the provincial borders such as interstate trade.

> While on the expenditure side the proportion of government spending that is decentralized is reasonably similar across federations, the extent of revenue decentralization varies widely. Indeed, from a budgetary perspective, differences in fiscal decentralization are largely differences in revenue decentralization, or equivalently, differences in vertical fiscal gaps. The main distinction between centralized and decentralized fiscal federal systems is the extent to which state governments have discretionary access to broad-based taxes. In federations such as Canada, India, Switzerland, and the United States, state-level governments have full access to broad-based taxes such as income, sales, and payroll taxes. In more centralized federations, such as Australia and Germany, much less own-source tax revenue is raised, although in both cases, revenue-sharing applies to federal taxes. (Boadway & Shah, 2007, p. xxix)

The country-wise features are given further.

For example, the Australian Constitution gives the national government (the Commonwealth) exclusive jurisdiction in areas such as foreign affairs, defence, immigration, trade, currency and several social programmes including pensions, unemployment insurance and family allowances. Provincial governments (the states) retain jurisdiction over the matters they controlled before joining the federation, including public security, urban development, housing and transportation. The Commonwealth and state governments share responsibility for funding health and education.

About the distribution of revenues, the Commonwealth is the sole occupant of the personal income tax and corporate income tax fields. Interestingly, state governments are not prohibited by the Constitution from collecting personal income taxes. Rather, they transferred this power to the Commonwealth at the time of the Second World War in return for grants from the Commonwealth. In 2000, there was a major tax reform about the GST collected by the Commonwealth and then transferred to the states. State and local governments are sole occupants of the property-tax field and dominant in payroll taxes. Revenue from the sale of natural resources belongs to the states, except where the resources are on Commonwealth lands or offshore (Boothe, 2003).

> The center emphasizes uniformity of public services across the nation and uses conditional grants to achieve that purpose. Tax administration and collection are central, representing 80 percent of revenues. Local governments are extensions of states but are given reasonable autonomy in local service delivery. (Shah, 2014, p. 49)

The strict separation of taxable sources avoids tax competition among governments; only fees and fines are employed by all levels of government. A separation of tax sources is also found in other federations, like the United States, Canada, or Switzerland, but, contrary to the latter, the prescript has led, under the conditions prevailing in Australia, to the federal government controlling virtually all lucrative taxes in the end.

In Canada, the federal responsibilities include national defence, foreign affairs, money, banking, shipping, railways and communications. Provincial responsibilities included matters such as provincial borrowing, the management and sale of public lands (and hence control of natural resources), hospitals and education. Over time, the federal government became involved in areas of provincial jurisdiction such as health care. Municipal governments are responsible for public transportation, fire protection, local police, local land use, libraries, parks, community water systems, roadways, parking and so on. The division of spending responsibilities in Canada shows a pattern where provinces are much more important actors than their Australian counterparts. Provincial and local governments are overwhelmingly dominant in the areas of health and education.

The Canadian federal government is dominant in the collection of both personal and corporate income taxes, while provincial and local governments are dominant in the fields of payroll and property taxes. The sales-tax base is shared between federal and provincial governments even though sales-tax systems and collection are not fully harmonized for seven of the ten provinces. Revenue from the sale of natural resources is included in the other revenue category and belongs to provincial governments if the resources are found on provincial lands, and the federal government if the resources are found on federal lands or offshore (Boothe, 2003).

In Germany, the Basic Law for the Federal Republic divides authority between the federal government and the states with the general principle governing relations articulated in Article 30: 'The exercise of governmental powers and the discharge of governmental functions shall be incumbent on the Länder insofar as this Basic Law does not otherwise prescribe or permit.' Thus, the federal government can exercise authority only in the areas specified in the Basic Law. The Basic Law divides the federal government's legislative responsibilities into exclusive powers (Articles 71 and 73), concurrent powers (Articles 72, 74 and 74a) and framework powers (Article 75). The exclusive legislative jurisdiction of the federal government extends to defence, foreign affairs, immigration, transportation, communications and currency standards. The federal and state governments share concurrent powers in several areas, including civil law, refugee and expellee matters, public welfare, land management, consumer protection, public health and the collection of vital statistics. In the areas of mass media, nature conservation, regional planning and public service regulations, framework legislation limits the federal government's role to offering general policy guidelines, which the states then act upon by means of detailed legislation. The areas of shared responsibility for the states and the federal government were enlarged by an amendment to the Basic Law in 1969 (Articles 91a and 91b), which calls for joint action in areas of broad social concern such as higher education, regional economic development and agricultural reform.

Switzerland has a relatively low degree of centralization, the federal government accounting for roughly 30 per cent of expenditure and tax revenues, whereas 70 per cent of expenditure and revenues are under the responsibility of the federated cantons and the local communities. A key feature of the Swiss system is its high degree of diversity among the regions and cantons. 'Although Switzerland is one of the most prosperous countries in the world (and the wealthiest country in terms of accumulated wealth per capita), it is also one of the least egalitarian, with regard both to persons and to regions' (Bessard, 2013). Over time, the political process had led to many tasks being carried out by both levels of government, with the consequence of reducing the autonomy of the cantons and weakening the accountability and efficiency of the public sector. Of the 31 functions where tasks were carried out jointly, 15 were placed under exclusive cantonal jurisdiction, and 6 under federal jurisdiction. The new repartition of tasks is not yet fully completed but first evaluations have identified positive results, such as lower costs for national roads ... (Bessard, 2013, p. 48).

THE PRE-TRANSFER FISCAL IMBALANCE EXPERIENCES

The inadequacy of resources to meet their expenditure functions makes the SNGs dependent on the central government, and this dependency is likely to continue if a proper transfer system is not in place from the beginning.

Vertical Fiscal Imbalance

Among the countries that adopted the federal systems, it is a well-known feature that the VFI is mostly in favour of the federal government.

> Almost invariably, countries assign more expenditure functions to subnational governments than can be financed from the revenue sources allocated to those governments (if seldom fully under their control). The result of this mismatching of functions and finances—sometimes referred to as 'vertical imbalance'—is that subnational governments are generally dependent upon transfers from higher levels of government, and the more so the more significant the expenditures with which they are charged. (Bird, 1990, p. 278)

The extent of VFI (the ratio of transfers to total revenue) varies widely among federations: in 2000–2001, federal transfers accounted for 45 per cent in Australia, 44 per cent in Germany, 30 per cent in

Brazil and the United States, 25 per cent in Switzerland and 20 per cent in Canada (Viswanathan, 2007). For example, as is well known, the Australian Federation has one of the largest VFI measured by the international agencies. Nearly 69 per cent revenue accrues to the Commonwealth government, while its expenditure responsibilities form about 55 per cent. The states collect 25 per cent of revenues but spend about 39 per cent of the total. The local governments collect only about 5 per cent of revenues and spend 7 per cent of expenditure. Thus, the states and local governments rely very heavily on Commonwealth government for funds (Searle, 2001, p. 8, Figure 1). In terms of direct programme spending, the Commonwealth spends about 54 per cent of the total, leaving 46 per cent for the combined state and local governments. In the case of the constituent six states in the Australian Federation, the revenue share is 29 per cent with 41 per cent expenditure responsibility and in the case of local governments, the revenue share is just 3 per cent and expenditure share is about 5 per cent.

In Canada, the VFI is comparatively less as the provincial governments collect 53 per cent of the revenues and spend about 63 per cent of the combined expenditure. The VFI is more of structural in the sense, the more productive and fast-growing revenue sources are allocated to the federal government while the expenditure functions allocated to the states such that the expenditures will grow faster. In other words, the problem lies in the allocation of revenue resources itself. Such high structural VFI necessitates increasing transfers from the federal to SNGs. Provincial and local spending is a much larger proportion of the total. Looking at the individual components of spending, one sees that only in the area of social services is the federal government dominant—and then with approximately 36 per cent of the total delivered by the provincial and local governments.

Horizontal Fiscal Imbalance

The problem of 'horizontal fiscal balance' has to do with the fact that geographical areas usually differ with respect to resource capacity and needs. For instance, the tax base per capita often differs substantially among different provinces. Furthermore, the needs for public services may differ because some areas, for example, have a higher percentage of schoolchildren and/or elderly people than others (Wolman, 1990). In many countries, income inequality is due to differences among individuals within a local authority or province rather than to differences among the local governments or provinces themselves. Therefore, by providing poorer provinces with additional resources will affect only one aspect of the equity problem. Ravallion (1999) reports that evidence from India and Indonesia shows that even dramatic redistribution across regions will have limited results unless targeting is improved within regions themselves. This, in turn, depends on the ability and willingness of the subnational jurisdictions to engage in redistribution.

An important aim of the Australian Federation is 'to transfer fiscal capacity to the states and municipal government, and to do so in a way that gives each jurisdiction, when added to their own revenue raising capacity, equal capacity to provide services' (Searle, 2001, p. 5).

> Independent assessments by the Commonwealth Grants Commission indicate that states' revenue capacities vary from about 75 per cent of the per capita Australian average to about 114 per cent of that average, largely due to variations in capacities arising from Payroll Tax, Land Revenue, Stamp Duty on Conveyances and Mining Revenue. (Searle, 2001, p. 10)

The HFI within the municipal sector is even larger than that at the states level, because of the different per capita capacities of local authorities to raise revenue.

As a federal system of government, there is also a commitment to fiscal equity within the Canadian economic union. Fiscal equity is an extension of the principle of horizontal equity to federal systems of government: individuals in similar economic circumstances should be treated in a like manner by provincial government, regardless of province of residence. If different provinces are able to provide different levels of NFBs to their residents, the principle of fiscal equity will be violated.

FEDERAL FISCAL TRANSFER MANAGEMENT INSTITUTIONS

As mentioned earlier, the federal fiscal transfers are managed either through intergovernmental negotiations and consultations or through an independent institution.

In Australia, the federal fiscal transfers are managed by the Commonwealth Grants Commission (CGC)—a small, independent, advisory body with no more than three or four members and around 40 supporting staff. The CGC has no constitutional status but is regarded as an integral part of Australia's federal structure. Members of the commission are appointed by the Commonwealth (on either a full-time or a part-time basis) after discussion of prospective candidates with the states. The states have an informal veto power over nominees. Commissioners are appointed for their expertise and experience and do not represent any jurisdiction or organization when working on commission business. Appointees are usually drawn from academia, retired civil servants or business, and they cannot be public sector employees. Their appointment can be up to five years. All proceedings of the commission's inquiries are open to the public, and it freely discloses the detailed calculations behind its results and findings. Every five years, coinciding with newly available census data, the commission reviews all aspects of its data and method of calculating the relative shares of general revenue funds to go to each state. In the intervening years, methods are unchanged and annual updates of the calculations incorporate the latest available data.

Both 'revenue needs' and 'expenditure needs' were assessed comprehensively for all recurrent revenue/expenditure categories. This was different from the formula governing German *Finanzausgleich*, for instance, which essentially emphasizes aggregate fiscal capacity, leaving expenditure functions aside. The Australian model also defines own 'tax effort' relative to standard 'tax effort'. The Commission's detailed reports on tax sharing led to a great deal of controversy in Australia. There were two main reasons for the controversy. First, a full review of state relativities was to define losers and winners of the proposed redistribution exercise. Second, the report was so specific in many ways that people started to wonder what it had to do with the transfer of general revenue to states—although it has to be acknowledged that a systematic assessment would have to include all state revenue and expenditures. Despite some criticism, the Commission's work is regarded as impressive. An important lesson to be learned from the grants commission's tax-sharing exercise is that too specific horizontal redistribution formulae for a substantive amount of general revenue are likely to meet political resistance. Nevertheless, the basic methodology developed by the Commission with the assistance of the states and the Commonwealth Treasury—the equalization model for assessing general revenue grant relativities—has now been accepted by all parties.

The grant distribution model that has been used in Australia since 1981, replacing the special grants arrangements, embraces all states and territories and determines the distribution of the total amount of Commonwealth general revenue grants. It involves the calculation of grant relativities by reference to the relative per capita revenue-raising capacities for all recurrent own-source revenues, the relative per capita expenditure needs (costs of providing standard services) for all recurrent expenditures, and the differential per capita amounts of most recurrent specific-purpose grants (those for the expenditures that have been equalized). In effect, each state's or territory's share of the total Commonwealth general revenue grants depends on its standardized deficit, which is the product of its population and its per capita grant relativity. The latter is assessed as its per capita standardized expenditure minus its per capita standardized own-source revenues, plus (or minus) its differential per capita specific-purpose grants. Separate assessments are made for 19 revenue categories, 41 expenditure categories and several grant categories. The grant relativities are assessed following a major review every five years. Methodological issues are also reviewed between the major inquiries. Of all federal countries, Australia is best noted for its balanced emphasis on expenditure need and revenue means factors in determining state relativities for the distribution of unconditional equalization transfers. Section 13(3) of the states (Personal Income Tax Sharing) Act of 1970 contains general guidelines concerning equalization as follows: ... respective payments to which the states are entitled under this act should enable each state to provide, without imposing taxes and charges at levels appreciably different from the levels of the taxes and charges imposed by other states, government services at standards not appreciably different from the standards of government services provided by the other states. Total equalization pool is determined by 39.87 per cent of personal income tax collections for the previous year. The CGC is entrusted with the task of developing state relativities based upon the above principle for use in grant allocation. These relativities are defended in open adversary proceedings by the commission, and a final report is presented to the Commonwealth cabinet for review. The cabinet occasionally revises the recommended relativities based on its own view of relative fiscal needs. Following this review, a final determination is made in the Annual Premiers' Conference.

In Canada, the primary vehicles used by the federal government to address the VFI are its transfer payments for health under the Canada Health Transfer, and its transfers for post-secondary education and various social services under the Canada Social Transfer. These transfers are conditional and include both a cash payment and the 1977 tax transfer. Equalization payments are made by the federal government to ensure that reasonably uniform standards of services and taxation are kept between the richer and poorer provinces. The federal equalization programme, established in 1957, is the main policy tool for reducing the fiscal disparities among provinces. The purpose of the programme was entrenched in the Canadian Constitution in 1982: 'Parliament and the government of Canada are committed to the principle of making equalization payments to ensure that provincial governments have sufficient revenues to provide reasonably comparable levels of public services at reasonably comparable levels of taxation' (Subsection 36(2) of the Constitution Act, 1982).

Concern with grants has played a major role since the inception of the Canadian federation. Traditionally, it has followed the FCE rationale adopted by Canada's Rowell-Sirois Commission in 1940, legislated in the Fiscal Arrangements Act of 1977 and given constitutional status in 1982. This principle was rejected by the Economic Council of Canada, which adopted the HEE principle in its 1982 proposal for fiscal reform. However, the Council continued to use an FCE type formula for determining grants, with funds to be given unconditionally. (Mieszkowski & Musgrave, 1998, p. 1)

Grants based on the FCE formula are the best that can be done.

The meaning of fiscal equalization, as used in the context of federalism, differs depending on the observer's perspective. A traditional interpretation, widely used in the United States, Canada and other federal countries, such as Australia, Germany and Switzerland, has called for grants to equalize fiscal performance at a common rate of tax.

TRANSFER ARRANGEMENTS EMPLOYED TO REDUCE FISCAL IMBALANCES

The meaning of fiscal equalization, as used in the context of federalism, differs depending on the observer's perspective. A traditional interpretation, widely used in the United States, Canada and other federal countries such as Australia, Germany and Switzerland, has called for grants to equalize fiscal performance at a common rate of tax (Mieszkowski & Musgrave, 1998, p. 1).

Fiscal decentralization inevitably leaves states and municipalities with different financial abilities to provide public services to their citizens. Different jurisdictions will have different needs and costs of providing public services and different revenue-raising capacities with which to finance them. As a consequence, intergovernmental transfers usually have an equalizing element to them, with higher per capita transfers going to jurisdictions with lower fiscal capacities. The form and extent of equalization differ considerably across nations, and there may or may not be one general transfer that is dedicated to equalization. But where no single equalization transfer is made, equalizing elements are typically built into more specific transfers, including shared-cost ones (Boadway & Shah, 2007, p. xxix).

Arrangements to Reduce VFI

Tax Sharing

Tax sharing or tax devolution could be by way of either tax power sharing, tax base sharing or tax revenue sharing. In Nepal, as in many countries, the division of tax powers is already done in the Constitution. There are other forms of tax sharing: tax revenue sharing and tax base sharing.

There are two forms of tax sharing, which differ in the extent of discretion given to the states. Revenue-sharing systems stipulate a share of given revenue sources that are allocated to the states. These schemes can be based on constitutional dictate or legislated by the federal government. The allocation of shares among the states can be based on state financial needs or simply on population or the principle of derivation. Revenue sharing provides some predictability to the states, but it gives them no discretion over their own revenues. Moreover, the revenue source being shared may not be a buoyant one, and revenue sharing may discourage the federal government from using the shared base or administering it efficiently. Some of these problems can be overcome by giving states the discretion to determine how much revenue to raise from a shared tax base while allowing them to take advantage of centralized tax administration. For example, states may simply piggyback onto federal taxes by imposing a state surtax on the federal base or on federal tax revenues collected by the state. These schemes preserve a harmonized tax system while affording the states the discretion to determine their own revenues. This presumably enhances accountability. (Boadway & Shah, 2007, p. xxxix)

In some countries, the tax base sharing is in vogue. Tax base sharing could occur when the federal and provincial governments tax the same base with different rates. This has become common especially in the case of value-added tax or GST as in Australia, Canada and India.

For example, in Australia, three important measures relating to tax sharing were undertaken at different times. The first was the sharing of the payroll tax revenue; the second was when states stopped collecting excise duties on tobacco and alcohol products by a court order and the Commonwealth government replaced the revenue; and third when goods and service tax was introduced in 1999, the revenue was transferred to the states as a measure of compensating their revenue losses. In Canada, Australia and more recently in India, the value-added tax base is shared between the federal and provincial governments.

In Germany, the main taxes (VAT, income tax) are shared among all three layers of government. The vertical distribution of shared taxes is as follows: The income tax (including wage tax) is allocated to the federation, the Länder and local governments in the ratios of 42.5, 42.5 and 15 per cent. The final withholding tax on interest and capital gains is shared in ratios of 44, 44 and 12 per cent. The corporation tax is shared among the federation and the states in equal parts. The shares of income taxes are relatively stable since they emanate from provisions in the Constitution. The share of VAT, however, is subject to federal legislation (with the participation of the Länder) and may significantly vary over time in response to VFIs that may emerge on the expenditure side. For the year 2009, the shares were: Federation, 53.9 per cent; Länder, 44.1 per cent; municipalities, 2.0 per cent. The variation of the VAT share is hence thought to establish 'vertical fiscal balance', so each level of government is expected to be financially self-sufficient in the aggregate. This may, of course, need adjustments among subnational jurisdictions at the horizontal level.

Grants

The primary aim of the transfer system in the Australian Federation is to transfer fiscal capacity to the states and municipal governments, in a way that gives each jurisdiction, when added to their own revenue raising capacity, equal capacity to provide services.

Transfers to deal with vertical imbalances take two basic forms: conditional grants (called SPPs in Australia) that have specific conditions attached to how they can be spent, and unconditional grants (called General Revenue Assistance grants). Apart from these, there are GST loss compensation grants during the transition period of GST introduction. Total Commonwealth transfers dealing with vertical imbalances were roughly equally split between conditional and unconditional grants. Since the tax reform of 2000, the unconditional grants have been replaced with an allocation to each state of a portion of the proceeds of the Commonwealth-levied GST (Boothe, 2003).

Most transfers from the Commonwealth to the local bodies are in the form of untied grants passed on to the states on condition that they establish a state Grants Commission that acts independently of the government to recommend the distribution to municipal government. The Commonwealth government requires the state local government grants commissions (local government GCs) to distribute the funds in three parts:

- About 20 per cent shared between each of the 730 local councils in Australia on an equal per capita basis;
- About 30 per cent shared between each council 'on the basis of the relative need of each local governing body for roads expenditure and to preserve its roads assets'; and
- About 50 per cent on the basis of fiscal equalization.

One of the conditions attached to this transfer is that the Commonwealth has to approve the assessment methods of the local governments. Grants from states to local governments are very low and form about 7 per cent of local government revenues. Most of them come under the category of tied grants. Earlier, most of the GRA grants to states were determined by mutual discussions between the Commonwealth prime minister and the premiers of the states. As regards the SPPs, they served the purpose of equalization objective as well.

By far the most important single revenue source of sub-central governments in Australia is grant money. These grants are mainly paid in the form of general purpose financial assistance, which is explained by their historic roots as 'income tax reimbursements' following the implementation of uniform income taxation in 1942. The Tax Reimbursement Act provided the legal basis for grants to any state that abstained from levying income tax. 'The states were thus not prohibited from exploiting this tax base; yet they were encouraged to refrain from doing so' (Mathews & Jay 1972, p. 175).

In addition, more than half of Commonwealth assistance is in the form of tied or conditioned grants (for health, education, roads and public housing). In 1992–1993, the total of transfers from the Commonwealth to the states was $31.7 billion in gross terms, whereas state expenditures amounted to $51.8 billion. The various categories of grants are shown in Figures 3.1–3.5 (Shah, 2014, p. 56).

The more recent history of general revenue assistance to the Australian states falls into three phases: from 1959 to 1976, when general revenue funds were given to the states under the label of 'financial assistance grants'; from 1976 to 1985, when such revenue was transferred to the states through revenue sharing; and from 1986 onward, when financial assistance grants were reintroduced.

Financial assistance grants were increased annually (from 1959 to 1976) by a formula stressing, for each state, three factors: population changes, average wage increases and a so-called 'betterment factor' designed to allow the states to expand their relative level of services. On their reintroduction, these grants have been determined by fiscal equalization factors based on revenue/expenditure disabilities for different states while the size of the pool is determined by a percentage growth rate set to reflect specified real (inflation-adjusted) changes in assistance which can be negative when fiscal restraint is called for. Since 1990 the Commonwealth has agreed to maintain the real value of such grants in order to provide greater certainty in the funding of state budgets. The Premiers' Conference of March 1994 extended this commitment in per capita terms for the following three years.

The revenue-sharing interlude had been initiated by Fraser's 'New Federalism' policies. Sharing was first adopted for the income tax alone. The pool was formed by applying first a fixed proportion and later an increasing proportion of the tax proceeds collected in the states. This led to the states' revenues being determined by factors similar to those used for financial assistance grants before. Later, revenue sharing was extended to federal tax receipts as a whole, which somewhat lowered the rate of growth of the states' revenue pool (since revenue elasticities of other Commonwealth taxes are typically lower than for the income tax). As noted before, the revenue-sharing experiment was abandoned largely because of uncertainties about the Commonwealth's planned tax policies and for political reasons—since the states had found themselves to be 'more vulnerable to unilateral federal decisions on tax policy' (Shah, 2014, p. 59).

General revenue assistance is given for recurrent and for capital purposes in Australia. The latter reflect the fact that the Commonwealth used to borrow on behalf of the states and distribute the funds through the Loan Council. This programme, however, has become an anachronism, and the Premiers' Conference decided to abolish this type of grant in 1994.

Specific-purpose grants in the form of recurrent and capital grants are given for specific state functions such as social services (health and education), social security and welfare, economic services (roads, transport, industry assistance, water resources) and other services (like housing and urban renewal, regional development, disaster relief and debt charges). Three types can be distinguished: (a) payments 'to' states for funding direct state outlays, (b) payments 'through' states to be passed on by the states to other bodies or individuals and (c) direct payments to local governments. The conditions attached to these grants vary widely. One category simply requires the payment to be made for a specified activity, with varying degrees of budgetary discretion available to the states; another entails programme stipulations (for instance, for a hospital funding grant, that free public hospital treatment to Medicare patients is provided). Or grants may hinge on the observance of principles of service provision and programme delivery mechanisms as established by Commonwealth state agreements (1994–1995 Budget Paper No. 3, p. 31). From a political point of view, specific-purpose grants are a way to 'signal' the grantor government's concern for specific public functions that lie outside its own realm of competence. This may pay off in national elections, yet it may also be resented by state legislators and governments (as well as 'informed' voters).

Arrangements to Reduce HFI

Any good transfer system should distribute funds based on a formula. Discretionary or negotiated transfers are always undesirable. The essential ingredients of most formulae for general transfer programmes are needs, capacity and effort. Often, needs may be roughly but adequately proxied by some combination of population and the type or category of local government. A more difficult problem is usually to include some measure of the capacity of local governments to raise resources. Equalization grants is a very popular method of fiscal transfers. The methods, however, differ slightly among the countries.

Australia introduced a formal system of horizontal fiscal equalization in 1933 to compensate states/territories which have a lower capacity to raise revenue. The objective is full equalization, which means that, each of the six states (and the Australian Capital Territory and the NT) would have the capacity to provide services and the associated infrastructure at the same standard, if each state/territory made the same effort to raise revenue from its own sources and operated at the same level of efficiency. At present, only GST revenues are distributed to achieve equalization. The distribution of GST required to achieve HFE is recommended by the Commonwealth Grants Commission (CGC). The equalization grants are unencumbered and can be used for any purpose. Accordingly, the grants seek equalizing fiscal capacity, not fiscal policies of the states. These grants do not result in the same level of services or taxes in all states, direct that the states must achieve any specified level of service in any area, nor impose actual budget outcomes. The principle the commission follows in arriving at its conclusions is that of horizontal fiscal equalization, a principle it first enunciated in 1936. It is that each state should be given the capacity to provide the average standard of state-type public services, assuming it (a) operates at an average level of efficiency and (b) makes the average effort to raise revenue from its own sources. Thus, the states are given the capacity to achieve interpersonal equalization of revenue imposts and receipt of services, but are left with the ultimate decisions of what levels of service are to be provided and what revenue efforts are to be made.

The first step in the commission's application of the fiscal equalization principle is to decide what range of state-type services and areas of revenue raising should be considered in the equalization assessments. A number of conclusions follow from the implementation of the fiscal equalization principle, and some aspects of its application are worth noting.

- CGC deals with capacity and not performance equalization. This is because in Australia the states are considered to have sovereign rights in functions they retained when the Constitution was written, and the Commission is concerned with untied grants. The Commonwealth has no power to direct the states except through SPPs.
- Capacity equalization means that a state may choose to levy low taxes and have a reduced standard of public services compared with other states; or a state may choose to have high-quality public

services in some functions, even at the cost of lowering the standard of other services, higher taxes overall or an increase in its debt.

- A state that is less careful about the efficiency of its operations will not be able to provide services at average standards unless it has higher than average tax rates or increased debt.
- The commission's recommendations attempt to be policy neutral—as far as possible, the commission tries to make sure that a state cannot get a larger share of the general revenue funding by changing its priorities or its policies.

Central to the commission's work is the need to measure or estimate 'disabilities'. These are influences beyond a state's control that require it to spend more (or less) to provide the same service as other states, or mean that it cannot raise as much revenue as other states from the same tax rates.

A traditional interpretation, widely used in Canada, Australia, Germany and Switzerland, is to provide grants to equalize fiscal performance at a common rate of tax. This model, also referred to as FCE, calls for transfers from states with high per capita income and low per capita needs to those of opposite characteristics (Mieszkowski & Musgrave, 1998). An alternative view seeks to apply the rule of horizontal equity across the states and the fiscal treatment should be the same for individuals in equal positions, independent of the jurisdiction in which they reside. That perspective, referred to as HEE, was first proposed by James Buchanan and has been resumed later especially in the Canadian debate.

> Concern with grants has played a major role since the inception of the Canadian federation. Traditionally it has followed the FCE rationale, adopted by Canada's Rowell-Sirois Commission in 1940, legislated in the Fiscal Arrangements Act of 1977 and given constitutional status in 1982. This principle was rejected by the Economic Council of Canada which adopted the HEE principle in its 1982 proposal for fiscal reform. However, the Council continued to use an FCE type formula for determining grants, with funds to be given unconditionally. (Mieszkowski & Musgrave, 1998, p. 2)

In Germany, after taxation became the federal government subject in 1919 and the states lost their ability to generate income, the state tax law of 1920 provided for equalization payments among the states which ensured that no state would have less than 80 per cent of the average state tax revenue. Sections 106 and 107 of the Constitution of the Federal Republic of Germany provide for the distribution of tax revenues (horizontal and vertical equalization). This includes reducing the revenues of richer states in favour of the poorer ones.

The local share of income taxes is basically by origin (residence principle), with a formula allocation of taxes on corporations. VAT is principally allocated on a per capita basis although up to 25 per cent of the Länder share is apportioned with respect to the lack of revenue-generating capacity of a state. While the allocation of taxes is hence reflecting both revenue-generating capacities (which tends to entail inequalities) and population (which is equalizing to some extent), the original distribution of taxes is highly unequal—especially between East and West Germany. Hence, there is need for further equalization. Under Article 107(2) of the Basic Law, it must be ensured by law that the varying financial capacities of the Länder are reasonably balanced; and that due regard be given to the financial capacity and financial needs of municipalities when allocating resources among local governments (which is effected within each state without cross-border transfers).

As regards the interstate horizontal equalization, it is carried out in a 'brotherly' fashion among the states themselves—without interference of the federal government (although based on a federal law requiring the consent of the Bundesrat, the states' national assembly). The federation complements the system through asymmetrical vertical grants (Bundesergänzungszuweisungen). In Switzerland, the equalization system was introduced in 1938 in the form of conditional grants, which varied according to the tax capacity of the cantons. The broad features observed with regard to the federal fiscal transfers in selected countries can be summarized in Table A1.

Table A1 *Summary of Federal Fiscal Transfers Features in Selected Countries*

Feature	Australia	Canada	Germany	Switzerland
Objective	Build capacity to provide services at same standard with same revenue effort and same operational efficiency	Achieve reasonably comparable levels of public services at reasonably comparable levels of taxation across provinces	Equalize differences in financial capacity of states	Provide minimum acceptable levels of certain public services without much heavier tax burdens in some cantons than others
Legal status	Federal law	Constitution	Constitution	Constitution
Legislation	Federal parliament	Federal parliament	Federal parliament, initiated by the upper house (Bundesrat)	Federal parliament
Paternal or fraternal	Paternal	Paternal	Fraternal	Mixed
Total pool determination	Ad hoc	Formula	Formula	Ad hoc
Equalization standard determines pool and allocation	No	Yes	Yes	No

Allocation	Formula	Formula	Formula	Formula
Fiscal capacity equalization	Yes, representative tax system	Yes, representative tax system	Yes, actual revenues	Yes, major macro tax bases
Fiscal need equalization	Yes	No	No (only population size and density)	Some
Program complexity	High	Low	Low	Medium
Political consensus	No (?)	Yes (?)	Yes (?)	Yes
Who recommends	Independent agency	Intergovernmental committees	Solidarity Pact II	Federal government
Sunset clause	No	Yes, five years	No	No
Dispute resolution	Supreme Court	Supreme Court	Constitutional Court	Supreme Court

Source: Shah (2014).

APPENDIX B: EVOLUTION OF THE FEDERAL FISCAL RELATIONS IN INDIA

The present centre–state relationship in India can be analysed only after considering the evolution of the system of resource transfers in the Indian federal governance.

By 1833 the Indian empire under British rule was divided into two parts—the provinces that were directly administered by the governments of India and the princely states, with financial autonomy. As regards the provincial governments, all the financial powers were in the hands of governments of India. All the revenues of the provinces were paid to the Government of India with detailed control on their expenditure. All the provincial spending was financed by fixed grants from the central governments (Jather & Beri, p. 585). Thus, the government in India was completely centralized (Hemming, Mates & Potter, 1997, p. 527). This has led to extravagance, rigidity and friction in the finance of provinces, and uncertainty in central finance.

After the first war of independence (1857–1859), the power to rule over the country shifted from the hands of East India Company to the British Crown and with this transfer came a sense of stability in the British rule. In 1870, Lord Mayo took steps to organize the administration and finance in the country which hitherto was centralized. Lord Mayo initiated powers to facilitate decentralized administration. He realized the necessity of some measures of financial decentralization to enlist greater interest and more cooperation on the part of the provincial governments in generating the public revenues and managing them in economical manner (Ambedkar, 1925). In 1871, he initiated the system of provincial settlement, under which some heads of local expenditure were handed over to the provinces, such as police, education, roads and civil works, registration, medicines and jails and so on. For management of these departments, their sources of revenue were transferred to provinces, while remaining provincial expenditure continued to be financed by grants from the central government. However, actual experience revealed various defects of this system: First, the revenue grants are far below the needed expenditure of a province; second, even the quantum of the imperial grants for any year depended on the surplus funds available after the needs of the central government are met; and, third, the allocation of grants was arbitrary. Thus, this system did not provide any real motive for economy in the provinces, as the provinces were empowered to levy additional taxation.

Later, Lord Lytton (1877), Lord Rippon (1882), Lord Curzon (1904) and Lord Harding (1912) all contributed in expanding this trend of decentralization of finance in the country. In 1877, Lord Lytton, as a further step in decentralization, transferred some of the heads of expenditure that were provincial in character, such as land revenue, excise, stamps, general administration, law and justice, to the provinces. He introduced revenue sharing of major taxes by transferring certain heads of revenue to the provincial governments such as excise, stamps, law and justice. Under this arrangement, the heads of revenue were divided into central and provincial, and the Government of India reserved to themselves 50 per cent of the net increase in the yield of the provinces. However, provinces showed no enthusiasm in the collection of the revenue from those taxes in which they got no share.

In 1882, Lord Ripon, with the help of his finance member, Major Baring, abolished the fixed lump-sum grants all together and revised the allocation of revenues as follows:

- *Imperial heads:* opium, salt, customs, commercial undertakings and so on.

- *Provincial heads:* civil department, provincial works and provincial rates.
- *Divided heads:* excise, assessed taxes, stamps, forest, registration and so on.

Instead of giving fixed grants to the provinces to make up their deficit, a certain percentage of land revenue was given to them, together with fixed cash assignments under the same head. However, the main defect of the revision of the provincial settlement every five years was the appropriation of the provincial surpluses by the central government for its own needs when settlement expired. Moreover, if any province economized, the reduced expenditure was taken as the basis of the next settlement. This killed all motives for provincial economy.

To remove this defect and uncertainty, Lord Curzon made the settlement quasi-permanent in 1904, that is liable to revision only if there was a substantive change in the original condition or in the event of emergencies like war and famine. The provincial governments also secured lump-sum grants—doles as they were called—from the windfall of central revenues or central surpluses, for specific objects like police reform, education and sanitation and so on. The settlements, which were quasi-permanent, were declared permanent.

The striking features of these settlements were: On the revenue side—the central government retained all the revenues for its use, revenues which could not be allocated or traced to any province. These were opium, railways, customs, salts, mint and exchange, post and telegraphs, military receipts and tributes from natives' states. Heads of revenue wholly provincial were forest, excises (except Bombay and Bengal) registration and the departmental receipt—education, law and justice. Divided heads of revenue receipts from these heads were divided between imperial and provincial governments in stated proportions, generally equal, but determined separately for each province. On the expenditure side, a somewhat similar arrangement prevailed, and there was a special arrangement for the sharing of expenditure on draughts.

The pre-reform federal finance system suffered from a number of defects:

1. Divided heads of revenue in which both the parties were interested were a source of a constant interference on the part of central government and hampered provincial development.
2. The occasional 'doles' given by the central government to the province out of its surpluses had a disturbing influence on provincial finance.
3. Serious interprovincial financial inequalities were created.
4. The provincial government had no independent powers of taxation and borrowing.
5. Too detailed control was exercised over the provincial budget and expenditure by the central government.
6. The provinces could not budget for a deficit nor could they spend their balances freely.

GOVERNMENT OF INDIA ACT, 1919

The roots of the present form of fiscal federalism in India basically go back to the Government of India Acts of 1919 and 1935. The Government of India Act, 1919, that was the result of the Montague–Chelmsford Report (1918)[1] marks the beginning of the modem federation in India. As a step towards autonomy, the 'divided heads' were abolished, and a clear-cut separation between the central and provincial heads of revenue was affected. The reforms of 1919 made the provincial executives to be responsible for the fundamental functions of government, the enforcement of law and order, and the maintenance of an upright administration. The 1919 Act and the devolution rules allowed the provinces considerable autonomy in financial matters. The provinces were also given the power to float loans both in India

[1] The Montagu–Chelmsford Reforms or Mont–Ford Reforms were introduced by the colonial government in British India to introduce self-governing institutions gradually to India. The reforms take their name from Edwin Samuel Montagu, the secretary of state for India during the later parts of the First World War and Lord Chelmsford, Viceroy of India between 1916 and 1921.

and abroad on the security of their revenues. The provinces could withdraw from the same public account; and any amount overdrawn was to be reimbursed before the close of the financial year. So, the 1919 Act was a half-way house between control and autonomy.

GOVERNMENT OF INDIA ACT, 1935

While the 1919 Act provided for a separation of revenue heads between the centre and the provinces, the 1935 Act allowed for the sharing of the centre's revenues and for the provision of GIA to the provinces. The 1935 Act had not only embodied the basic principles of federal finance but had also endowed the provinces with financial power and authority to proceed on the way of all round development. The Act 1935 gave full control over provincial administration to elected legislatures and popular ministers subject, however, to control and regulation in vital matter by the British using the agency of the Governor-General and Governors who were invested with special responsibilities.

The provisions for fiscal federalism including the fiscal transfers provided under the Constitution of 1950 drew heavily from the 1935 Act. The Act was the first attempt of the British government to bring in an arrangement of federalism in the Indian subcontinent, which was till then categorized into British-ruled areas and the fiscally independent princely states. Through the Act of 1935, a scheme of fiscal integration of the princely states into the proposed Indian federation was mooted. The Act mandated that the federating states shall surrender their right to levy certain taxes such as the income tax, the excise duties, export duties and duties on salt. In turn, the states were to receive a share in the federal revenues by way of tax sharing and grants. These arrangements were applicable to both the federating Indian states and the provinces under the direct administrative control of the British government. The classification of the functional domain was made into three parts, the Federal List, the State/Provincial List and the Concurrent List, similar to the Seventh Schedule of the Constitution, 1950. The financial arrangements provided in the Act of 1935 insofar as these related to the princely states did not come into operation, as the states did not join the federation. However, these provisions were implemented in relation to the centre (the federation) and the provinces.

The provincial governments no longer derived their authority, political and fiscal, by devolutions made by the centre but obtained it as a direct grant from the crown. In the central field also, the Act provided for a partial transfer of responsibility to a ministry, but only when the federal provisions of the Act became operative and it had retained the supervisory control of the secretary of state over India's administration. Regarding the federal provisions becoming operative, the Act 1935 provided that the federation comprising the governor's provinces, the states which have acceded or would accede later to the federation and the chief commissioner's provinces, would come into existence only when a proclamation of inauguration was issued by the Majesty.

The sharing of revenue authority between the federation and the provinces provided that the major sources of revenue for the centre were to be the duties of customs including the export duties, duties of excise except on alcoholic and narcotic substances and on medicinal and toilet preparations that contained such substances, corporation tax, taxes on income other than agricultural income. For the provinces, the major revenue sources were the land revenue, sales tax, forest and irrigation receipts, mining receipts and so on. On the expenditure side, the major responsibilities assigned exclusively to the centre included the defence, armed forces, external affairs, a few central universities and institutions of research, census, foreign trade, shipping and ports, airways, petroleum and other inflammable products, federal pensions, labour safely in mines, banking and so on. The major responsibilities assigned exclusively to the provinces included law and order, courts, police, prisons, public works, roads, inland waterways, irrigation, agriculture, land rights and records, forests, fisheries, unemployment, provincial pensions, public health and sanitation and so on. The Concurrent List had few significant expenditure items such as welfare of labour, invalidity and old age pensions, electricity and unemployment insurance. The net fiscal position of the centre vis-à-vis the provinces was expected to be a surplus for the centre and a deficit for the provinces, both of a small order. Land revenue, which used to contribute more than half of the total tax revenues and was thus the major resource base for the provinces, had lost much of its buoyancy consequent upon introduction of permanent settlement or similar long-term settlements in most parts of the British India. By 1930–1931, land revenue was contributing less than a quarter of the total tax revenues.

The plan for fiscal transfers under the 1935 Act had provided for a structure wherein some of the federal taxes and duties were assigned to the provinces, some were made sharable either unconditionally or under certain conditions, while some others were prohibited from sharing. Besides the devolution of taxes and duties, the Act had provided for extension of GIA of the revenue of such of the provinces and states that were in need of assistance by the federal government. Such need was to be decided at the discretion of the His Majesty in Council. These arrangements can be explained in terms of the following groups:

Taxes and Duties Levied and Collected by the Federation but Assigned to the Provinces and Federated States

Section 137 of the Act provided that succession and estate duties in respect of non-agricultural properties, terminal taxes on goods or passengers carried by railway, sea or air, and taxes on railway fares and freights, shall not form part of the federal revenues but shall be assigned to the provinces and to the Federated states, if any, within which that tax is leviable in that year, and shall be distributed among the provinces and those states in accordance with such principles as may be prescribed the federal legislation.

Federal Taxes That Were to Be Shared with the Provinces Mandatorily

This group includes the income tax on non-agricultural incomes, which was a shared tax, and the export duty on jute and jute products which was an assigned tax. For these purposes, the relevant provisions were contained in Sections 138 and 140(2), respectively, of the Act, which read, inter alia, as follows:

> 138(1) Taxes on income other than agricultural income shall be levied and collected by the Federation, but a prescribed percentage of the net proceeds in any financial year of any such tax, except in so far as those proceeds represent proceeds attributable to Chief Commissioner's provinces or to taxes payable in respect of Federal emoluments, shall not form part of the revenues of the Federation, but shall be assigned to the provinces and to the Federated states, if any, within which that tax is proper to be levied in that year, and shall be distributed among the provinces and those states in such manner and from such time as may be prescribed.

> 140(2) One half or such greater proportion as His Majesty in Council may determine, of the net proceeds in each year of any export duty on jute or jute products shall not form part of the revenues of the Federation, but shall be assigned to the provinces or Federated states in which jute is grown in proportion to the respective amounts of jute grown therein.

Federal Taxes That Could Be Shared with the Provinces If the Federal Legislature Chose to Do So

Section 140 of the 1935 Act provided for sharing of certain taxes with the provinces and the Federated states only if the federal legislature provided for such sharing by enacting a legislation for the purpose. Such legislation was, however, never enacted and during the entire period of British rule, these duties were not shared with the provinces. The relevant part of this section is quoted below:

> 140(1) Duties on salt, Federal duties of excise and export duties shall be levied and collected by the Federation, but, if an Act of the Federal Legislature so provides, there shall be paid out of the revenues of the Federation to the provinces and the Federated states, if any, to which the Act imposing the duty extends, sums equivalent to the whole or any part of the net proceeds of that duty, and those sums shall be distributed among the provinces and those states in accordance with such principles of distribution as may be formulated by the Act.

Non-sharable Union Levies

The 1935 Act had retained the custom duties and the corporation taxes as non-sharable. However, with regard to the latter tax, a special provision was made under Section 139 to say that corporation taxes shall not be levied in any federated state until ten years and thereafter, if the ruler of a federated state chooses so, that tax would not be levied in such state but the ruler shall have to compensate the federation suitably for the same.

Grants-in-Aid

The 1935 Act provided for GIA to the needy provinces. Section 142 stated that such sums as may be prescribed by His Majesty in Council should be charged on the revenues of the Federation as GIA of the revenues of such provinces as His Majesty may determine to be in need of assistance, and different sums may be prescribed for different provinces. This was to be 'charged' expenditure for the centre (Section 142).

The 1935 Act had not prescribed the exact ratios for vertical and horizontal sharing of the sharable taxes and duties, leaving it to be decided by the His Majesty in Council, that is, the federal government in its absolute discretion. The Act did not provide for the intermediation or recommendation of any advisory institution such as the FC in respect of discretionary aspects of the transfers.

Yet, the British government appointed a one-man committee comprising Sir Otto Niemeyer to make recommendations in regards to the discretionary parts of the fiscal transfers. The Niemeyer Committee (1936–1947) was responsible for making recommendations to the government on the matters which come under Sections 138(1) and (2), 140(2) and 142 of the 1935 Act[2] subject to the approval of both houses of the British Parliament, and on any ancillary matters arising out of the financial adjustments between the Government of India and the provincial governments regarding which the government might desire a report. Effectively, the committee was asked to make recommendations only on limited items, namely, vertical and horizontal

[2] Section 138(1) and (2) related to the income taxes, Section 140(2) to the assignment of the net proceeds of the jute export duty and Section 142 to the grants-in-aid to the revenues of the provinces.

sharing of the net proceeds of income tax and of the export duties on jute or jute products and GIA of revenues of the needy provinces. The issue of devolution of the revenues from the export and excise duties including the salt duties, mentioned for optional sharing in terms of Section 140(1) of the Act, was not referred to the committee.

Negotiations initiated with the provinces to secure their assistance were protected and had not made much progress when the war intervened in 1939 to interrupt their continuance. The federal provisions of the Act, therefore, were put into hold. The provisions relating to them, however, came into force in 1937. The relations of provinces with the centre were regulated thereafter in accordance with provisions. In this way, although the act executed, the facade of federations is retained the essentials of a unitary form of government. The reservation of usual powers to the government answerable to the Governor-General and his overriding authority over the entire field of India's administration including the demarcated sphere of provincial jurisdiction did little to change basically the centralized feature of administration. The purpose of the provisions which served this position was to retain British control over the Indian government even after a responsible ministry had been installed at the centre, so the 1935 Act was a half-way house of federations. At best, it may be said, because of its comprehensiveness, the 1935 Act was admirably suited for adoption as the interim constitution.

The federal provisions of the 1935 Act were to come into force only when the rulers of the native states aggregate population whereof amounted to at least one-half of the total population had acceded to the federation. This condition could not be met as the rulers of the states kept delaying. Thus, the Federation of India could not come into being as envisaged in the Act. However, the other parts of the Act impacting the fiscal, legislative and administrative relationship between the centre and the provinces were brought into operation in 1937. Implementation of even those provisions was subject to considerable stress from time to time owing to the outbreak of the Second World War and the engagement of the British authorities as well as the native political leaders with the freedom movement.

Despite its halting and partial implementation, the provisions in the 1935 Act proved to be a significant step in defining the boundaries of the legislative and executive domain for the centre and the provinces. These arrangements were conducive for fiscal stability of the centre and the provinces and laid the legal foundation for fiscal federalism in the country. These provisions indeed influenced the drafting of the Constitution of 1950 to a good extent. The deliberations of the Constitution Drafting Committee and the Constituent Assembly Debates indicate that particularly for defining the fiscal contours of federalism for the united India, the framers of the Constitution found merit in several of the features of the 1935 Act. Also, the ToR for the Niemeyer Committee, though brief, found their imprint on the ToR of the FCs of the post-Independent India.

NIEMEYER AWARD (1936–1947)

The report of Sir Otto Niemeyer, officially titled as The Indian Financial Enquiry Report, and popularly called the Niemeyer Award (April 1936),[3] made 69 specific recommendations with regard to the vertical and horizontal sharing of the sharable taxes and duties as well as for GIA for those provinces that it determined to be in need of assistance owing to their financial weakness. It also made recommendations for debt relief, in relation to the outstanding debts of the provinces to the centre.

THE MESTON AWARD

The abolition of divided heads of revenue and clear-cut separation of heads of revenue between central and provincial governments resulted in a central deficit of ₹983 lakhs, which had to be provided for by a scheme of provincial contributions to the central exchequer. A committee was appointed under the chairmanship of Lord Meston in 1920 to consider and recommend a scheme of provincial contribution to the central government and other related questions. The

---

[3] Sir Niemeyer, The Indian Financial Enquiry Report, presented by the secretary of state for India to the Parliament of the United Kingdom in April 1936.

Table B1 *Provincial Surpluses or Deficits in the First Year of Reform: 1921–1922 as Estimated by Meston Award*

| | Increased Spending Power under New Distribution of Revenue | Standard Contribution in 1921–1922 | Percentage of Standard Contribution to Deficit | | | Meston Committee's Estimation of Spending Power after the Contribution in 1921–1922 | Actual Surplus/ Deficit in 1921–1922 |
			Percent Contribution to Deficit in 1921–1922	Recommended by Meston Committee	Finally Adopted (000)		
Madras	576	348	35.50	17	17–90	288	–99
Bombay	95	56	5.50	13	13–90	37	–191
Bengal	104	63	6.5	19	19–90	41	–215
United Provinces[a]	397	240	24.5	18	18–19	157	–148
Punjab	289	175	18	9	9–90	114	–171
Burma	246	64	6.50	6.50	6.5–90	182	14
Bihar and Orissa	51	0	0	10	0	51	–15
Central Provinces[b]	52	22	2	5	5–90	30	–24
Assam	42	15	1.5	2.5	2.5–90	27	–24
Total	1,850	983	100%	100%	90%	867	–887

Notes: [a] The United Provinces was a province of British India corresponded approximately to the combined regions of the present-day Indian states of Uttar Pradesh and Uttarakhand.

[b] The central provinces covered parts of present-day Madhya Pradesh, Chhattisgarh and Maharashtra states.

Meston committee maintained that the provinces would acquire large revenues including income tax because of the abolition of divided heads of revenue. Therefore, provinces should make contribution to the central government out of their revenue surpluses. There was an 'initial contribution' based upon the increased spending power of the provinces due to the new distribution of the revenue heads and was fixed in such a way that provinces should not be confronted with a deficit or compelled to resort to new taxation. Then there was also a 'standard contribution' to be determined separately for each province on the basis of its financial conditions.

The new allocation of revenue and expenditure was as follows:

- *Imperial heads of revenue:* opium, salt, customs, income tax, railway, post and telegraphs, military receipts.
- *Provincial heads of revenue:* Land revenue (including irrigation), stamps (judicial and commercial), registration, excise and forest.

The Meston Award did not please anybody and caused much provincial discontent. The 'initial contributions' were considered arbitrary. Industrial provinces such as Bombay and Bengal could never reconcile themselves to the virtual loss of the income tax revenue. On the other hand, agricultural provinces such as Madras, Punjab and United provinces resented what they considered their excessive initial contributions, the contributions became burdensome when the provincial governments were faced with a series of heavy deficits in place of comfortable surpluses, which the Meston Committee had envisaged. The revenues assigned to them, such as land revenue, were inelastic and inadequate, to carry out its functions.

The financial development in the subsequent years resulted in gradual improvement in the finances of the central government as compared to that of the provinces. The central government in 1925–1926 provided some relief to the provinces. Out of a total surplus of ₹324 lakhs, ₹250 lakhs were utilized to grant permanent remissions of contribution to Madras (₹126 lakhs), United provinces (₹56 lakhs), Punjab (₹61 lakhs) and Burma (₹7 lakhs). This facilitated the task of reducing the provincial contributions and by 1928–1929 they were totally abolished.

The final abolition of the provincial contributions, however, did not end all controversy regarding the division of revenue between the central and provincial governments. The main grievance of the provinces was that the central government had taken for itself sources of revenue like income tax and customs, which were expanding or were capable of expansion and provinces were left with inelastic and stagnant sources like land revenue and excise, although the needs of the provincial government were rapidly expanding. The provinces were responsible for nation-building departments such as education, medical relief, and agriculture, on which heavy outlay was essential. Famine expenditures had also been put on the shoulders of the provincial governments. The Bombay Legislature Council in their representation to the Government of India in March 1925 pointed out that the distribution of surplus revenue assigned to the provinces under the reform was determined in haphazard manner. And there is no relation to the needs of provinces or to total taxation derived from them.

The Montague–Chelmsford Report urged that if self-government was to become a reality, the provinces should be in a position to calculate their resources with certainty and to a certain extent be free to develop their own taxable capacity. The history of federal and provincial finance elsewhere, however, shows that an absolute clear-cut division between central and provincial revenue is not possible. The principal source of revenue in different provinces and the new allocation of revenue all resulted in provincial inequalities. The fundamental defect of the system, as pointed out by the Simon Commission Report (1928),[4] was that, while it professed to follow the theoretical ideal of federal finance, in practice it left inadequate resources to the provincial government. Furthermore, it was even more surprising that the Government of India Act of 1919 left the residuary power of taxation in the hands of the central government. Provincial autonomy is a meaningless phrase without arming the provinces with adequate spending power. The Indian financial problem is largely one of harmonizing the distribution of functions with the allocation of the sources of revenue of the provinces and the centre, respectively.

---

[4] In November 1927, the British government appointed the Simon Commission to report on India's constitutional progress for introducing constitutional reforms.

Vertical Sharing of the Income Tax

The Niemeyer Committee turned out to be rather conservative in making recommendation on the transfer of the proceeds of income tax to the provinces. On the face of it, it recommended sharing of 50 per cent of the net proceeds of income tax with the provinces. However, it also put a rider to the effect that for the first five years after the award was put into operation, the share for the provinces shall be reduced by such amounts as would make the central government's share in the divisible pool of ₹13 crore. For the next five-year period, the sum retained in the last year of the first period would be reduced by a factor of 1/6 every year.[5] The result of the Niemeyer formulation was that the provinces received far less than the figure of 50 per cent recommended by Niemeyer.

No doubt, the gross collections were to be reduced by the proceeds attributable to the chief commissioner's provinces, taxes on federal emoluments and the cost of collection. Exact figures for these three factors for the aforesaid years are not available, but these generally amount to about 10 per cent of the gross collections.[6] Therefore, the actual transfers to the provinces remained far less than 50 per cent. Niemeyer justified this on the grounds of financial stability and credit of India as a whole being of paramount consideration, for which it was essential to maintain the solvency of the central government.[7]

Sharing of the Sharable Proceeds of Income Tax

For the sharing of the sharable proceeds of income tax among the provinces, Sir Niemeyer indicated that he had adopted two factors, namely, population and the source of collection for some reference

[5] The rider was permissible under Clause (2) of Section 138 of the Government of India Act, 1935.

[6] The Niemeyer report (Para 26) has given an indication in this respect as follows. The estimated net proceeds of income tax for 1936–1937, net of the cost of collection and proceeds attributable to Burma, would be ₹13.4 crore. In that figure, the estimated amount pertaining to corporation tax, chief commissioner's provinces and federal emoluments would be about ₹1.4 crore, leaving a residuum of about ₹12 crore divisible between the centre and the federating units.

[7] The Niemeyer Report, Para 3, 1936.

year, and determined a fixed percentage share for each province. He did not indicate the relative weights assigned to the two factors citing uncertainty of some of the statistical data. Obviously, Niemeyer used his discretion in the matter.[8]

Assignment in Respect of Jute Export Duties

In respect of the jute export duties, the 1935 Act had provided for assignment of at least 50 per cent of the net proceeds to the jute-growing provinces in proportion to the respective amounts of jute grown therein.[9] It had also provided that such assignment could be more than 50 per cent, if the federal government so decided. The federal government, in turn, referred this matter to Sir Niemeyer, who recommended that 62.5 per cent of the net proceeds be assigned to the provinces. The 1935 Act had also provided that the inter se sharing of the sharable proceeds of the jute export duties should be distributed among the jute-growing provinces/states in proportion to the respective amounts of jute grown therein. Niemeyer was not happy about this provision and stated in his report that:

> In my opinion, it is doubtful whether the argument that the incidence of this particular duty falls wholly on the producer can be maintained and even if such proof can be produced, it may be doubted whether it would be valid in a changing market.[10]

Having noted such opinion, Niemeyer did not pursue the matter further.

GIA to Provinces

The ToR for Sir Otto Niemeyer included the issue of GIA for the provinces, in line with Section 142, the substantive provision of which stated:

> Such sums as may be prescribed by His Majesty in Council shall be charged on the revenues of the Federation in each year as grants in aid of revenues

[8] The Niemeyer Report, Paras 34, 139.

[9] Section 140(2) of the Government of India Act, 1935.

[10] The Niemeyer Report, Para 22, 140.

of such provinces as His Majesty may determine to be in need of assistance, and different sums may be prescribed for different provinces.[11]

A similar provision exists in the Constitution of India and all the FCs have made recommendations. Comparing the approaches of the FCs with those of Niemeyer, it appears that Niemeyer took a very limited view of the matter, in defining the 'needs' of the respective provinces. He took the estimates of the revenue receipts and expenditure as were presented to him for the year 1936–1937 as the primary basis for determining the 'needs'. On that, he imposed certain specific requirements of the individual provinces.

For instance, for Sindh, he examined only the cost and returns from the Lloyd Barrage and the need for another sum of ₹5 lakh for providing a jail at Shikarpur. For the newly created province of Orissa, the central government had, in the preceding year, provided a grant of ₹50 lakh, which included ₹40.5 lakh towards revenue expenditure, ₹7.5 lakh for non-recurrent expenses relating to famine and so on and ₹2 lakh as untied funds. Niemeyer made an *ad hoc* increase in this sum to ₹57 lakh for the first year, ₹53 lakh annually for the next four years and ₹50 lakh per annum thereafter. For Assam, Niemeyer recommended an assistance of ₹45 lakh towards revenue deficit and ₹7 lakh towards maintenance of the Assam Rifles, for the North-West Frontier province (NWFP), and the Government of India had already extended an annual subvention of ₹100 lakh. Niemeyer enhanced it by ₹10 lakh annually for period of five years, subject to a review at the end of that period. For the provinces of Bengal, Bihar, central provinces and the United provinces, Niemeyer recommended annual grants of ₹75 lakh, ₹25 lakh, ₹15 lakh and ₹25 lakh, respectively, without explaining the reasons for arriving at the individual figures. Having assessed the needs of the provinces for revenue assistance, Niemeyer first considered meeting part of that need by way of debt cancellation and consequent reduction in debt servicing expenditure. For the remaining sums, he recommended GIA under Section 142 of the 1935 Act, amounting to sums ranging from ₹25 lakh to ₹110 lakh

[11] The Niemeyer Report.

per year to each of the provinces.[12] It needs to be appreciated that the initial FCs in India did not depart drastically from the approach of Niemeyer, though they made certain improvements by way of broad basing and refining the methodology.

THE 1947–1950 PERIOD

During the period commencing with the Independence and until the promulgation of the Constitution in 1950, the principles being followed until 1947 in respect of the devolution of central revenues, based upon the Niemeyer Award, were broadly continued by the executive decisions of the Government of India. Thus, 50 per cent of the net proceeds of income tax were transferred to the states. The Government of India Act continued to be in operation until the 26th January 1950, that is, until it was repealed by Article 395 of the Constitution. Further, under the 1935 Act, it was permissible to share the proceeds of the union excise duties too. However, the Government of India chose not to extend any such share to the provinces/states, as was the practice prior to 1947. For the inter se sharing of the divisible share of income tax, the Government of India took an executive decision in regard to the shares attributable to the divided parts of the provinces of Punjab and Bengal as well as the NWFP, which had gone to the newly created Pakistan. The provincial shares were revised after distributing the quota of such transferred territories among the provinces of the Indian union according to population with some adjustments in favour of West Bengal and Assam.

The Krishnamachari Committee

To examine such issues, the Indian States Finances Enquiry Committee was set up in October 1948 with Shri V. T. Krishnamachari as chairman, with the primary focus on the Part B states[13] and of Baroda's

---

[12] Ibid, Paras 13, 14 and 19–24.

[13] The Constitution of 1950 distinguished between three main types of states and a class of territories:

merger with Bombay.[14] The report of the committee was discussed by the union government with the states concerned and with certain agreed modifications, incorporated in the agreements entered into by the union government with the states. The main feature of the agreements between the Government of India and the Part B states was that the centre would make good difference between the loss of revenue and savings on expenditure responsibilities, for a transitional period, as 'revenue gap grants'. For this purpose, the revenue receipts and expenditure figures were determined based upon an agreed period immediately preceding the integration. The revenue gap grants were guaranteed in full for the first five years and on a gradually diminishing scale for a further period of five years at the end of which the grants would reach the level of approximately 60 per cent of the original figure. It was also agreed that the Part B states would get either a share in divisible sources of revenue like the income tax, or the 'revenue gap grant', whichever would be higher.

It was also agreed that the share of each Part B state should be 50 per cent of the net proceeds of the taxes on income other than agricultural income levied and collected by the Government of India in that state in each year. Four Part B states, namely, Hyderabad, Mysore, Travancore-Cochin and Saurashtra, qualified for the 'revenue gap

Part A states, which were the former governors' provinces of British India, were ruled by a governor appointed by the president and an elected state legislature. The nine Part A states were Assam, Bihar, Bombay, Madhya Pradesh (formerly central Provinces and Berar), Madras, Orissa, Punjab (formerly East Punjab), Uttar Pradesh (formerly the United Provinces) and West Bengal.

Part B states, which were former princely states or groups of princely states, governed by a Rajpramukh, who was usually the ruler of a constituent state, and an elected legislature. The Rajpramukh was appointed by the President of India. The eight Part B states were Hyderabad, Jammu and Kashmir, Madhya Bharat, Mysore, Patiala and East Punjab States Union (PEPSU), Rajasthan, Saurashtra and Travancore-Cochin.

Part C states included both the former chief commissioners' provinces and some princely states, and each was governed by a chief commissioner appointed by the President of India. The ten Part C states were Ajmer, Bhopal, Bilaspur, Coorg, Delhi, Himachal Pradesh, Cutch, Manipur, Tripura and Vindhya Pradesh.

The sole Part D territory was the Andaman and Nicobar Islands, which were administered by a lieutenant governor appointed by the central government.

[14] Report of the First Finance Commission, Government of India, Chapter II, 1952.

grants', whereas the others did not as the expenditure saved to them by integration was more than the revenue lost to them. The issue of financial burden caused to some of the Part A states by merger of the former princely states with them was also addressed. It was provided that all Part A states affected by the merger would receive 50 per cent of the net proceeds of the taxes on income other than agricultural income levied and collected in the merged territories within the state each year or the 'revenue gap grant', whichever was higher. Accordingly, four Part A states received such grant, namely, Bombay, Bihar, Madhya Pradesh and West Bengal.

Deshmukh Award (1950–1952)

While the constitutional provisions relating to federal fiscal transfers were brought into force with effect from 26 January 1950, an interim arrangement was followed by the Government of India till 31 March 1952 when the decision in pursuance to the award of the 1FC came into force. During this period, that is, until 31 March 1952, the arrangements followed till then, which were in turn broadly on the lines of the Niemeyer Scheme, were continued. Accordingly, 50 per cent of the net proceeds of income tax, exclusive of the proceeds attributable to Part C states and the proceeds of the taxes payable in respect of union emoluments, were assigned to the states. As for the horizontal transfers, a need was felt to make certain interim arrangements, to take care of the situation arising out of the partition of India that had led to transfer of some of provinces (or parts) to Pakistan and the share of such provinces (or parts) was to be redistributed among the Indian states.

To address these issues, a committee under the chairmanship of Shri C. D. Deshmukh[15] was constituted towards the end of 1949

[15] Chintaman Dwarakanath Deshmukh (1896–1982) of the Indian Civil Service was the first Indian Governor of the Reserve Bank of India (from 11 August 1943 to 30 June 1949). In 1950, he joined the Union Cabinet as the Finance Minister and held that office with distinction till he resigned in July 1956. He was Vice-Chancellor the University of Delhi from March 1962 to February 1967, Chairman of the University Grants Commission from 1956 to 1960, President of the Indian Statistical Institute (ISI) from 1945 to 1964, President of the Institute of Economic Growth, New Delhi, from

to examine the matter and make suitable recommendations. Shri Deshmukh, in his report, recommended for redistribution of the aggregate quota available for redistribution largely on the basis of population, with two adjustments, one for the purposes of rounding off and the other for giving a small weight in favour of the weaker states. The Deshmukh Award was not expected to deal with the matter of sharing of union duties of excise, nor did it make any reference to that matter. The award also made recommendations regarding GIA to the jute-growing provinces in terms of Article 273. The award was accepted by the Government of India and remained the basis for fiscal transfers from 1 April 1950 until 31 March 1952, after which the scheme pursuant to the recommendations of the FC came into force.

DRAFTING OF THE CONSTITUTION

The principles based upon the Niemeyer Award for the distribution of income-tax receipts were in the practice during the period 1936–1947, were adopted for the initial years after the Independence, that is, till the promulgation of the Constitution in 1950, but with some amendments in the inter se sharing of the divisible share of income tax to consider the territories transferred to Pakistan.

N. R. Sarkar Committee

The President of the Constituent Assembly had, in the meanwhile, referred the issue of financial provisions to be incorporated in the Constitution to an expert committee headed by Nalini Ranjan Sarkar, a former member of the Viceroy's Executive Council and with two other members, V. S. Sundaram and M. V. Rangachari (Member Secretary), who were senior officers of the Indian Audit and Accounts Service. The committee consulted various opinions including the draft prepared by B. N. Rau, the Constitutional Adviser, memoranda of the provinces and the union finance ministry, and made various suggestions including

1965 to 1974 and so on. It was during the period when he was both the President of the ISI and the Union Finance Minister that the National Sample Survey (NSS), to be conducted by the ISI, was instituted (1951–1952), and the Central Statistics Office (CSO) was established.

the setting up of an FC for making recommendations relating to fiscal transfers and sharing.

The financial arrangements recommended by the Expert Committee mooted significant departure from the provisions of the 1935 Act. For instance, the Expert Committee had recommended that 60 per cent of the net proceeds of the income-tax collections, except the proceeds attributable to the chief commissioner's provinces and to the federal emoluments, should be transferred to the provinces, and of that 60 per cent, 20 per cent should be on the basis of population, 35 per cent on the basis of collection and 5 per cent as a balancing factor to mitigate any hardship that might arise for some provinces in implementing the other two factors.

The Expert Committee had further recommended that the net proceeds of the corporation tax should also be included in the divisible pool and that 50 per cent of the net proceeds of the excise duty on tobacco be assigned to the provinces and distributed among them on the basis of estimated consumption. The Committee recommended for continuation of the arrangements in regard to the assigned taxes (federal stamp duties, terminal taxes on goods and passengers and so on) but made a limited departure by recommending that the centre should retain 40 per cent of the net proceeds of the estate and succession duties.

The suggestions of the Expert Committee were discussed by the Drafting Committee for the Constitution and later in the Constituent Assembly and were incorporated in the Constitution after some amendments. In certain respects, the Drafting Committee did not accept the recommendations of the Expert Committee. For instance, the Drafting Committee did not accept the recommendations of the Expert Committee relating to devolution and chose to retain the provisions on the lines of the 1935 Act. Thus, in the draft placed before the Constituent Assembly, the provisions for devolution included a mandatory sharing of income tax without indicating any specific number, optional sharing of excise duties, and no sharing of the remaining central taxes including the corporation tax, and that was adopted by the Constituent Assembly.

In most other respects, the Drafting Committee favoured and accepted the recommendations of the Expert Committee, with some modifications in some cases. Among the most significant provisions accepted was the provision relating to the FC.[16] The Expert Committee had recommended the aforesaid principles for devolution and so on only for a limited period. For the long term, it had recommended setting up of an expert body, FC, to make periodic recommendations on three broad issues:

1. Allocation between provinces of the centrally administered taxes assigned to them;
2. Considering applications for GIA for provinces and recommending thereon; and
3. Considering and reporting on other matters referred to it by the President.

The basis for allocation of revenues between the provinces was to be reviewed by the FC every five years, or, in special circumstances, earlier. In this respect, the Drafting Committee concurred with the recommendations of the Expert Committee and the provisions relating to constitution and functions of the FC were, with some drafting changes, incorporated in the Constitution.

The Constituent Assembly had adopted the Constitution of India on 26 November 1949. A few of Articles, namely, Articles 5 to 9, 60, 324, 366, 367, 379, 380, 388, 391 to 393, were brought into force on that day itself, whereas the majority of the provisions, including those relating to the financial matters, were brought into effect from 26 January 1950. The Constitution of India, as it was adopted by the Constituent Assembly on 26 November 1949, had recognized the necessity and the significance of specifying the powers and functions of the union and the states and their mutual relationship at the interface. The main features of the federal structure envisaged in the Constitution are as discussed further.

---

[16] The Framing of India's Constitution, a study commissioned by the Indian Institute of Public Administration, New Delhi, with B. Shiva Rao as chairman (1968), and the Report of the First Finance Commission, Government of India, 1952, Chapter II.

The distribution of functional domain, which includes the powers to make laws, between the union and the states by virtue of the lists contained in the Seventh Schedule. List I contains the list of functions in the exclusive domain of the union, List II, of the states and List III, concurrent.[17]

The power was given to the Parliament to legislate on exclusively state subjects in situations such as: first, with respect to the matters in the State List in national interest, but for a limited period (Article 249); second, in respect of any matter in the State List if the proclamation of emergency is in operation (Articles 250 and 353); third, with respect to two or more states by consent of those states (Article 252); fourth, the executive power given to the union to give directions to the states in the normal circumstances (Article 257) and during the operation of a proclamation of emergency (Article 353); fifth, superiority of union laws over state laws in cases of overlap or conflict (Article 254); sixth, a residuary power of legislation vest with the centre (Article 248).

While the Constitution has indicated the broad framework for the ToR of the FC, it allows the FC to determine its own principles for making recommendations in relation to the tasks assigned to it. The Constitution also permits the FC to follow its own procedure in the matter. In addition to the constitutional provisions, Parliament has enacted the Finance Commission (Miscellaneous Provisions) Act, 1951, which prescribes the qualifications for the chairman and members of the FC and also the procedure that the FC should follow to perform its duties. The ensuing paragraphs review the principles adopted by the FCs for assessment of the finances of the centre and the states and for the tax devolution, GIA and other items of the transfer of resources.

COMMISSION AND COMMITTEES ON CENTRE–STATE RELATIONS

Discussions about the centre–state relations have been marked by recommendations of committees and commissions. More prominent among them are the Administrative Reforms Commissions (1969), the

---

[17] Constitution of India, Seventh Schedule.

Rajamannar Committee (1971) and the Sarkaria Commission (1983), all of which made many important recommendations for reconstructing the centre–state relations.

Administrative Reforms Commission (1969)

The Administrative Reforms Commission held firmly that the Indian Constitution is a federation with a strong centre. It stated that the Constitution is so well balanced that while providing maximum possible autonomy to the states, it places in the hands of the centre adequate powers to ensure the unity and integrity of the country. The following are the key recommendations of the Administrative Reforms Commission:

1. The FC may be asked to make recommendations on the principles which should govern the distribution of plan grants to states.
2. The appointments of the FC may be so timed that when making its recommendation it will have before it an outline of the forthcoming FYP.
3. In order to secure effective coordination of the FC's recommendations, a member of the PC may be appointed to the FC.
4. The FC should include two persons, one having experience of financial administration at the centre and the other having such experience in state.
5. The unit of the Plan Finance Division of the ministry of finance at the centre may be strengthened.

Rajamannnar Committee (1971)[18]

The government of Tamil Nadu constituted this committee to examine the entire question regarding the relationship that should subsist between the centre and the states in India's federal set-up, with reference to the provisions of the Constitution so as to secure to the states the utmost autonomy. The bases for the devolution of revenues on the states should be widened by including corporation tax, custom and

---

[18] P.V. Rajamannar was the chairman of the 4FC (1964).

export duties, and tax on the capital value of assets in the divisible pool to be shared by the centre and the states.

All excise duties and cesses which are sharable at the option of the union should all be made compulsorily divisible between the union and the states. Grants by the centre to the states, both for plan expenditure and for non-plan expenditure, should be made only on the recommendation of the FC or a similar statutory body. Recommendations of the FC shall be binding on all the parties—centre as well as the states. PC should be placed on a statutory basis and the existing PC should be abolished. This committee had observed that the assistance to be given by the centre for plan projects is practically dependent on the recommendations of the PC and, therefore, a body like the FC cannot operate in the same field.

Sarkaria Commission (1983)

The Sarkaria Commission was constituted in June 1983 to examine and review the working of the existing arrangements between the union and the states in regard to powers, functions and responsibilities in all spheres and recommend such changes and other measures as may be appropriate. The Commission made a large number of recommendations, the more important of which relate to finance.

1. Corporation tax should be made sharable with states;
2. Certain other levies, loan procedures and foreign exchange entitlements should be liberalized in favour of the states;
3. Municipal bonds should be tax exempt; and
4. CSS should be strictly limited.

The Sarkaria Commission had also discussed setting up of an expert committee to recommend restructuring of taxation and resource distribution from the centre to the states. It was proposed that an advisory subcommittee of finance be set up in the NDC, and that the FC itself work under the member-in-charge of financial resources in the PC. The recommendations of the Sarkaria Commission have been widely acclaimed across the political spectrum. But most of the crucial recommendations which constitute the sentinel of a federal restructuring are yet to be implemented. The clamour by the state governments for more powers vis-à-vis the centre is sought to be modified by appointments of such commission without any pragmatic intention of really implementing their recommendations. Meanwhile, the old theory persists that a strong centre is needed to preserve the unity and integrity of the country. Now, the moot question is whether the old theory is capable of tackling all the federal problems or a radical federalism that aims at securing more powers to the states is to be put on the agenda. And the choice for a new federalist balance has to trace the problems right from the constitutional provisions to the present practices.

EVOLUTION OF THE FINANCE COMMISSION

Guided by the recommendations of the Sarkaria Committee, the Constitution Drafting Committee had proposed setting up of FC at a maximum interval of five years for the purposes of making recommendations in respect of the following:

1. Devolution of central taxes and duties to the states and distribution of the same among the states;
2. Extension of GIA to the revenues of the needy states;
3. Extension of GIA to the states for the development and welfare of the scheduled tribes and scheduled areas; and
4. Any other matter in the interest of sound finance.

The Constituent Assembly had found these proposals generally acceptable[19] and adopted the proposed clauses with minor changes. Accordingly, the provisions of the Constitution relating to FC were brought into effect on 26 January 1950. The FC is constituted under the provisions of Article 280 of the Constitution, and the Finance Commission (Miscellaneous Provisions) Act, 1951. Under these provisions, the President constitutes the FC and appoints its chairman and members, at the interval of no more than five years. The FC makes recommendations relating to the distribution of the net proceeds of taxes between the union and the states, the principles which should govern the GIA of the revenues of the states out of the Consolidated Fund of

[19] Proceedings of the Constituent Assembly dated 9 and 10 August 1949.

India and the measures needed to augment the Consolidate Fund of a state to supplement the resources of panchayats and municipalities. In addition, any other matter may be referred to the Commission by the President in the interests of sound finance.

The provisions for constituting the FC are contained in Clause (3) of Article 280. In the original form of the Constitution (1950), this clause prescribes five broad themes for the FC to make recommendations about

1. The distribution between the union and the states of the net proceeds of taxes which are to be, or may be, divided between them under Chapter I of Part XII of the Constitution (i.e., vertical transfers or devolution);
2. The allocation between the states of the respective shares of such proceeds (i.e., the inter se or horizontal distribution);
3. The principles for making GIA of the revenues of the states from the Consolidated Fund of India;
4. The continuation or modification of the terms of any agreement entered into by the Government of India with the government of any state specified in Part B of the First Schedule under Clause (1) of Article 278 or under Article 306; and
5. Any other matter considered by the President to be in the interest of sound finance.

The 1FC was set up in November 1951 and was required to give its report covering five fiscal years commencing 1 April 1952. So far, 15 FCs have been set up.

Of the five themes, the fourth theme was deleted by the seventh amendment (1956), which had also omitted Article 278. Subsequently, a set of new terms were added in Article 280(3) by the 73rd and 74th Amendments (1973), requiring the FC to also make recommendation in respect of measures needed to enable the states extend financial help to local bodies, panchayats and municipalities. While the constitutional provisions for the FCs have been fairly cryptic, the ToR assigned for the successive FCs have been far more elaborate and extensive. The various tasks/issues referred to the FCs by way of the ToR can be broadly classified into mandatory and non-mandatory considerations. The evolution of both the considerations in the ToR for successive FCs is analysed in subsequent chapters.

TRENDS IN CONSTITUTIONAL DEVELOPMENTS IN INDIA

Initially, the governmental levels recognized in the Constitution were two: the union and the states. But the two constitutional amendments carried out in 1992 have accorded constitutional status to the panchayats and municipalities, although the exact demarcation of their powers and functions is left to the state governments to be specified through their respective legislatures. With all these provisions, the Indian Constitution has been characterized as 'quasi-federal'. In several respects, unitary elements have clearly overshadowed the federal attributes, with the centre assuming a more dominating role than what even the constitution-makers had visualized (Dandekar (1987). Although the powers of the union and the states are enumerated in separate lists in a schedule appended to the Constitution, the 'ownership' of powers cannot be said to be clear-cut. The Concurrent List covers fairly wide areas wherein the union government is vested with powers to dismiss an elected state government on the grounds of breakdown of normal constitutional arrangement. The adoption of planning in the country in 1951 and the establishment of the PC through an administrative order of the Government of India gave further powers of control over the states by the centre through its strategy of development and planning. The institution of all-India services provides another mechanism for exercising control over the states. The centre's sway over the economy was widened further by public ownership of large industries and nationalization of major banks in the country. The ambit of central control over state subjects was further extended through a number of CSS to be implemented by the state and local governments.

As in other federations, the Constitution of India mandates that, subject to the provisions made in the Constitution, 'trade, commerce and intercourse throughout the territory of India shall be free' (Article 301). Comparable to the 'commerce clause' of the US Constitution, these provisions should have helped to secure the free functioning of a common market in India. The Indian Constitution, however, stipulates that Parliament may impose restrictions on freedom in 'public interest'. Invoking public interest, both the centre and the states imposed controls on the movement of commodities that play a vital role in the life of the common people like food grains, edible oils, and cotton, severely impeding the emergence of an integrated market in the country. The states on their part used 'public interest' to create barriers segmenting the country's market, Maharashtra's Cotton Monopoly Procurement Scheme of 1971 being a glaring example. The centre is clearly a party to this segmentation which continues even now as the continuation of the scheme requires centre's approval periodically. There was often a multiplicity of control orders imposed on the same commodity and notifications were issued for the same item by both the centre and the states.

Financial Emergencies

The Indian Constitution contains a unique provision to deal with a financial emergency. Article 360(1) provides that if the president is satisfied that a situation has arisen whereby the financial stability or credit of India or any part of the territory thereof is threatened, he may by proclamation make a declaration to that effect. The proclamation ceases to operate at the expiration of two months (and can be revoked or varied earlier by the President). If it is approved by both Houses of Parliament, it can be continued longer.

The effect of issue of proclamation under Article 360(1), known as the Proclamation of Financial Emergency, is that during its subsistence, the executive authority of the union shall extend under Article 360(3):

1. To the giving of directions to any state to observe such canons of financial propriety as the case may be; and
2. To the giving of such other directions as the President may deem necessary and adequate for the purpose.

Directions of the nature mentioned in (2) notwithstanding the apparent width of language must be connected with the financial propriety (not the words 'for the purpose'). Subject to this requirement, it would appear that the union can give directions even of an administrative nature, that is, directions to reduce or modify certain types of administrative action by the state government, in order to avert the threat to financial stability or credit. It is further provided in Article 260(4), which begins with a non-obstinate clause, that the directions issued under Article 360 may include a requirement to reduce salaries and allowances of 'all or any clad of persons serving in connection with the affairs of a state' as provided in Article 360(4)(i).

It is further provided in Article 360(4)(ii) that the directions may include a provision requiring all money bills or other bills to which the provisions of Article 207 apply to be reserved for the consideration of the President after they are passed by the legislature of the state. It is finally provided in Article 360(4)(b) that the President may (while the Proclamation of Financial Emergency is in operation) provide directions for the reduction of salaries and allowances of all or the union including the judges of the Supreme Court and the High Courts.

A little analysis will show that the most important effect of a Proclamation of Financial Emergency is that it empowers the President to modify the constitutional scheme of division of financial powers inasmuch as the union can give directions vitally affecting the manner in which the executive power of the state may be exercised. The provision regarding money bills has a similar consequence. Another notable feature of Article 360 is that it empowers the issue of directions for reducing the salaries and allowances not only of persons employed in connection with the affairs of a state, but of persons serving in connection with the affairs of the union including the judges of the Supreme Court and the High Courts. Here is an example of power to modify rights conferred by the Constitution. It is also worth pointing out that the scope of the power to issue directions under Article 360 regarding salaries and so on of employees is also wide enough to affect contractual rights. To sum up, a proclamation under Article 360 of the Indian Constitution has at least three important consequences temporarily modifying:

1. The federal scheme of distribution of power;
2. Constitutional rights of individuals (particularly judges); and
3. Contractual rights.

Modification of the federal scheme. The first point touches not merely the exercise of the executive authority but also, as regards money bills, the legislative authority. These important consequences of a Proclamation of Financial Emergency did not go unnoticed in the Constituent Assembly. When, in mid-October 1949, Dr Ambedkar introduced into the Constituent Assembly the last of the emergency provisions—new Article 280A (now Article 360)—Pandit Kunzru disliked this provision. Dr Ambedkar contended that the proposed provision was similar to the National Recovery Act of 1935 (United States). But this did not satisfy Pandit Kunzru, who said that the National Recovery Act was a temporary measure. Kunzru pointed out that only three days earlier (13 October 1949) Jawaharlal Nehru had said that the Indian Constitution was federal and was based on the American Constitution. In Pandit Kunzru's view, the proposed Article 280A was not consistent with that statement of Nehru. Dr Ambedkar's explanation was that the provision was necessary in view of the present economic and financial situation in the country.

It needs to be pointed out there must be satisfaction on the part of the President of India that there is a threat to the financial stability or credit of India or any part thereof. The part may, of course, extend over more than one state. The proclamation will be issued, varied or revoked only on the bona fide. There does not appear to be any scope for legal valence to the issue of the proclamation. As regards the measures taken by government in pursuance of the proclamation, they must have some nexus with the threat to financial stability of credit. No doubt, the courts will make a presumption of the constitutionality of such action.

While the Constitution clearly recognized the needs for coordination among different levels of government in the matters of governance, and made provision for the creation of a forum for consultation among governments in the shape of interstate council (Article 263), the council was constituted as late as 1990, despite strong recommendations by high-powered commissions—the Administrative Reforms Commission and the Sarkaria Commission. The entire gamut of centre–state relations was considered in depth by the Sarkaria Commission, but its recommendations are yet to be fully acted upon.

The initiation of economic reforms in 1991 has reduced centre's role in controlling the economy, and recent changes in the political configuration in the country have broken the monopoly of the political party that had ruled at the centre and the states in the initial 40 years after Independence, and has replaced it by the coalition government at the centre. There has been the emergence of governments in several states run by regional parties, leading to the demand for greater regional autonomy to the states and vesting of constitutional status to local bodies, consequent upon the enactment of constitutional amendments. All these developments led to the demand for 'cooperative federalism' in the country, to guard against the emergence of monopoly at the centre. Cooperative federalism accords primacy to lower tiers of the government in providing public services, and contemplates the most decentralized form of governance. But a change from quasi-federalism to cooperative federalism needs lot of changes—political, legal and constitutional. A Constitution Review Commission has been set up recently by the Government of India to consider different aspects of changes demanded in the Constitution.

The above presentation shows that federation is not just a structure but a process and, therefore, it is more important to activate the forum for interaction than going in only for formal arrangements that divide the powers between the union and the states and the state and the local bodies. Federalism is poised for acquiring new dimensions, with world economy getting globalized and integrated and the paradigm of desirable arrangements of functions and finances at the subnational levels undergoing changes, old ideas of sovereignty are fast facing obsolescence, as nations agree on their own to abide by internationally accepted conventions and standards (Bagchi, 2000).

Relevant Constitutional Amendments

The Constitutional Amendment Act, 1992, by making a provision for the constitution of state FC, under Article 243(i) and 243(y) after the expiry of every five years, for recommending devolution of resources from the state government to local bodies, has altered the erstwhile fiscal arrangement between the state government and local bodies and has tried to rectify the imbalance. The Constitutional Amendment Act gives local bodies a constitutional status, assigns them a number of functions, ensures them stability, provides a suitable framework to function with greater freedom and also makes institutional arrangements for devolution of finances from the state government to local bodies.

It is for the first time that, unlike its predecessors, the 11FC was assigned certain ToR relating to local bodies and their finances. The inclusion of certain issues relating to local finances in the ToR of the Commission has added a new dimension to the character of fiscal federalism in India and also demonstrates the fact that the nation as a whole should feel interested in the financial health of local bodies and have a stake in the task of restructuring and strengthening local bodies as units of self-government.

The 80th and 88th constitutional amendments brought in major changes in the scheme of fiscal relations between the centre and the states. The 80th amendment, brought in June 2000, made all the central taxes and duties sharable with the states as per the recommendations of the 10FC. However, it excluded the cess and surcharges from sharing, even though the 10FC had not recommended so. The 88th Amendment, brought in January 2004, gave a formal place to the service tax in the Union List, which was all along a residuary taxation. The amendment also took the service tax outside the purview of the FC but empowered the Parliament to make laws for bringing about the sharability of this tax.

The 80th amendment substituted the entire wording of Article 269 and retained only two items under this Article, namely, taxes on interstate sales/purchases of goods and taxes on interstate consignment of goods. Despite this amendment, Parliament still has the power to levy these taxes as the Seventh Schedule remains unchanged by this amendment. However, the effect of the amendment is that the taxes that are not mentioned in Article 269 remain mandatorily sharable with the states[20] along with all other taxes, in terms of Article 270.

[20] In India, currently there are 28 state governments and 7 union territory governments. The finances of union territories are the direct responsibility of the central government. The 29 state governments are classified in two categories: special-category

Present

The Indian Constitution carried these provisions a step forward by providing for an FC to determine the distribution, between the union and the states, of the net proceeds of taxes and the GIA to be provided to the states which are in need of assistance. While the constitutional provisions relating to the functions of the FCs have remained unchanged, one notable change in the framework of federal fiscal arrangements was brought out by the 80th amendment which broadened the ambit of the sharable central taxes. The enlargement of the sharable pool to cover all central taxes, except those listed in Articles 268 and 269 and earmarked cesses and surcharges, has enabled states to share in the overall buoyancy of taxes. It has also provided greater stability to resource transfers as fluctuations in individual taxes are evened out. With the 73rd and 74th amendments to the Constitution, which have provided constitutional support to the process of decentralization, the FCs are also required to suggest measures to augment the resources for the panchayats and municipalities.

In the economic sphere, liberalization has necessitated greater fiscal decentralization. On the political front, factors such as the end of single-party rule, emergence of coalition government at the centre and increasing importance of regional parties in the political affairs of the country have forced greater decentralization. Finally, the amendment of the Constitution in 1992 to empower local government is yet another enabling factor in the evolution of a more decentralized federalism in India.

states and non-special-category states. There are 11 special category states and the rest are non-special-category states. The special-category states are given special central assistance in the form of 90:10 plan grants and loan. The same ratio for the non-special-category states is 30:70.

APPENDIX C: VERTICAL FISCAL IMBALANCE

The vertical fiscal balance is said to be ensured when the revenues and expenditures of each level of government are approximately equal. 'For many purposes, however, it is useful to think of vertical fiscal balance as being achieved when expenditures and revenues (including transfers) are balanced for the richest local government, measured in terms of its capacity to raise resources on its own' (Bird, 1993, p. 207). Among the countries that adopted the federal systems, it is a well-known feature that the VFI is mostly in favour of the federal government.

> Almost invariably, countries assign more expenditure functions to subnational governments than can be financed from the revenue sources allocated to those governments (if seldom fully under their control). The result of this mismatching of functions and finances – sometimes referred to as 'vertical imbalance' – is that subnational governments are generally dependent upon transfers from higher levels of government, and the more so the more significant the expenditures with which they are charged. (Bird, 1990, p. 278)

MERITS AND DEMERITS OF DECENTRALIZATION

Before discussing the measurement of VFI, it is useful to recapitulate the debate over the broad principles involved in determining the assignment of spending and taxing responsibilities to different tiers of government. It is widely accepted that some degree of fiscal devolution is desirable to allow local considerations to be taken into account in macroeconomic policy decisions. Further, there are theories about the optimal assignment of spending and taxing responsibilities to different tiers of government. There are advantages and disadvantages of decentralizing the various functions of government from higher levels to lower levels.

ARGUMENTS FOR VFI

Advocates of VFI make the following claims. First, the central government is best placed to determine 'national' interests as distinct from narrower state interests. For example, the central government should have resources to help reduce cyclical fluctuations in the macroeconomic activity. Second, the central government should be able to influence the allocation of resources in the economy by its spending and revenue decisions for meeting equity objectives through the taxation/welfare system. Its greater access to revenue allows it to pursue horizontal fiscal equalization, that is, to ensure that each state has the capacity to provide services at national average levels of efficiency. 'A centralised fiscal policy is tantamount to an insurance contract where the higher level government promises to even out income variations across regions that result from regionally asymmetrical shocks' (Spahn, 1997). Third, a centralized tax administration is more efficient than a decentralized one. Further, centralized administration reduces the scope for 'tax competition' whereby states match tax cuts with other states. Also, some claim that the alleged adverse effects of VFI are overstated. Although VFI has often been criticized, it has not been demonstrated from a national interest point of view that a pressing problem exists. The states do conduct substantial revenue-raising activity in their own right.

CRITICISMS OF VFI

Critics have argued that VFI reduces government accountability. The underlying argument is that governments should be accountable for both spending and raising revenue. This principle is undermined when one tier of government raises revenue but another tier spends it.

Essentially, the accountability argument is that if a government does not raise all the revenue that it spends, it will not be fully accountable to its taxpayers, and its spending decisions are likely to be inefficient. Accountability in this sense refers to the need to explain, justify, convince or demonstrate to the taxpayers that the revenue is indeed necessary and that the funds raised will be spent responsibly. The political cost of revenue rising consists of these obligations on the part of the governments, and generally varies not only between taxation and intergovernmental grants, but also between different types of taxes and grants. Thus, in comparison with taxation, intergovernmental grants are likely to create the impression of zero political costs for the recipient government, and thereby result in a loss of accountability and efficiency. If, however, grants are given for specific purposes and carry with them at least some obligations towards the government which gives them, accountability is comparatively enhanced. Thus, on the criterion of accountability, specific purpose grants should be ranked higher than general revenue grants, which in turn are superior to taxation.' (Grewal, 1975, p. 10)

A second criticism is that VFI forces the states to rely on narrowly based taxes for own-source revenue. A taxation principle is that the tax base—such as land or consumption—should be as broad as possible, that is, with minimal exemptions. The central government imposes the main broadly based taxes—for example, the central excise and income tax—leaving the states with only a few such taxes, namely sales tax, state excise, stamp duties, motor vehicles tax, entertainment tax and land taxes.

Third, it is argued that the central government's financial power diminishes the political power of the states. This argument holds that the states are best placed to determine priorities in the areas for which they are responsible. But the central government uses its financial power to override state priorities, for example, by requiring the states to spend more on a function than they would prefer. A related argument is that VFI is likely to distort the pattern of public spending away from state functions towards central government functions, and therefore from areas such as economic infrastructure and community services.

Fourth, it is argued that the negotiation of agreements between the central government and the states involves unnecessary policy duplication and waste of resources. Also, 'when centralised control is exercised through the vehicle of financial transfers instead of direct provision of services, the lines of responsibility for each level of government are blurred' (Grewal, 1975, p. 12).

A distinction can be made between 'desired' and 'excess' components of VFI. The arguments for and against described above obviously pertain to the desired or consciously built VFI in the federal system. It is the persistence of excess or undesirable VFI that is proving to be a difficult assignment. This could be attributable to several factors.[21]

1. The nature and extent of fiscal autonomy;
2. Impact of greater state autonomy on federal powers to achieve stability and growth objectives;
3. Clash of federal and state priorities (for example, housing, social welfare, infrastructure expenditures);
4. The absence of, or defects in, existing revenue-sharing arrangements;
5. Failure of the central government to contain inflation and its effect on state budgets;
6. Constitutional barriers on the use by the states of certain taxes (coupled, perhaps, with a refusal of the central government to collect taxes on behalf of the states);
7. Shortcomings in machinery for intergovernmental coordination;
8. Pursuit of centralist policies by some national governments; and
9. Political power conflicts.

MEASUREMENT OF VFI

The concept of VFI is premised on the notion that in the ideal situation each level of government should be able to raise from its own sources all the revenue required to finance its expenditure.[22]

---

[21] As Hunter (1977) puts it, 'The persistence of these large imbalances in some federations can, in part, be put down to sheer inertia, allied with a feeling that it is not really a problem anyway. But a full explanation is much more complex and would go to the very heart of intergovernmental relations' (p. 38).

[22] For example, in an attempt to institutionalise this requirement for fiscal balance, the Commonwealth Government enunciated in 1926 a 'basic principle of national finance' according to which 'every government shall have the responsibility of raising the revenue which it is expending' (Prest, 1974, p.188). But such a perfect balance

Complexities in the measurement of VFI arise because of the diverse degree of command exercised by the provincial governments over different components of transfers. In this note, we intend to review the different methods of measuring the VFI and use them to measure the VFI in India.

Federal transfers differ in terms of the control and command exercised by the federal and provincial governments, the liabilities and conditionalities involved, as also the structural effects on the economy. For example, the control and command exercised over tax revenue sharing is not the same as tax assignments. Similarly, the liabilities involved in lendings are not the same as grants. The specific-purpose grants differ from general grants in terms of conditionalities. The structural effects of tax power sharing are not the same as those of tax revenue sharing. Consequently, measurement of VFI differs basically on account of methods of inclusion and exclusion of different components of transfers in the formula.

Measures of VFI suggested in the literature are of three types: The first type of measures is based on actual or realized revenues, expenditures and transfers.

A variant of this type is to base the measurement of VFI not on actual or realized fiscal components but on the basis of 'permanent' or even 'normative' components.

The second type of measures aim at taking into account the structural factors such as the inherent productivity of the tax instruments assigned that have the potential to cause VFI. For example, in India income tax is assigned to the central government while sales tax is in the states' list. In the face of inflation, the productivity of income tax is more because of its progressive nature. Sales tax being not progressive

remains only a benchmark, and has not been achieved in Australia since Federation. Even in its heyday, the leading economists, including Giblin and Mills, regarded the principle neither so basic nor so universal as its advocates claimed (Prest, 1974, p. 189). At the same time, Giblin and Eggleston stressed, in the third report of the Grants Commission in 1936, the need to avoid excessive imbalance, observing that if a government raises less revenue than it needs, its services are likely to be starved, but equally a government becomes extravagant if it has more money than it needs (Prest, 1974).

may not be as productive. The tax power assignment to the centre and states has structural VFI built into it.

The third type of measures aim measuring the VFI that takes into account the welfare implications.

MEASURES BASED ON ACTUAL FISCAL COMPONENTS

Ratio of Transfers to Subnational Expenditures

One way of measuring the VFI is simply as ratio of central transfers to subnational expenditures. Alternatively, *ratio of own-source revenue of a government to its total outlays.*[23] Prest (1974, p. 189) suggested that a ratio of tax revenue to outlays which is short of equality but well in excess of 50 per cent would be desirable. This ratio slightly underestimates the (VFI) ratio, as the denominator includes transfer payments to other governments and to the public trading enterprises.

Hunter's Modifications

Recognizing this problem, analysts have developed more refined measures of VFI. Hunter (1974, 1977), for instance, proposed three such 'coefficients of vertical imbalance'. Essentially these measures took into account to varying degrees, net borrowing by SNGs, 'shared taxes', and the degree to which federal transfers were 'conditional'. His intent in constructing these measures was to define more precisely the extent to which the basic allocation of revenues and expenditures conforms to the principle enunciated by Mathews (1980, p. 10) that 'governments at each level...'. In other words, what Hunter was attempting to do was to distinguish between revenue sources that were under federal control and those that were under state control. He did so by assuming in one measure that unconditional transfers did not reduce state autonomy, in another that they did, and in a third that not only

---

[23] Committee of Inquiry into Revenue Raising in Victoria (1983).

such transfers (and borrowing) compromised state autonomy but so also did shared taxes to some extent.[24]

Difference between Own-Source Revenue and Own-Purpose Expenditure Commitments

Hunter's idea that government at each level should command financial resources necessary for them to carry out their expenditure responsibilities can also be simply defined[25] as difference between own-source revenue and own-purpose expenditure commitments of a level of government.

The above conventional ratios used for measuring the degree of fiscal imbalance, although simple to calculate, often divert attention from the qualitative aspects of the imbalance.[26] These measures have the virtue of being easy to calculate. But they do not take into account the extent to which transfers, own revenues of SNGs and indeed even the subnational expenditures reflect federal or subnational policy decisions. Conceptually, focusing on actual deficits and surpluses at different levels of government is obviously a very limited approach to the broad problem of VFI. In order to look beyond the simplistic ratios, where indeed the real nature of the problem of fiscal imbalance may be revealed, it is important to consider additional measures that capture the relevant features of the structure of state revenue systems. Recognizing this certain alternative measures are suggested.

[24] Hunter's judgments as to how to assess such 'autonomy' could of course be questioned and soon were (for example, Thimmaiah [1976]. Nonetheless, despite its inherent subjectivity, variants of this approach are still used in the literature (Rezk, 1998).

[25] The Working Party of Commonwealth-state Treasury officers in 1990–1991 also defined VFI in the same way.

[26] 'The problems caused by vertical fiscal imbalance cannot always be solved through revenue sharing. Conventional ratios often used for measuring the degree of fiscal imbalance divert attention from the qualitative aspects of the imbalance. Complementary measures that help focus on the tax structure issues are also needed' (Grewal, 1975, p. 5).

Bird's Measures

Type 1: Unrestricted budget balances for the central, local, regional and SNGs (sum of regional and local governments):

$$SVI_j^I = [(\text{Revenue} + \text{Grants})_j - (\text{Expenditure} + \text{Lending})_j]$$
$$/[\text{Expenditure} + \text{Lending}]_j,$$

where j is the consolidated central government, regional government, local government, or SNGs.

Type 2: Budget balances, excluding net intergovernmental transfers between the government of interest and other levels of government:

$$SVI_j^{II} = [(\text{Revenue} + \text{Grants})_j - (\text{Net Intergovernmental Grants})_j$$
$$- (\text{Expenditure} + \text{Lending})_j]/[\text{Expenditure} + \text{Lending}]_j^{NT}$$

where the superscript abbreviation NT indicates that figures are net of intergovernmental transfers.

Type 3: Budget balances, excluding intergovernmental transfers and intergovernmental net borrowing (the latter term, denoted in the formula as IGNB, is a negative of the net lending to other levels of government account as it is used in the IMF Government Finance Statistics Yearbook):

$$SVI_j^{III} = [(\text{Revenue} + \text{Grants})_j - (\text{Net Intergovernmental Grants})$$
$$- (\text{IGNB})_j (\text{Expenditure} + \text{Lending})_j]$$
$$/[(\text{Expenditure} + \text{Lending}_j^{NT} + (\text{IGNB})_j.$$

In addition, for each country we have calculated three alternative coefficients of vertical imbalance reflecting the shares of subnational expenditures that are covered with intergovernmental transfers (CVI 1) or intergovernmental borrowing (CVI 2), and not covered with own revenues (CVI 3).

CVI 1: Intergovernmental transfer share in SNG expenditure:

$$CVI_1 = (\text{Net Intergovernmental Grants})_{SNG}$$
$$/(\text{Expenditure} + \text{Lending})_{SNG}^{NT}.$$

In addition, two subcategory coefficients are calculated separately to reflect individual shares of net current and capital intergovernmental transfers that partially cover the total SNG expenditure:

$$CVI_1^{cur} = (Net\ Intergovernmental\ Grants)_{SNG}$$
$$/(Expenditure + Lending)_{SNG}^{NT}$$
$$CVI_1^{cur} = (Net\ Intergovernmental\ Grants)_{SNG}$$
$$/(Expenditure + Lending)_{SNG}^{NT}.$$

CVI 2: Intergovernmental transfer and intergovernmental net borrowing share in the SNG expenditure

$$CVI_2 = (Net\ Intergovernmental\ Grants)_{SNG} + (IGNB)_{SNG}$$
$$/(Expenditure + Lending)_{SNG}^{NT}.$$

CVI 3: Share of SNG expenditure that is not covered by the SNGs' own revenues:

$$CVI_3 = 1 - [(Revenue + Grants)_{SNG} - (Net\ Intergovernmental$$
$$Grants)_{SNG} - (IGNB)_{SNG}]/[(Expenditure + Lending)_{SNG}^{NT}.$$

It is important to recognize explicitly the defects of this approach. They are both conceptual and empirical. Conceptually, focusing on actual deficits and surpluses at different levels of government is obviously a very limited approach to the broad problem of VFI; however, the data are manipulated. Hettich and Winer (1983), for instance, argued years ago that ideally one needs a more logically consistent approach related to such fundamental concerns as the maximization of social welfare.

STRUCTURAL MEASURES OF VFI

Less ambitiously, an obvious refinement would be to focus not on actual but on 'structural' budget balances—that is, the balances inherent in current expenditure and tax policies at each level of government. A recent Canadian study by Matier, Wu and Jackson (2001) for example first projects expenditures and revenues at each level of government and various demographic and economic assumptions and then considers the extent to which the fiscal positions of each level are sustainable in the framework of an intertemporal budget constraint. Under this approach, VFI exists if one level has 'room' to reduce taxes or increase (programme) spending while satisfying its intertemporal constraint and another level would have to increase taxes or reduce spending to do so. Although more formal, the results of this approach seem very sensitive to both model specification and empirical assumptions and are hence are unlikely to be accepted by all.

Measures Based on Social Welfare

Bird and Tarasov (2002) discuss the concepts of vertical fiscal imbalance and HFI and use several statistics to measure these concepts for eight industrially developed federations: Australia, Austria, Belgium, Canada, Germany, Spain, Switzerland and the United States. Although the periods covered and the detail provided vary from country to country due to limitations in data availability, the overall coverage seems more complete and comparable than in previous studies. Bird and Taraso also outline briefly the types of intergovernmental fiscal transfers used to deal with fiscal imbalances in the eight countries and under consideration. Although this account is necessarily highly condensed, given the complexity of transfer systems in most countries, the frequency with which changes are made, and the difficulty of obtaining complete information, it is nonetheless broadly accurate.

If imbalance is the problem, then balance would seem to be the solution. It is thus not surprising that the concept of VFI—the 'fiscal gap' as it has been called (Boadway & Hobson, 1993) is often discussed as though in an ideal federation the own-source revenues of each level of government should be sufficient to finance the expenditure for which it is responsible without recourse to intergovernmental fiscal transfers. VFI, thus understood, seems to require that each level of government should have separate and independent revenue sources sufficient to finance the expenditure assigned to that level no more and no less. In other words, given the assignment of expenditures, revenues should, it is argued, be assigned so that there is no 'imbalance' between revenues and expenditures at a level of government.

To make this last point clearer, it is important to understand that the two concepts of fiscal balance mentioned above—VFI and HFI—cannot be cleanly separated. One way to think of VFI, for example, is that it might be considered eliminated—that is, VFI is achieved—when expenditures and revenues (excluding transfers) are balanced for the richest local government measured in terms of its capacity to raise resources on its own (Bird 1993, 207–227). Even if this is achieved, fiscal gaps or VFI will, of course, still remain for all poorer local governments. Generally, however, it is common to discuss such gaps instead in terms of HFI, that is, as a problem of achieving horizontal fiscal balance within the regional or local government sector rather than vertical balance between levels of government. In any case, however it is defined, whether and to what extent HFI is considered a problem is, of course, a highly political issue in most federal countries, as discussed below.

Before turning to how VFI may be measured, consider the ways in which it might be eliminated, assumed vertical balance is viewed as an appropriate or desirable policy goal. First, the assignment of expenditures can be taken as fixed and more revenue-raising powers devolved to subnational jurisdictions. Alternatively, revenue powers may be taken as fixed and some expenditure powers reassigned to the federal level. In Canada for example, this is how the gradually expanding social security system (unemployment insurance and old age pensions) was initially dealt with in the middle of the last century, through constitutional amendments to federalize these expenditure functions.

VFI may in principle be closed also simply by reducing subnational expenditures or raising subnational revenues from existing sources, just as federal governments may rectify any inverse imbalance or deficit (revenues exceeding expenditures) at the central level by increasing their expenditures or reducing their taxes. Like all governments, federal governments are seldom reluctant to expand their own expenditures or less commonly to lower their taxes. Often, federal governments also argue that SNGs can both spend more efficiently and increase their 'fiscal effort'. No doubt there is at least as much room for improvement in these respects at the subnational level in most countries as at the federal level.

Social Welfare Measure of VFI

Hettich and Winer (1983) for instance argued that ideally one needs a more logically consistent approach related to such fundamental concerns as the maximization of social welfare.

VFI Based on Structural Budget Balances

Less ambitiously, an obvious refinement would be to focus not on actual but on 'structural' budget balances—that is, the balances inherent in current expenditure and tax policies at each level of government. Recently, Matier, Wu and Jackson (2001), for example, first project expenditures and revenues at each level of government and under various demographic and economic assumptions and then consider the extent to which the fiscal positions of each level are sustainable in the framework of an intertemporal budget constraint. Under this approach, VFI exists if one level has 'room' to reduce taxes or increase (programme) spending while satisfying its intertemporal constraint and another level would have to increase taxes or reduce spending to do so. Although more formal, the results of this approach seem very sensitive to both model specification and empirical assumptions and hence are unlikely to be accepted by all.

In any event, we cannot undertake such an ambitious dynamic analysis, so we are constrained to work only with actual past data. Even then, we have to be aware of important differences in the real significance of numbers purporting to measure.

More than the tax revenue sharing, tax power sharing could also cause VFI. It depends upon the degree of discretionary change to tax rates or tax bases required for generating additional revenue. This point can be illustrated by contrasting two governments, one of which (central government) raises its revenue from progressive income taxation and the other (say, a state government) from sales tax. In a period of high inflation accompanied by correspondingly high increases in money incomes, but little growth in output, the central government would experience high and automatic growth in its tax revenue without having to increase the rate of tax or broaden the tax base while the state's revenue would remain static.

MEASUREMENT OF VFI IN INDIA

The measure of VFI should be such that it preserves the basic idea that 'government at each level can command the financial resources necessary for them to carry out their expenditure responsibilities'. Given the constitutional division of revenue and expenditure responsibilities, a measure of VFI can be defined as the positive difference between the central- and state-level fiscal balances as follows:

$$\text{VFI} = (R_c - E_c) - (R_s - E_s) \geq 0,$$

where R_c and R_s denote revenues of the centre and states before devolution and transfers, and E_c and E_s are respective total expenditures.

As Bird (2002) puts it, if *imbalance* is the problem *balance* is the solution. Therefore, the transfer needed from the centre to states should be such that VFI = 0. Let T be such transfers so that

$$(R_c - E_c) - T = (R_s - E_s) + T$$

and

$$T = [(R_c - E_c) - (R_s - E_s)]/2.$$

This measure needs to be refined by distinguishing between revenue sources and expenditure commitments that were under federal control and those that were under state control. For example, some revenue sources such as central sales tax and stamp duties are partly under the control of the central government in that the powers to change the rate structure lies with it, although the revenues are collected and retained by the states. Similarly, certain expenditures are conditioned by central government through either plan process or other national requirements. To that extent, the states are not entirely free to manipulate their pre-transfer fiscal gaps. In other words, a part of the VFI is inherent in the fiscal structure.

India has a high degree of VFI. The central government's own-source revenue—about 66 per cent of total central government and state revenue—exceeds its own-purpose outlays of around 45 per cent of central government and state spending combined.

VFI is attributable to a number of interrelated factors. First, the central government's financial power has increased through time at the states' expense. A major factor was the central government's taking control of income tax. Second, the states are constitutionally responsible for major areas of spending such as health and education.

APPENDIX D: MEASUREMENT OF HFI—AN ILLUSTRATION OF THE NMBF METHOD

As an illustration, consider a simple log-linear revenue and expenditure functions of states.

$$R = Y^\beta e^{(\alpha+u)},$$
$$E = P^\psi Y^\xi e^{(\gamma+v)}.$$

The main capacity variable considered for revenue determination is the GSDP at current prices. The need factors are represented by the population size. State-specific factors representing revenue efficiency, cost disability and so on are assumed to vary across the states but relatively invariant over time within a state.

The fiscal gap can be expressed as either ratio R/E or difference $R-E$. The ratio form is convenient if one wishes to estimate the combined fiscal gap function. It would be easier with the ratio.

$$G = R/E = P^\psi Y^{(\beta-\xi)} e^{(Z-u-v)},$$

where $Z = \alpha - \gamma$.

Alternatively, if the fiscal gap needs to be expressed in the difference form, it is convenient to estimate the revenue and expenditure functions separately due to their non-linear specification. Estimation of two functions separately also reduces the problem of multicollinearity. Accordingly, we prefer separate estimation. We estimated the model using panel data for 14 major states and ten years 1990–1991 to 2000–2001.

THE FE VARIANT

Perhaps, it would be prudent to prescribe certain behavioural norms of efficiency in both revenue raising and spending by imposing uniform values for the parameters involved. One way to impose such norms would be to set the parametric values at some average or consensus levels and derive the corresponding fiscal gap. Clearly, it would mean that the actual fiscal gap of a state exceeding the normative level will not be considered for computing its share of transfers. On the other hand, if the actual fiscal gap of state falls below the normative level, the state will be rewarded by considering its normative level.

The most acceptable set of values for the behavioural parameters involved in the revenue and expenditure functions would be the averages or means across the states. In the representative tax system also, it is the average or mean effective tax rate that is used as a norm for tax effort. However, it is not easy to derive the average value set for the multiple parameters involved because of stochastic factors.

Although the normative approach calls for assessing the fiscal efficiency of states on common scale, certain state-specific disability factors either on the revenue raising or in expenditure efficiency need to be taken cognizance while imposing the norms. Considering these aspects, we specify the two component functions with common response parameters for the main determinants but allow the constant term to capture the state-specific factors using the FE estimation method. The results are as shown in Table D1. As can be seen, in the revenue function the norm is derived for the buoyancy coefficient as 0.937 while the constant term or 'fixed effects' are allowed to be state specific. Similarly, the response coefficients of population and GSDP are restricted to be the same for all states while the constant term is left to vary across the states.

Table D1 *FE Results of the Own Revenue and Total Expenditure Functions for Each State*

State	Revenue Function: $\log R = \alpha + \beta \log Y$		Expenditure Function: $\log E = \gamma + \psi \log P + \xi \log Y$		
	α	β	γ	ψ	ξ
Andhra Pradesh	−1.6496	0.9372	−2.7770	3.7899	0.4156
Bihar	−1.7796		−3.7928		
Gujarat	−1.5717		−1.0581		
Haryana	−1.6396		1.8154		
Karnataka	−1.5054		−1.4027		
Kerala	−1.6719		0.1152		
Madhya Pradesh	−1.6291		−3.3117		
Maharashtra	−1.5991		−2.9020		
Orissa	−2.0675		−0.3275		
Punjab	−1.5929		1.3814		
Rajasthan	−1.7882		−1.4814		
Tamil Nadu	−1.5972		−1.9889		
Uttar Pradesh	−1.9097		−5.3253		
West Bengal	−2.1730		−3.1088		

THE ADJUSTMENT FOR USING THE 1971 POPULATION

While estimating the model, an important determinant of the fiscal gap is the population. It basically represents the expenditure needs of a state. However, it has been mandatory for the FCs to use the 1971 population figures, instead of the current period figures.[27] The idea is to keep the pattern of population size across the states to be the same as in 1971. Since the expenditure function is specified to be

[27] 'In making its recommendations on the various matters aforesaid, the Commission shall adopt the population figures of 1971 in all cases where population is regarded as a factor for determination of devolution of taxes and duties and grants-in-aid' (ToR of the FC).

sensitive to the size of the population, we escalated the 1971 population of each state uniformly using the escalation factor, namely, the all-India population growth. Accordingly, in deriving the fiscal gaps and transfer shares, we could preserve the 1971 size distribution of population across the states (more about the use of population later).

DERIVATION OF THE TRANSFER SHARES

The fiscal gap estimated with the FE method (common behavioural patterns with respect to the main determinants but with state-specific behaviour captured by the constant terms) and the resultant shares

Table D2 *Estimated Fiscal Transfer Shares by the NMBF Method*

State	Normative Shares Derived Using the Estimates of Fiscal Gap by the FE Method	Transfer Shares Recommended by the 11FC	Transfer Shares for the 12FC with 11FC Formulae
Andhra Pradesh	7.8	7.7	7.9
Bihar	7.3	14.6	14.9
Gujarat	5.4	2.8	3.0
Haryana	1.7	0.9	0.8
Karnataka	4.4	4.9	4.4
Kerala	4.9	3.1	2.4
Madhya Pradesh	9.3	8.8	7.7
Maharashtra	5.3	4.6	4.0
Orissa	4.8	5.1	5.8
Punjab	4.9	1.1	0.9
Rajasthan	6.3	5.5	6.0
Tamil Nadu	6.5	5.4	4.6
Uttar Pradesh	16.1	19.8	22.2
West Bengal	7.9	8.1	7.8

Note: The sum of the shares of the 14 major states works out to be 92.5 per cent of the total. Accordingly, the FE shares are adjusted to sum to the same level to make them comparable.

are shown in Table D2 and Figure 3.1. A comparison of the transfer shares with the FE method of explaining the fiscal gap shows that the share patterns could be notably different from those obtained by the formula of the 11FC gives the estimated fiscal transfer shares with FE method as compared to those recommended by the 11FC and those derived using the 11FC method for the 12FC period.

ADVANTAGES OF THE MODEL

The model has several advantages over the conventional intuitive formula-based determination of the horizontal shares. The main advantage is that the transfer shares are determined on the basis of rational fiscal behavioural framework keeping in view the basic motivations of the federating units for coming together.

Second, the criteria and the weights for horizontal distribution of transfers in this model are derived from factors that are responsible for variations in the basic NMBF and not imposed from outside, as has been the case so far. The NMBF (proxied by the own revenue–expenditure gap) is subdivided into three components: (a) component that varies with factors common to all the states, (b) component that varies with state-specific factors and (c) component that varies with random factors. After removing the effect of random factors, the remaining two components of fiscal gap are made comparable by restricting the parameters of common factors to be uniform for all the states. The common factors are akin to the criteria, and their estimated uniform parameters are similar to the weights. In this way, whatever criteria emerge from the model are related to their respective NMBF, and the weights are in accordance with the degree of their relevance to the NMBF.

Third, while determining the shares, state-specific factors such as cost disabilities due to geographic and climatic conditions that influence the fiscal behaviour are fully taken into account in the form of state-specific 'fixed effects'. These factors are not easy to identify and not amenable for prescribing as quantifiable criteria. The model does away with the need to identify the state-specific factors, although their effect is fully taken into account.

Fourth, although it was well recognized in the past that the three considerations—needs, cost disability and fiscal efficiency—should form the basis in designing a suitable scheme of fiscal transfers, an objective way of striking a balance between them eluded the FCs so far. As a result, past FCs are led to devise exotic criteria such as the income–distance criteria, the inverse income criteria, the fiscal performance criteria, the tax effort criteria, poverty criteria and so on. Their form and their relevance are not easy to digest. In contrast, our model and estimation procedures automatically allow striking an optimal balance between the equity and efficiency objectives of the transfers.

POSSIBLE FURTHER IMPROVEMENTS

Within the framework, several alternative model specifications are possible. For example, the variables to be used as the determinants of the fiscal gap are largely based on intuitive reasoning and therefore are subject to change. However, once a few major factors are specified, the inclusion of other factors and their specific transformations depend not only on their association with the dependent variable but also on their covariance with the major factors. For example, if one is intuitively sure of the major role of population as a determinant of the fiscal need, the other factors such as income and poverty will qualify for inclusion only if they represent the other dimensions of influence. Other possible variants of the model can be specification in linear or non-linear form, inclusion of the state-specific factors as fixed or random, inclusion or non-inclusion of the time-trend variable and in alternative ways and so on. Some of these choices can be resolved on the basis of statistical tests involving extensive econometric work.

APPENDIX E: CRITERIA USED FOR HORIZONTAL TAX SHARING IN INDIA BY SUCCESSIVE FINANCE COMMISSIONS

FIRST FINANCE COMMISSION

The share of union excise collection was fixed at 40 per cent, and the sharable pool included excise revenues from tobacco, matches and vegetable oil only. The population criterion was based on the 1951 census (Government of India, 1952).

SECOND FINANCE COMMISSION

The vertical share of union excise duties was lowered to 25 per cent, but the sharable pool was expanded to include excise collection on tobacco, matches vegetable oil, sugar, tea, coffee, paper and vegetable non-essential oils. The population criterion was based on the 1951 census. A 10 per cent weight for horizontal distribution was unspecified, although the report mentioned that some adjustment factor was employed to benefit states, which were relatively less populated.

THIRD FINANCE COMMISSION

The vertical share of union excise duties was further reduced to 20 per cent but the sharable pool was expanded to include by and large all items on which union excises were being levied. The criteria for horizontal distribution were not specified but the report indicated that considerations relating to population, relative financial weakness of states, the disparity in the levels of development reached, the percentage of schedule castes and tribes and backward classes in their population were deliberated upon. The population criterion was based on the 1951 census.

FOURTH FINANCE COMMISSION

The 20 per cent weight assigned to economic backwardness included considerations on

1. Per capita gross value of agricultural production;
2. Per capita value added by manufacture;
3. Percentage of workers (as defined by census) to the total population;
4. Percentage of enrolment in classes I to V to the population in the age group 6–11;
5. Population per hospital bed;
6. Percentage of rural population to total population; and
7. Percentage of population of scheduled castes and scheduled tribes to total population.

The exact use of these considerations was not specified. The population criterion was based on the 1961 census.

FIFTH FINANCE COMMISSION

The 5FC was the first to use the distance criterion under which the beneficiary states were restricted to the ones below the all states' average of per capita income. All states' average was taken as the representative highest income. The backwardness criterion was employed using the integrated index of backwardness constructed on the following parameters:

1. Scheduled tribes population;
2. Number of factory workers per lakh population;
3. Net irrigated area per cultivator;
4. Length of railways and surfaced; roads per 100 square kilometres;
5. Shortfall in number of school-going children to those of school-going age; and
6. Number of hospital beds.

Items 2–4 and 6 were used as inverse. The population criterion was based on the 1961 census.

SIXTH FINANCE COMMISSION

The 6FC used the distance criterion in the presently familiar but unadjusted version. This resulted in the highest per capita income state not getting any share of the 25 per cent proceeds of union excise collection. The population criterion was based on the 1971 census, which since then has remained frozen for all the successive commissions.

SEVENTH FINANCE COMMISSION

The poverty criterion was constructed by taking the share of people below the poverty line of each state in the aggregate of all poor people. The revenue equalization criterion was constructed by measuring the distance of revenue potential of each state from the highest potential estimated among all states. The distance was multiplied by the respective population of the state and the share of this product obtained from the aggregate of all such products. The revenue potential was estimated by obtaining the average of states' own tax and non-tax revenue ratio to SDP and applying this average on the SDP of each state. The average ratio was determined by a cross-sectional regression exercise.

EIGHTH FINANCE COMMISSION

Out of the 45 per cent of union excise duties fixed as vertical share, 5 per cent was kept aside for distribution on the basis of post-devolution assessed non-plan revenue deficit of states.

NINTH FINANCE COMMISSION

The 9FC submitted its report in two parts: first, for the period 1989–1990, and second for the period 1990–1995. It also kept aside a certain proportion of union excise duties for devolution on the basis of deficit criterion.

TENTH FINANCE COMMISSION

The 10FC had recommended two schemes of horizontal distribution. The first was based on the conventional sharing of income tax and union excise duties and the second on the sharable pool, which included all union taxes as detailed in the 80th amendment to the Constitution.

ELEVENTH FINANCE COMMISSION

The 11FC had recommended sharing of all taxes collected by the centre except service tax and expenditure tax, which are not levied in Jammu and Kashmir.

BIBLIOGRAPHY

Alm, J., & Jorge Martinez, V. (2015, Winter). Re-designing equalization transfers: An application to South Africa's provincial equitable share. *The Journal of Developing Areas, 49*(1), 1–22.

Ambedkar, B. R. (1925). *The evolution of provincial finances in India.* New York: AMS Press.

Bagchi, A. (2001, 8 December). Fifty years of federalism in India: An appraisal. *Kale Memorial Lecture.* Pune: Gokhale Institute of Politics & Economics.

Bennett, S., & Richard, W. (2007). Specific purpose payments and the Australian federal system, Politics and Public Administration. Research Paper no. 17, Government of Australia, Canberra.

Beri, S. G., & G, J. (1937). *Indian economics.* Oxford University Press.

Bessard, P. (2013). Switzerland's reformed fiscal equalization system: Still substantial room for improvement. In J. Clemens & N. Veldhuis (eds), *Federalism and fiscal transfers* (pp. 43–54). Toronto: Fraser Institute.

Bird, R. A. (1990). Intergovernmental finance and local taxation in developing countries: Some basic considerations for reformers. *Public Administration and Development, 10,* 277–288.

Bird, R. M. (1993). Threading the fiscal labyrinth: Some issues in fiscal decentralization. *National Tax Journal, 46,* 207–227.

Bird, R. M., & Smart, M. (2002). Intergovernmental fiscal transfers: International lessons for developing countries. *World Development, 30*(6), 899–912.

Bird, R., & Tarasov, A. (2002). Closing the gap: Fiscal imbalances and intergovernmental transfers in developed federations. *International Studies Program, Working Paper 02 02.*

Boadway, R., & Shah, A. (2007). Overview. In R. Boadway & A. Shah (eds), *Inter-governmental Transfers: Principles and Practices.* Washington, DC: The World Bank.

Boothe, P. (2003). Taxing, spending, and sharing in federations: Evidence from Australia and Canada. In P. Boothe (ed.), *Fiscal relations in four countries: Four essays.* Ottawa: Forum of Federations.

Breton, A. (1965, May). A theory of government grants. *The Canadian Journal of Economics and Political Science, 31,* 175–187.

Dafflon, B., & Tóth, K. (2005). Fiscal federalism in Switzerland: Relevant issues for transition economies in Central and Eastern Europe. *World Bank Policy Research Working Paper 3655.*

Dogra, A. (2018, June 10). *An in-depth look at the advantages and disadvantages of federalism.* Retrieved 20 December 2012, from https://opinionfront.com/advantages-disadvantages-of-federalism

Eleventh Finance Commission. (2000). *Report of the Eleventh Finance Commission.* New Delhi: Government of India.

Form of Federations. (2019, 10 June). *Form of federations-countries.* Retrieved from http://www.forumfed.org/countries/

Government of Canada. (2017, 14 November). *Department of Finance.* Retrieved from https://www.fin.gc.ca/fedprov/tff-eng.asp

Government of India. (1952). *Report of the First Finance Commission of India.* New Delhi: Government of India.

———. (1970). *Report of the Fifth Finance Commission.* New Delhi: Government of India.

———. (1982, 30 September). D G Letter No. 23011128/82/PLY. Ministry of Health and Family Welfare.

———. (1984). Report of the Eighth Finance Commission. New Delhi: Government of India.

———. (1988). *Report of the Eigth Finance Commission.* New Delhi: Government of India.

———. (1990). *Report of the Fifth Finance Commission.* New Delhi: Government of India.

———. (1990). Report of the Ninth Finance Commission, second report.

———. (1990). *Report of the Seventh Finance Commission.*

———. (1995). *Report of the Tenth Finance Commission.*

———. (2009). *Report of the Thirteenth Finance Commission: Volume I.* New Delhi: Government of India. Retrieved from http://fincomindia.nic.in/writereaddata/html_en_files/tfc/13fcreng.pdf

———. (2015). *Constitution of India.* New Delhi: Ministry of Law and Justice, Government of India. Retrieved from www.constitution.org/cons/india/const.html

———. (2015). *Report of the Fourteenth Finance Commission.*

Government of Nepal. (2015). *Nepal Constitution_full English 2015.* Kathmandu: Government of Nepal.

———. (2017). *Inter-Governmental Fiscal Transfers Act.* Kathmandu: Government of Nepal.

Gramlich, E. (1987). Subnational fiscal policy. *Perspective on Local Public Finance and Policy, 3,* 3–27.

Grewal, B. S. (1975). *Centre-state financial relations in India.* Punjab University Press.

Guhan, S. (1995, 22 April). Report of the Tenth Finance Commission. *Economic and Political Weekly*, p. 877.

Hemming, R., & Mates, N. a. (1997). *Fiscal federalism: Theory and practice*. Washington, DC: International Monetary Fund.

Koutsogeorgopoulou, V., & Tuske, A. (March 2015). Federal-state relations in Australia. *OECD Working Papers, ECO/WKP(2015)16*.

Marchildon, G., & and Haizhen, M. (2014). A needs-based allocation formula for Canada health transfer. *Canadian Public Policy, 40*(3), 209–223.

Matier, C., Wu, L., & Jackson, H. (2001). Analysing vertical fiscal imbalance in a framework of fiscal sustainability. *Department of Finance Working Paper 2001–23*.

Mieszkowski, P., & Musgrave, R. A. (1998). Federalism, grants and fiscal equalization. *Rice University Working Papers 1*.

Oates, W. (1999). An essay on fiscal federalism. *Journal of economic Literature, 37*(3), 1120–1149.

Oates, W. E. (1972). *Fiscal federalism*. New York: Harcourt, Brace and Jovanovich.

———. (1977). An economist's perspective of fiscal federalism. In W. E. Oates (ed.), *Political economy of fiscal federalism* (pp. 3–20). Lexington Books.

———. (1999, September). An essay in fiscal federalism. *Journal of Economic Literature, 37*, 1120–1149.

OECD. (2018). *OECD public governance reviews: Paraguay: Pursuing national development through integrated public governance*. Retrieved in 2018, from https://www.oecd-ilibrary.org/sites/9789264301856-7-en/index.html?itemId=/content/component/9789264301856-7-en&mimeType=text/html

Policy Research and Development Nepal. (2009). *A Study on the Design of a Formula Based Grants System for VDCs and update grant system for DDCs in Nepal*. Kathmandu: Local Bodies Fiscal Commission, Government of Nepal.

Prest, A. (1974). *Intergovernmental Financial Relations in United Kingdom*. Canberra: Centre for Research on Federal Financial Relations research monograph no. 23.

Rao, M. G. (2012). *Changing contours in federal fiscal arrangements in India*. New Delhi: National Institute of Public Finance & Policy.

Rao, M. G., & Sen, T. (1995). *Fiscal federalism in India: Theory and practice*. New Delhi: National Institute of Public Finance & Policy.

Rao, M. G., & Singh, N. (2008). The assignment of taxes and expenditures in India. *Stanford University, King Centre on Global Development, Working Paper No. 30a*.

Rao, M., & Chelliah, R. (1991). *Survey of research on fiscal federalism*. New Delhi: National Institute of Public Finance and Policy.

Ravallion, M. (1999). Monitoring targeting performance when decentralized allocations to the poor areunobserved. *Policy Research Working Paper 2080*. Washington DC: World Bank, Development Research Group.

Sarkar, J. (1969, 9 August). A permanent finance commission? *Economic & Political Weekly*, pp. 1311–1315.

Sarma, J. (1997, 12 July). Federal fiscal relations in India: Issue of horizontal transfers. *Economic & Political Weekly*.

Sarma, J. V. (1997). Federal fiscal relations in India: The issue of horizontal transfers. *Economic & Political Weekly*, pp. 1719–1723.

Sarma, J., & Bhaskar, V. (2012). Indian Finance Commission: Need for revamping and restructuring. *National Seminar on Centre-State Relations in Indian fiscal context at CESS*. Hyderabad: Centre for Economic and Social Studies.

Searle, B. (January 2001). *Federal fiscal relations in Australia*. Torino, Italy: International Centre for Economic Research.

Shah, A. (1997). Fiscal federalism and macroeconomic governance: For better or for worse? *Decentralization, and Macroeconomic Governance in Brazil 16–17 June*. Brasilia: Government of Brazil.

———. (2003). *Inter-governmental fiscal arrangements - Lessons from international experience*. World Bank.

———. (2004). Lessons from International Practices of inter-governmenta fiscal transfers. *Fiscal management for better governance: Lessons from each other*. Chongqing, China: Joint Program of the Ministry of Finance, China, the Canadian Agency for International Development and the World Bank Institute.

———. (2006, October). Practitioner's guide to intergovernmental fiscal transfers. *World Bank Policy Research Working Paper 4039*.

———. (2014, 27 March). *Intergovernmental fiscal relations in Australia*. Retrieved from https://www.researchgate.net/publication/251826817

Singh, N. (2015). NITI Aayog and Indian Fiscal Federalism. *Yojana, 59*, 52–54.

Singh, N., & Srinivasan, T. (2013). Federalism and economic development in India: An Assessment. In N. Hope, A. Kochar, R. Noll, & T. Srinivasan (eds), *Economic reform in India: Challenges, prospects and lessons*. New York: Cambridge University Press.

South Africa Local Government Association. (2012, May). Analysis of the current local government equitable share formula. *Local Government Equitable Share Formula Review. Discussion Paper 2*.

Spahn, P. B. (1997). Decentralized government and macroeconomic control. *Infrastructure notes, World Bank Working Paper 38329*.

Srivastava, D. K. (2017). *Key features of India's fiscal transfer system*. New Delhi: Earnest & Young (India).

Tanzi, V. (2000). *On fiscal federalism: Issues to worry about*. Retrieved from https://www.imf.org/external/pubs/ft/seminar/2000/fiscal/tanzi.pdf

Thirteenth Finance Commission. (2009). *Report of the Thirteenth Finance Commission*. New Delhi: Government of India.

Tocqueville, A. D. (1838). *Democracy in America*. New York: Vintage Books Random House.

Twelfth Finance Commission. (2005). *Report of the Twelfth Finance Commission*. New Delhi: Government of India.

Viswanathan, R. (2007). *Fiscal federalism and regional equity*. Retrieved from http://www.forumfed.org/libdocs/IntConfFed07/Volume_2/IntConfFed07-Vol2-Viswanathan.pdf

Vithal, B. P., & Sarma, J. V. (2002, 24 August). Twelfth Finance Commission: Framing its terms of reference. *Economic and Political Weekly*.

Vithal, B. P., & Sastry, M. L. (2001). *Fiscal federalism in India*. New Delhi: Oxford University Press.

Watts, R. L. (1999). *Comparing federal systems*. Toronto: Queen's University.

Wolman, H. (1990). Decentralization: What it is and why we should care, in Bennett (ed.), *Decentralization, local government and markets* (pp. 29–42). Oxford: Clarendon Press.

Wurzel, E. (1999). Towards more efficient government: Reforming federal fiscal relations in Germany. *OECD Economics Department Working Papers No. 209*.

ABOUT THE AUTHOR

J. V. M. Sarma, former Professor at the School of Economics, University of Hyderabad, has been involved in public finance, statistical and econometric methods, tax policy research and teaching for more than three decades. He served as Economic Advisor to the Twelfth Finance Commission, Government of India. He has also been associated with several studies for national-, international- and state-level governments.

Before joining the University of Hyderabad, he was Senior Fellow at the National Institute of Public Finance and Policy, the Indian Institute of Management Bangalore, the Centre for Economic and Social Studies, Hyderabad, and the Institute for Social and Economic Change, Bengaluru. Throughout his career, Dr Sarma's basic research interests have been statistical and econometric methods and their applications in public finance, public policy design, corporate finance and international taxation.

Dr Sarma has been actively involved in public policy reforms in the country, having been a member of several committees such as the Andhra Pradesh Revenue Reforms Committee, the Andhra Pradesh Fiscal Reforms Implementation Committee, the Gujarat State Public Finance Reform Committee, the Central Excise Working Group and the Commission on Macroeconomics and Health, Government of India.

Dr Sarma has been Visiting Fellow of Ford Foundation (at Economic Growth Centre, Yale University, USA) and Indo-Canadian Foundation (University of Toronto, Canada) and Consultant to World Bank and Asian Development Bank. Presently, he advises the governments of Nepal, Bangladesh, Laos, Bhutan, Vietnam and Sri Lanka on matters relating to public finance management.

Dr Sarma has authored six books, undertaken several policy research projects and published numerous papers in reputed journals. His most recent work is the textbook *Public Finance: Principles and Practices*.

INDEX